STALINISM IN PRAGUE

STALINISM IN PRAGUE

The Loebl Story

by

EUGEN LOEBL

Translated by Maurice Michael

American Edition
Edited and with an Introduction by
Herman Starobin

GROVE PRESS, INC. NEW YORK

Library of Congress Catalog Card Number: 79-91443

First Printing

Manufactured in the United States of America

Contents

Part II. The Trial Proceedings

Part III. The Supreme Court

Preface

The trial discussed in this book took place seventeen years ago (1952). Its purpose was to put an end to the possibility of an independent Czechoslovak road to socialism. In addition to those convicted in the so-called Slansky trials, hundreds of additional Government and Communist Party officials were condemned in similar trials.

Both the Czechoslovak Communist Party and the Government had been deeply convinced that they were sovereign and, in fact, until the onset of arrests in 1949 they had been making their own decisions. Thus, although not all the members of the Government nor of the Party leadership were in the dock, the trial was in reality directed at all of them.

On August 21, 1968, another public trial took place, this time of all citizens of Czechoslovakia, and 14 million people were condemned to imprisonment. They have been deprived of their national and social rights and, in a sense, live in a jail whose guards at one time numbered half a million men.

Why did the invasion take place?

We were invaded in August 1968 because we sought to find our own road to socialism, and because we wanted to embark on a truly socialist road. Our aims were lofty: we were attempting to build a society based on the principles of humanism and democracy, a society in which people could truly realize their aspirations and their hopes. We tried to create a synthesis between the scientific-technical revolution of our time and a truly socialist revolution.

In the course of the twenty prior years, we had been able to see for ourselves that expropriation of the means of production does not by itself mean socialism. Social appropriation should have followed expropriation. It did not; in reality, the Party leadership retained in its own hands all the attributes of ownership. Their absolute monopoly was incredibly more concentrated than that which existed in capitalist countries.

In 1968 we were striving to transform this pseudo-socialism—our term for it in Czechoslovakia was "distorted socialism"—into a new and genuine socialism. Expropriation was not an end in itself, but merely the prerequisite for the democratization and humanization of society. We genuinely sought to give all the citizens of our country the same rights, with Communists not being favored in any way. As "committed" citizens, the Communists were not to expect advantages from their Party membership, but would have to be prepared to make greater sacrifices than others.

Czechoslovakia had to be occupied because it had been made into a mirror in which the true face of Soviet socialism and that of the other countries was reflected clearly in all of its nakedness and with all of its deformities.

In brief, this is the tragedy of Czechoslovakia.

EUGEN LOEBL

Spring 1969

Introduction

The treason trials in East Central Europe in the late 1940's and early 1950's, like those in the Soviet Union in the 1930's, have left many unanswered questions. In the parlance that has become so common in the Communist states, almost all of the defendants have been "rehabilitated" in the years following Stalin's death in 1953, particularly outside the USSR. Unfortunately, few of the major victims lived to benefit from the largess of the party leaders. One of the few is Eugen Loebl, onetime Deputy Foreign Trade Minister of Czechoslovakia and the first of fourteen arrested in that country in what became known as the "Slansky trial."

Treason trials and fratricide are not uncommon in the history of revolutions. But the socialist revolution in East Central Europe held the promise of a socialist humanism as an integral part of the new economic relationships being created in these countries. Neither the mood nor the aspirations endured for more than a few brief years. Starting in 1948, Stalin's insistence on the need for complete

Soviet hegemony in the new bloc of countries in the face of what he conceived to be the urgent threat of war wrought deep-seated changes in the expectations and plans of other Communist leaders.

The first victim was the until then universally accepted dictum among practitioners of Marxism that each country would create its own path to socialism. In Marxian terms this made great sense, since each country had evolved in a differing set of historical circumstances and each had attained a level of economic development that varied from that of others. To Czechoslovak Communists this interpretation of Marx's writings made particular sense. Their country was technologically the most advanced in the socialist bloc and, therefore, was not subject to the pressures for rapid economic development and the concomitant social compulsions that might be the lot of other Communist-led governments.

Second, the victims were, of course, the leading Communists in the Party apparatus and in Government, who attempted to carry out in practice the implications of diverse paths to socialism. By charging them with treason and either executing them or jailing them, nonbelievers in Soviet hegemony could be removed and the trials would serve as an object lesson to others.

Despite the fact that the Czechoslovak Communist Party as a whole, including the President of the Republic and Chairman of the Party, Klement Gottwald, had agreed to what had become known as "the specific road to socialism," the Party readily accepted the Soviet leaders' conclusions. Further justifications for the execution or imprisonment of Communists by Communists was Stalin's theory, now widely echoed in the newer socialist countries, that the class struggle intensifies after power is taken away from the capitalists. This conception, abandoned since Stalin's death, served to justify treason trials in the Soviet Union and to explain how tried and true old Communists in each of the new socialist states could be charged with committing such heinous crimes, including treason.

Since Krushchev's speech denouncing Stalin, there have been a number of attempts to set the record straight. But whatever de-Stalinization took place in the Soviet bloc, the details of the treason trials, either in Russia or in Eastern Europe, were never completely and publicly disclosed. Nor have the defendants, particularly those who remained alive, ever been fully "rehabilitated." As Loebl remarks, to have done so "it would inevitably have been necessary to disclose the true and primary reasons for all the things that were done."

Unavoidably, the treason trials that took place in all countries calling themselves socialist created considerable doubt in the outside world, as they did internally. After the spate of trials of leading old Communists in the Soviet Union in the 1930's, Arthur Koestler sought to explain in a novel why people who committed no crime readily confessed to wrongdoings that had never taken place. Psychological in nature, his interpretation was based on loyalty to the party and an acceptance by the defendants of the overriding political need for the confessions.

As one of the few major survivors, and an articulate one at that, Eugen Loebl provides a completely different frame of reference. That the trials were organized and rehearsed to the last detail and the specific victims chosen by the Soviet secret police becomes clear in his personal account of his encounters with them. That all this was known by those whom the agents of the Soviet super-secret-policeman, Lavrenti Beria, had spared is also made abundantly clear.

The story that emerges in these pages, in the pertinent excerpts of the trial, and in Loebl's own "rehabilitation" proceedings of 1963 is a dreadful tale of both ingenious and far less subtle pressures. The author does not seek lofty explanations, nor does he deny how he was cynically used to broaden the scope of the trial. What emerges is the oversimplified, rigid, and doctrinaire carrying out of Stalin's instructions to make certain of the security of the bordering countries. The victims were broken before they became pliant tools in the hands of their inquisitors.

In choosing the defendants, it was no accident that eleven out of the fourteen were of Jewish origin. Most of the arms used by Israel to defend itself at the time of its establishment in 1947 came from the Skoda plant in Czechoslovakia. However, by the late 1940's and early 1950's, the fear of dual loyalties on the part of those who happened to be of Jewish origin became a matter of concern. The same was true of those who had been in the West during the German occupation of Czechoslovakia and the war, or who had been members of the International Brigades in Spain. All the defendants were in one of these categories, some in two, others in all three.

Even after de-Stalinization set in in Eastern Europe, the Czechoslovak Communist leaders were the last to accept it. Loebl, for example, remained in jail for five years after Krushchev's attack on Stalin and was not returned to grace for another two years. His story of these events is not merely that of a man who spent some of the prime years of his life in jail—from the age of 42 to 54. It points up what was done to vitiate the principles on which the system claimed to be based.

The Soviet invasion of Czechoslovakia on the night of August 20-21, 1968, marked a further step toward re-Stalinization. There can be little doubt now that the Soviet leaders feared most of all the example to Czechoslovakia's neighbors of a possible humanist socialist society and the revelations concerning violations of "socialist legality" by Soviet, as well as Czech, officials and Party leaders. The Czechoslovaks had revealed more about such violations in eight and one-half months than the Russians have since 1956. And much more was in the offing.

By invading Czechoslovakia and putting an end to the new liberalization taking place there, the Soviet leaders effectively destroyed what remained of its once enormous legacy of love and respect for the USSR. To the people of Czechoslovakia, open discussion was neither antisocialist nor anti-Soviet. Frankness, on the contrary, would only serve the interests of socialism, something the Soviet leaders had apparently long since rejected. Toward the end of his account, Loebl asserts: "We can no more allow the period of the fifties to be identified with socialism, than international socialist relations can accept Stalin's concept of the hegemony of the Soviet Union."

Loebl's report of the Czechoslovak treason trial is part of the discussion of differing views of socialist development. Written initially for the people of his own country, the author insists that truth will vindicate socialism. This message is directed at both socialists and nonsocialists. It suggests to the former the need to learn from the past and from the effects of the imposition of a monolithic form of socialist practice. To the latter it seeks to explain how and why people like Loebl continue to be socialists, despite failures of the system in practice and the personal suffering to which many like himself were subjected. To both it counsels that democracy, humanism, and socialism are not contradictory.

Whether one agrees or disagrees with the author's conclusions, the record presented in the following pages should not be ignored in piecing together what has happened in the socialist world and where the countries that constitute it are going. In Eugen Loebl's view, his continuing belief in socialism made it necessary for him to relate the story of the trial.

HERMAN STAROBIN

STALINISM IN PRAGUE

Part I

The "Slansky Trial"

Genesis of a "Traitor"

In September, 1949, I was summoned before the Central Committee by Karel Svab and Ladislav Kopriva, then heads of the Security and Cadre Departments of the Communist Party, respectively. They told me they were going to interrogate me. My future would depend on my telling the unadulterated truth without any reservations.

I was taken into a room which happened to be that in which the Party's Economic Commission, of which I had been a member, used to sit. Jarmila Taussigova, B. Doubek, and another comrade, whose name I did not know, arrived. This unidentified person and Doubek later interrogated me. Taussigova invited me to write a precise and self-critical account of my background. I was provided with a typewriter and paper and began to write. I had no idea what they had against me. To be on the safe side, I detailed all my activities both before and after joining the Party, and I tried to be objective about both myself and my work. I made no secret of my mistakes and I think that, if anything, I presented myself in too poor, rather than too good a light.

When evening came I still had not finished but was then taken into another office, which the Economic Commission had also used previously. It was now not an office but a prison cell. A bed had been set up, I was not allowed to turn out the light or to leave the room, and there was a guard at the door. Every half hour the door was opened and someone looked in to see what I was doing. Thus as early as the fall of 1949 the Secretariat of the Party Central Committee had its own little prison in its building on Prikopech Street.

The next day I continued writing about my background. The finished document was collected that afternoon and toward evening Taussigova and Doubek arrived and discussed it with me. There was a long argument about the exact date of my joining the Party. They had "now learned" that I was not of working-class family, that I had been in the West and that I had dealings with Western journalists, politicians, and economists. These were "sins," and they discovered quite a number of similar ones. I was expecting them to arrest me and was pleasantly surprised when Taussigova informed me that the Party agreed that I was to continue to function as First Deputy Minister for Foreign Trade, but I was not to leave Prague and not to mention to anyone where I had been and what I had been doing. Any violation would lead to expulsion from the Party and immediate arrest.

I obeyed this order scrupulously, but nonetheless on November 24, 1949, a man entered my apartment and, having identified himself as a member of the Security Service, handed me a summons from the Minister of the Interior, Vaclav Nosek, requiring my presence. There was a car waiting outside. In the car sat two more men whom you could tell at a glance were plainclothesmen. The car drove in the direction of the airfield at Ruzyne. When I objected that that was not the way to the house where Nosek lived, they reassured me that he was waiting for me in another house. We stopped in front of a large building where uniformed members of the Security Service awaited us. One of them announced: "In the name of the law, you are under arrest!"

Immediately I was made to put on the clothes prescribed for those under arrest, consisting of little more than rags. Evidently this was supposed to act as a psychological shock.

For four days nobody paid any attention to me; then on the fifth, I was sent for.

My interrogation was conducted by Captain V. Kohoutek, who was promoted to major after the trial. The secretary was a young lieutenant, a former carpenter from Martin, and the group which supervised the interrogation, taking it in turns of one or two hours, was headed by Doubek; also there was the man unknown to me, who, along with Doubek and Taussigova, had previously interrogated me in the Secretariat of the Central Committee.

Those in charge were Doubek and Kohoutek. They told me that neither they nor any other officers of the Security Service were responsible for my arrest. One who held so high an office and who was so well known in the West could only be arrested with the agreement of the Central Committee. There was no use trying to make them believe that the Central Committee had had me arrested without definite proof of my guilt. I must realize that my arrest meant that sentence had already been passed on me and that only a frank confession and the revelation of the names of my accomplices could induce the Party to make allowance for extenuating circumstances.

I replied that I was not aware of having done anything culpable or inimical to the Party; I had always tried to act honestly, and if I had made mistakes, I had never done so intentionally. I asked to be told exactly what I was accused of and to be given the opportunity to prove my innocence.

They denounced this as a typical "Jewish trick": I only

wanted to find out how much they knew about my crimes so as to confess only that much and keep silent about all the other things of which they did not yet know. As far as I was concerned, they told me, they had so much material that any objective court would sentence me to death. Their only concern was to make it possible for me to compensate for at least some of the harm I had done by giving a frank confession. Above all, I should tell them on whose orders I had been acting, who had helped me, and with what Czechoslovak and foreign enemies of the people I had worked.

At that early stage I was naive enough to believe that there had been some denunciation of me, so I told them the only explanation I could think of was that our enemies were making false reports in an attempt to get rid of faithful comrades and those with expert knowledge in order to weaken the Party. It soon transpired, however, that they had nothing against me, not even false accusations. Their only document was the background statement I had written for them. What they wanted to do was turn that into an indictment.

And that was all too easy. For example, I had stated that I had been head of a section in the Ministry of Foreign Trade at the time when Hubert Ripka * was Minister. They only needed to add a short sentence to the effect that I was his agent and had betrayed the Party on his instructions. When I said that I maintained contact with Western journalists, they demanded that I should add that I had provided them with information that should have been kept secret "in the interests of the Republic." Also that I had concluded a trade agreement with Yugoslavia as Tito's agent and one with the Soviet Union to its detri-

*Hubert Ripka was a leader of the non-Marxist Czech National Socialist Party and a member of the Cabinet until the Communist Party's seizure of power in February, 1948. He fled the country shortly thereafter.—*Ed.*

ment, and so on. I shall explain this kind of technique by declaration later. First, however, I should like to show how I came to confess to so many crimes.

There are many different accounts of how confessions are obtained for such trials. Most of them explain confession by the use of political pressure. Others talk of drugs and physical torture. In reality the method used is so simple that one could call it a thing of genius. That is to say, the Communist official under arrest is persuaded that his confession will benefit the Party, that it will help the Party to overcome certain political difficulties.

Having finally committed to paper a much more detailed background statement than the one I had written for the Central Committee, I not only failed to admit my guilt, but even denied the suggestion that there had been any hostile intent in any of my actions. I was labeled an "obdurate enemy," that is, one who is not prepared to reveal the identity of those who were damaging the Republic, and as such I was subjected to "harsh treatment."

Prison is always associated with sitting, but in my case sitting was not allowed. I had to stand all the time I was being interrogated and was not even allowed to sit when in my cell. The interrogations lasted an average of sixteen hours a day, with breaks of two hours. Thus I had to stand or walk to and fro in my cell for a total of eighteen hours a day, which left six hours for sleep. One was not allowed to have one's hands under the blanket. The cells were under constant observation and if a prisoner was seen with his hands under the blanket he was shouted at and cursed.

This in itself kept me in a state of constant tension. I was scarcely able to sleep during the few hours available because every ten minutes the guard banged on the cell door and one had to jump to one's feet, stand at attention, and report: "Detention prisoner 1473 reports: Number in cell, one. All in order." For the first few nights I invariably found it impossible to get to sleep again after being roused in this way; later I became so exhausted that I fell asleep again the moment I had made my report. Thus I was dragged out of deep sleep thirty or forty times a night. If I failed to hear the bang on the door, the guard would come in and kick me until I awoke.

Another means of exerting pressure was by hunger. The food was so totally inadequate that you never had had enough, but were always aware of being hungry. That, of course, was endurable. Often the interrogation was deliberately made to continue beyond mealtime—sometimes at midday, sometimes in the evening. When you returned to your cell the guard told you that the food had already been served and that he could not alter the prison rules and regulations just for your sake. He could not wait with the food until you deigned to put in an appearance. This combination of continual hunger, repeated interruption of sleep, and of having to stand or walk in small, hard leather slippers throughout the day caused indescribable physical distress.

After about three weeks my feet were swollen and my skin had become tender to the slightest touch. Washing them had become torture and every step I took caused pain.

Interrogation was conducted by three men, each taking his turn, and consisted of a never-ending flood of insult, humiliation, and threats. Often I had to spend the day standing with my face to the wall. The systematic repetition of the same question got on my nerves. When an interrogation achieved nothing, the prisoner would be "put on ice," which meant being left alone all day in the cell.

I was not allowed to sit. I even had to eat standing up. You could not even sit on the toilet, since what was provided was a so-called "Turkish closet." Walking for sixteen hours a day, however slowly, meant covering fifteen or twenty miles—on swollen feet. Such a day seemed endless and the prisoner could scarcely wait for night.

Yet lying down itself caused more pain than anything else. The sudden change in pressure brought such violent pain to my feet that sometimes I had to scream out. There was no real relief either. The process of regularly being roused to report just increased the pain and the nervous tension. You must remember the atmosphere in which we lived. There were always sounds: a limp body being dragged along, despairing cries from men and women under torture, the bellowing of interrogators—the interrogation rooms were just above my cell—and often the sobs and weeping of the interrogated. Add to this the brutality of the guards and the consciousness of being perfectly innocent, yet powerless. The worst, perhaps, was the knowledge that one was the victim of one's own Party, for which one had lived and given everything.

I could see no way out. There was not even a charge from the Public Prosecutor committing me to prison for interrogation; if there had been, I would have been able to lodge an appeal within twenty-four hours. In fact I did not receive the charge until just before my trial, after I had been under arrest for three years. It was not possible to get in touch with my defending counsel, and when I asked to be allowed to send a complaint to the President of the Republic, they laughed in my face. Kohoutek "enlightened" me. Klement Gottwald,* he said, had been against my arrest, but it had been decided on by the "Teachers" and I should face up to the fact. (Later I shall return to these "Teachers"—from the Soviet Secret Police.)

After resisting for several months, I was given drugs, though not until later did I realize this. Suddenly I had a feeling as if a hand had thrust itself through my forehead into my brain. It was the same sensation that you get from analgesic gas and thus not unpleasant. I do not know how long the sensation lasted, perhaps only a few seconds, per-

*Chairman of the Communist Party and President of the Czechoslovak Republic.—*Ed.*

haps minutes. The moment I was no longer aware of the "hand" in my head, I felt perfectly normal. As long as I was in this state, I could not hold anything in my hands and if I happened to be walking I had to stop. The state was not unpleasant in itself; what was nasty was the fear I had that I must be going mad. I was continually watching myself to see if "it" was coming back, how long the intervals were between "attacks," and how many I had a day. Fear of ending in a madhouse was worse than the fear of death. It was only after I had been sentenced that I learned from my fellow prisoners Artur London * and Sefcik Kevic, Yugoslav vice-consul in Bratislava, that they too had been in the same state. After sentence, when I was working in the garden of Ruzyne Prison, fellow prisoners who cleaned the prison hospital told me that they found empty ampules, the contents of which had been administered to prisoners in their soup. They had also heard the prison doctor, Josef Somer, asking the prison governor to be allowed to observe the behavior of prisoners who had eaten the drugged soup. Apparently, Dr. Somer had been in a concentration camp during the war. But I feel he could have outdone quite a lot of Gestapo doctors.

Suicide was the only way out, but one that scarcely anyone was able to attempt. The prisoners, especially the "prominent" ones, were very strictly watched. For example, our handkerchiefs were only two inches square, because in one prison a man had succeeded in strangling himself with an ordinary handkerchief. In the new prison at Ruzyne the windows were so high up that it was impossible to break the glass and get a piece with which to cut an artery. I did bite through the skin of a finger and rub dirt into the wound hoping that would finish me, but all that happened was that the wound festered and hurt. London told me later that he too had tried to take his

*With Loebl, one of the three to survive.

life. There was a rumor in the prison that Rudolf Slansky* had also attempted suicide, charging head first into the stone steps of the Turkish closet, after which the steps had been covered with some spongy material.

We were allowed no contact with our families. My family had their first letter from me after I had been under arrest for fourteen months, and only then did I get a reply from my wife and son. Illness was a catastrophe. The brutality of Dr. Somer exceeded that of the interrogators and guards, and this I found much more difficult to accept. It was, of course, to the doctor's advantage, because prisoners did their utmost to avoid coming under him.

They used a cunning procedure for dental treatment: prisoners were led blindfolded into the dentist's room, seated in the chair while still blindfolded, and their hands were then tied to the arms of the chair. Only then was the blindfold removed from their eyes. To sit with your hands tied was torment. However, the dentist—I never knew his name—was a very decent person and a good dentist. He was at pains not to hurt his patients and I shall never forget the humanity in his eyes and in the way he stroked my hand on one occasion when no one was watching.

Prisoners were blindfolded and led by the hand whenever they left their cells. That must have happened to me more than a thousand times during the four years I was in Ruzyne, but I always felt it degrading, as if I were a cow being taken to slaughter.

The authorities organized fake executions. On six or seven occasions I was awakened in the night, led blindfolded to the basement and into the chancery to listen in on a telephone conversation. As they were always threatening that they could not go on indefinitely feeding me at

*Secretary-General of the Czechoslovak Communist Party until his removal in 1951. Slansky became the principal defendant in the trial.—*Ed.*

the expense of the State, nor let me ruin their nerves or waste much more precious time on me, I was on each occasion convinced that "this was it," especially since they never tired of telling me that they did not need a court sentence before they executed me. Apparently they attached great importance to anything one said while in the agitated state this put one into. Before each of my "executions," I concentrated on how I was going to behave, whether I would speak and, if so, what my last words should be. I managed to keep relatively calm; but back in my cell, there was the inevitable reaction which took the form of shivering and a feeling of utter despair, which could last for hours. The saying that man even grows accustomed to the gallows is not true as far as my experience goes.

After my confession, when Kohoutek was being friendly, I asked him why they did all this. He replied that he did not know what I was talking about; that I must have imagined it. Later, fellow prisoners told me that it was indeed normal practice; executions were regularly faked in order to break the resistance of those under interrogation.

The things I found worst, however, were not being allowed to sit, the interruptions of sleep, and the boredom. I often thought that it would be ideal to be condemned to life imprisonment as long as one was allowed to sit and read. However, a sentence, whatever it was, would have been a release. I knew that after sentence, unless I was executed, I would be sent to a labor camp ("We're not going to feed criminals like you for nothing!") and there I would be able to end my life if I wished. But when would I be brought to trial? In one year's time, or two, or three?

That is the atmosphere in which the unsentenced prisoner lived. He was aware that he had only to sign a confession and he would be free of pressure. To be allowed to sit seemed the acme of freedom. Once a confession was signed, the prisoner would be allowed to read books, to buy extra food, and so free himself from the perpetual nagging feeling of hunger and thinking about food. He would be able to write to his family; he would even be taken out for exercise. (In the first two years I was in the prison yard on only four occasions and for only fifteen minutes each time.)

Not only his interrogators urged a prisoner to confess, but he himself. What was the point of letting yourself be mentally and physically destroyed when you would be found guilty whether you confessed or not? What would be involved in making a confession in open court? Did it matter what your relatives, comrades, and others who believed in you thought afterward? What was the point of clinging to ideals when everything had been sullied, become pointless, when such atrocities, such Gestapo methods, were possible in a socialist state? There were other moments when I tried to convince myself that no one had a right to deny man's great ideals; the truth would come out, I told myself, and my innocence would be established.

It was a never-ending dialogue with yourself, like Shakespeare's Launcelot Gobbo. If they had ever taken me for interrogation at one of those moments when I had talked myself into capitulation, I would have admitted whatever they wanted; but when I was taken before my inquisitors, I had a strong feeling to live up to the ideals that had caused me to join the Party and I resisted any such suggestion.

But in the end I did confess. I imagined that if I did so, I would be put on trial and in court I could retract everything. Having confessed, I was able to sit, was given books, but I was not brought before a court. When I had recovered somewhat, I withdrew my confession and applied for permission to send a complaint to Gottwald. That was refused and it all began again. I was afraid they might beat me up, but I was never once struck. During the entire time I received only one slap on the face and that was dealt me by Deputy Minister [Karel] Svab, who ended up in the same trial as I and was condemned with me.

Kohoutek, who was said to have started life selling shoes, had become filled with self-importance. He was greatly impressed by the fact that he now had power over those whom he would have fawned upon in the past. He made a great thing of all the people he knew and how important he was. As long as I denied the accusations and insisted on being an honorable citizen, he was thoroughly unpleasant; but, scarcely had I confessed to being scum, than he became friendly and chatty. We discussed every conceivable thing and he often spoke of matters that would have cost him his head if the Teachers had learned of it. London has told me that he had the same experience.

Kohoutek revealed to me the tactics of these Teachers: beating and physical torture were only to be employed when time was short. For example, it was to be used when an agent had been caught and one had to discover immediately who his accomplices were so that the Security people could arrest them before they had time to escape. In those cases physical torture must be applied sufficiently to break down resistance immediately.

Later I had opportunities to talk with men who had been subjected to this. In addition to the "classic" beating-up method, they used immersion in icy water, crushing the genitals, bandaging the head with wet material which shrank as it dried, causing fearful pain. All this was accompanied by interrogation that went on day and night. None of those with whom I spoke had been able to endure more than two days of it. In their cases it made no difference if they subsequently retracted their statements.

Kohoutek explained that different methods had to be used in preparing political trials. They had to have a guarantee that in court the accused would stick to their confessions in detail. They could not risk anyone retracting his confession during a public trial. Thus in these cases there was no point in forcing a confession by the use of physical force. ("Pain passes and the confession will be withdrawn.") The interrogators had to break those concerned and they must be so conditioned that they would not dare to withdraw their confessions, even if invited to do so by the Prosecutor himself.

In the end I confessed to every conceivable crime. I did not even toy with the idea of retracting later; in fact I did not even feel sorry or ashamed that I had given in, that I was lying. It is not easy to explain that state of mind.

Before the trial I had to learn my statements by heart. A question-and-answer statement was drawn up, giving all the questions the judge and prosecutor were going to ask me and the answers I was to give. When I had memorized them I was tested by one of the officials, a miner from Ostrava, named Josef Drozd. He was now a lieutenant-colonel and a decent fellow. He asked the questions and I answered as if I were actually in court. Drozd "directed" me, telling me if I was speaking loudly enough, too slowly, or too quickly. It appalls me now to think that I was not even aware of the idiotic, degrading position I was in. I had lost all sense of human dignity. All that man has inherited down through the ages, what he values most highly, what has become part of his nature, what it is that makes him human—all that had ceased to exist for me.

I often talk about my experiences in prison. Time creates distance and small amusing episodes come more and more to the fore. I no longer get agitated when telling about those eleven years in prison or when I think of them; yet I try to avoid speaking of *this* state that I got into, and even now, after all these years, I get very agitated when I remember the time when I had ceased to be human.

One must remember that with the help of doctors and psychologists they had worked out a system for depriving man of his humanity. Party members and high officials implemented the system in the name of the humanist ideal of socialism. I cannot imagine the mentality of those who were responsible for this, who approved of it and glorified it and were perfectly satisfied, indeed, even claimed to pass judgment on their victims. I feel guilty that I was not strong enough to stand up to the terror. I was not justified in acting against my ideals, and I believe that to the end of my life I shall not be able to forgive myself that weakness.

My confession was in no way an expression of depression or of mental decline. After I had confessed, I was allowed books, even given books that my wife sent me. I had plenty to read, mainly books on philosophy, or the natural sciences, and, of course, economics. These included a number of works by West European scholars, which had been sent to me by relatives living abroad. It was at this time that I had the idea for a book, worked it out in my mind, and finally wrote it on my release.* I was a completely normal person, apart from the fact that I had ceased to be human.

Cui bono?

Slansky's treasonable [alleged] Center, like the Titoites in Yugoslavia, [allegedly], invented the so-called theory of a specific Czechoslovak road to socialism in order to conceal its true aims. Under the cloak of this theory—which really meant the restoration of capitalism

*Published in German as *Geistige Arbeit: Die Wahre Quelle des Reichtums*, 1968, by Econ-Verlag, Wien and Düsseldorf, translated from the original Slovak; to be published in English as *The New Source of Wealth: The Revolution of the Intellectuals*, by Grove Press.—Ed.

in the Republic—the Center was [said to be] preparing for a reversal of conditions in Czechoslovakia along the Tito pattern and under the guidance of English and American imperialists. (*Proceedings of the Trial*, p. 401.)

In fact, the main protagonist of the specific way to socialism in those days was Gottwald, as can readily be shown by his speeches and articles on the subject. The idea itself was that of the collective Party leadership and it was adopted at the Party conference. The Party then held the view—a view that is again finding acceptance—that in the building up of socialism the specific problems of the country in question must be taken into consideration; socialism cannot otherwise be successfully established. Today, for example, each socialist country has its own specific economic control system.

It is obvious that the trial condemned one of the Party's basic political concepts, that of giving expression to the interests and the necessity of a socialist organization in Czechoslovakia, an idea that, incidentally, was incompatible with those held by Stalin, Beria,* and perhaps others too.

I was accused of having seen to it that, even toward the end of the First Five-Year Plan, our foreign trade was to be divided between the West and the socialist states in the proportion of 55 percent to the former and 45 percent to the latter.

In the Five-Year Plan Law, foreign trade was only mentioned in one short section. It had been the subject of much discussion. In the Party's Economic Commission, in which I had suggested this division, I had argued that we had to maintain contact throughout the entire world so as

*Lavrenti Beria had been Minister of Internal Security in the USSR under Stalin and head of the dreaded secret police. He was executed shortly after Stalin's death following secret proceedings against him, and charges that he was plotting the seizure of power in the Soviet Union.—*Ed.*

to be able to benefit from the dynamics of technical and economic development. This was not only in the interests of the Czechoslovak economy, but also in the interests of the other socialist states, because that was the only way in which we could be sure that the quality and price of our exports to those countries would be on the same level with those of the rest of the world. After the heads of the Economic Commission had agreed on this, Ludvik Frejka,* Jaromir Dolansky,** and I consulted with Gottwald, who accepted the idea. It was also adopted by the Party Presidium, the Government, and Parliament. To condemn this concept as tantamount to a return to capitalism was to condemn the Party's own policy, though in fact it was only we, the "members of the Center," who were on trial.

In view of the fact that what really was on trial was a law passed by the Government and Parliament, the answer to the question *cui bono?* is obvious.

Part of the case against me was that I had advocated paying compensation to the owners of concerns that had been nationalized. These included Great Britain and the U.S., and, among individuals, the firm of Unilever by reason of the nationalization of the Schicht Works. The law stated that there was an obligation to pay compensation in cases of nationalization and the Czechoslovak Government had repeatedly affirmed its intention to compensate owners whose property had been appropriated. Prior to February, 1948,*** the Government had in fact paid Switzerland a relatively large sum for this very reason.

*At the time of his arrest, head of the Economic Department of the Chancellery of the President of the Republic and head of the Party's Economic Commission.—*Ed.*

**Minister of Finance and later head of the State Planning Commission.—*Ed.*

***The Communist Party seized power in February, 1948, charging that the nonsocialist parties and the West were engaged in a plot to remove them from the Government.—*Ed.*

The events of February brought the question of nationalization into the foreground. The Government wished to avoid nationalization being used as fuel to feed anti-Czechoslovak propaganda, especially in England and the U.S., where at that time there was a growing demand for economic sanctions against Czechoslovakia. The U.S. had placed embargoes on the supply of industrial equipment, including a broad-ribbon rolling mill on which we had already paid $20 million. (The Court laid the onus for this payment on me. In fact, at the time Dolansky had obtained Gottwald's agreement to it and the advance payment had been made on the latter's instructions.)

The Government had set up a commission which had to decide for which nationalized concerns compensation was to be paid. Members of the commission included Finance Minister Dolansky, Minister of Industry Gustav Kliment, Minister of Foreign Trade Antonin Gregor, and Minister of the Interior Vaclav Nosek. I was not even present at any of its meetings.

After the commission had decided that Unilever was justified in claiming compensation for its subsidiary in Czechoslovakia, the Schicht concern, I was given the job of implementing the transaction. In the draft that I drew up, I adopted the principle used in commerce, that the master is the one who makes the payment: that is to say, the debtor. Thus we could well decide for ourselves the conditions on which we would make payment.

Unilever, as one of the largest manufacturers of artificial fats in the world, owned not only plantations on the Gold Coast in West Africa, but also a network of stores as well. I proposed that these stores obtain their supplies of glass, jewelry, porcelain, toys, and such from us. Unilever was to pay us 80 percent of the cost of these purchases and credit 20 percent to our account. The total amount to be paid was to be agreed upon once there was a large enough amount on the credit side of the account. It would be much easier to negotiate at that stage. The advantage for Unilever was that they would obtain compensation; for us, that we would get foreign exchange for goods that were very difficult to sell to hard-currency countries. Also, we would be paying the compensation not in pounds sterling but in goods, jewelry, etc.

The suggestion was enthusiastically received by Gottwald and accepted. Unilever agreed to it and the Government approved it. A similar kind of agreement was entered into with Great Britain.

Early in 1949 an American delegation came to Prague to discuss compensation for nationalized property. Minister of Finance Dolansky personally asked me to conduct the negotiations for the Government. Unlike Great Britain, there were no restrictions on imports into the U.S. and so we had to work out another idea. I suggested that we should tell the Americans that we preferred to pay compensation, but that, like other European countries, we did not have dollars at our disposal. If they would grant us a loan of $100 million and lift the embargo on the $40 million worth of goods we had already ordered, we would use the credit to buy equipment in the U.S. that would enable us to produce more goods for export. The dollars these exports earned would be used to pay the compensation.

This shocked the Americans at first. They had come to collect compensation and were met with a request for a loan. In the end, however, they agreed that it was a realistic proposal and promised to put it before their Government, which some time later announced that it was ready to continue negotiations. The Czechoslovak Government informed the U.S. that they would send a delegation to the States and appointed me to head it. During April and May of 1949 I negotiated with representatives of the U.S. Government along these lines. For technical reasons the negotiations were then adjourned until November, by which time I was already in prison.

Before we left for America I had long discussions with Dolansky and Vladimir Clementis * and then with Dolansky and Gottwald about the project, and the Government had also occupied itself with it. Thus, the agreement I made was neither a culpable act nor disadvantageous; above all, it was not a private act, not my personal doing, but something that I carried through on behalf of the Government. Basically, it was a question whether the Cold War was to be further stepped up or whether at least properly regulated trade relations were to be possible. The Czechoslovak Government was of the opinion that it was sensible and advantageous to our economy to maintain economic relations with Great Britain and the U.S.; but our Teachers and their bosses evidently held different views.

Another crime laid at my door was what was called "categorization." I was accused of introducing categorization into our trade relations with Romania. In actual fact this question came up in discussions with Bulgaria.

In 1948 Georgi Dimitrov, the Bulgarian Party and Government head and former General Secretary of the Comintern, and Boris Kollaroff came to Prague to discuss the basic questions of our economic relations and other matters. Before negotiations started, Gottwald invited Clementis and me to a preliminary talk. There were two opposing schools of thought about the two countries' trade relations. The Bulgarians took the view that trade relations between socialist states should be on the basis of each giving what it has. I, however, took the view that there must be categories and suggested four of these. For example: Category I included machinery (from us) and raw materials (from Bulgaria); Category IV included jewelry (from us) and attar of roses (from Bulgaria), and so on. Dimitrov's idea was that we should send them our machinery and get attar

*Dr. Clementis succeeded Jan Masaryk as Foreign Minister, having been Under-Secretary prior to the latter's death. He was a principal defendant in the same trial as the author.—*Ed.*

of roses in return. Gottwald was entirely in agreement with the idea of categories and he told me to put the idea forward during our negotiations and to champion it. It was interesting to see the great respect Gottwald had for his former chief in the Comintern and how unpleasant it was for him to have to refuse Dimitrov's proposal.

At the joint meeting, which Gottwald attended, I put forward the idea of categories and this led to a violent argument with the two Bulgarians. In the end the idea was adopted. Here again I must emphasize that I was acting on Gottwald's instructions and that these were wholly in accordance with the interests of our economy. However, they were certainly in conflict with the efforts being made to abolish the economic frontiers of Czechoslovakia and to subordinate our country to the hegemony and politics of Stalin. This later concept can be seen running like a red thread through the entire trial, appearing in everyone's testimony. It was obviously the "personality cult" adapted to the field of international relations.

As far as my own testimony is concerned, you do not have far to look to find the thread. Our Teachers had no inhibitions about speaking frankly and they told me several times in the presence of Kohoutek and Doubek that Anastas Mikoyan * had "unmasked" me as an enemy of the Soviet Union. This occurred during the treaty negotiations with him in Moscow in the autumn of 1947 when I had insisted on our being paid world market prices, that is to say, "capitalist" prices, for our exports to the USSR. That made me a *Vrag* (enemy). I also wanted to sell uranium to the Americans. In other words, things were even worse because I had stood up for the economic interests of Czechoslovakia.

The implications here are of such importance that I

*Soviet Foreign Trade Minister at the time and a leading member of the Party's Politburo.—*Ed.*

would like to go into the background of these charges in greater detail.

It Began with the Marshall Plan

When the American Government announced the Marshall Plan in June, 1947, our Government was one of many which deliberated whether or not to accept it. Voices were raised in the Party's Economic Commission against its acceptance. At this critical time, Hilary Minc, Polish Minister for Industry and the man virtually in charge of Polish economic policy, arrived in Prague. He was the guest of our Minister of Foreign Trade, Ripka, who was unable to meet him at the station, and this I did instead. I spent the afternoon with Minc at the Polish Embassy discussing the Marshall Plan. He emphasized Poland's economic difficulties, especially those arising from the need to repair war damage, and he regarded the Marshall Plan as an important aid in doing this. I put forward my views, which I had already aired during the discussion at the Economic Commission and during talks with the editors of our Party press: as our economy was essentially consolidated to a far greater extent than those of the other European countries which had taken part in the war, the greatest "assistance" we could be given was to be allowed to exploit the world trade situation for ourselves. For this we required a free hand, no ties that might restrict our freedom to maneuver. In addition we had uranium which had now become so valuable. Minc was a supporter of the Marshall Plan; he advocated it to the Polish Government and it was accepted. This, of course, carried considerable weight with our Government, which also agreed to the Plan, though with certain reservations.

Gottwald and most of the members of the Politburo and

Government were attending a reception for Minc when it became known that Stalin had invited our Government to send a delegation to the Soviet Union. Gottwald knew that we owed the invitation to our acceptance of the Marshall Plan. During the reception, he decided that I should go to Moscow and prepare that part of the discussions concerned with our foreign trade as head of a team of experts from the Ministry of Foreign Trade. The Czechoslovak delegation arrived shortly afterward. It was headed by Gottwald and included Foreign Minister Masaryk, Prokop Drtina * (in place of Ripka, who was ill), and Josef Kopecky (Catholic People's Party).

The delegation went to its rooms in the house where we were quartered. While Gottwald rested after the journey, the other members of the Government and some of the experts seated themselves in the drawing room. Time dragged on, but there was no sign of Gottwald. Masaryk became nervous and kept sending Pavel Reiman, head of Gottwald's Chancellery, to see what was happening. On each occasion, Reiman reported that Gottwald was still asleep. Then suddenly Gottwald walked into the room, still in his hat and coat, and said: "Everything is all right. I've just come to an agreement with Stalin. We're to see him this evening."

This was a bombshell. The members of the delegation were annoyed with Gottwald for presenting them with a *fait accompli*, thus reducing them to a merely decorative role; but they accepted it and went to the talks with Stalin. Masaryk declared that under no circumstance would he allow the Government's decision to join the Marshall Plan to be changed.

I did not take part in the discussions with Stalin and know of them only at second hand from Gottwald's report and from what Masaryk told me. Stalin insisted that the

*Minister of Justice in the pre-1948 coalition government and a leader of the non-Marxist Czech National Socialist Party.—*Ed.*

Czechoslovak Government reject the Marshall Plan. He even threatened us. After that Masaryk felt that he could not prevent the Government's decision being altered and so should try to get from Stalin a decent exchange, that is to say, appropriate economic help to compensate for the damage we would suffer. I know that people were calling Prague all night, that the Government held a meeting in the middle of the night, and that in the end Stalin's decision was accepted.

Gottwald then sent for me, told me that there were going to be important economic negotiations, and that he was putting me in charge of them. He also gave me the job of drawing up that part of the communiqué dealing with foreign trade policy. I produced a communiqué that embodied our requests to the USSR, but did not specify what our deliveries were to be, so that it was clear that the agreement was to be based on equivalent exchanges.

Gottwald agreed entirely with this attitude and approved the wording of my part of the communiqué, which he personally showed to Stalin and, the two men agreeing, it was included in the final document. In September I returned to Moscow at the head of a Trade Delegation. This time, in order to stress the importance of the delegation, I was given the rank of Ambassador and Minister Plenipotentiary.

So we began negotiating with Mikoyan. Because of the catastrophically bad harvest we had had in Czechoslovakia, our main demand was for supplies of wheat and foodstuffs. The Soviet Union wanted mainly rolled iron and steel. The talks were held in committee and day by day the demands of the Soviets grew higher and higher and their readiness to meet our needs less and less.

On the thirtieth anniversary of the October Revolution, Molotov gave a reception and I took this opportunity to talk with the Soviet Trade Delegation assigned to Prague and Mikoyan's deputies, Karel Menschikov and General

Vladimir Yefimovich Semitschasny, "man to man." I told them of our difficulties and complained that we seemed as far from an agreement as we had been when negotiations began. This brought forth the suggestion that I ought to Meet Mikoyan "on Party level" as well as officially.

Such a meeting was arranged. As I was the official representative of what was then still a non-Communist government and we were to have a Party talk, the whole thing had to be done in secret. And it was done in the best tradition: I was told to wait in my hotel room for a telephone call and when that finally came, about midnight, I was met at the hotel entrance by a man who led me to a side street where a car was waiting. Gregory Biller, who was with me, acted as interpreter. He came originally from Czechoslovakia, but had lived in the Soviet Union ever since he was a child, had studied there, and joined the Party. Mikoyan received me about twelve-thirty. Our talk lasted about three hours. At the beginning it was very pleasant and friendly. I informed Mikoyan about the political situation in Czechoslovakia (this was around the time when Zdenek Fierlinger * had been removed from leadership of the Social-Democratic Party and replaced by Bohumil Lausman). I emphasized the exceptional importance of reaching an advantageous agreement with the Soviet Union in this situation and asked him to take into consideration my endeavors to obtain advantageous quantities and prices in that context.

We had scarcely gotten to concrete items when his tone changed completely. He told me that he was Minister of Foreign Trade and that it was his duty to conclude an advantageous agreement. Nothing else interested him. We were unable to agree on a single point. After three hours, I summed up by saying that he appeared to see it as his

*First postwar Prime Minister and leader of the left faction of the Czechoslovak Social-Democratic Party.—*Ed.*

duty as Minister of Foreign Trade to squeeze advantages out of the situation while I saw mine as endeavoring to conclude an agreement in the spirit of the arrangement already concluded between Stalin and Gottwald. I then left.

There was now a complete deadlock in our talks. I sent a written report to Gottwald and copies to Frejka and Reiman. I also had a number of telephone conversations, particularly with Frejka, whom I had told that I was not prepared to conclude an agreement on terms dictated by Mikoyan. However, as I was not empowered to break off negotiations, I requested that Ripka should come to Moscow.

Because of our disastrous harvest we needed not only large quantities of corn and foodstuffs, but we needed them by certain dates if we were to be able to hold out until the following harvest. Mikoyan wanted to make the USSR's delivery of grain coincide with our deliveries of rolled iron and steel and certain machinery. He wanted a scheduled, "timetable" agreement whereby for every delivery of iron and steel and machinery made by us, we would receive a delivery of Soviet corn and foodstuffs of equal value. Inevitably, most of what we were to deliver could not be ready until the last quarter of 1948, while we would need their agricultural produce in the first six months of the year.

There were further differences of opinion on prices. The year 1947 was one in which bad harvests were general in Europe and the world prices of agricultural produce were rising daily. That is why Mikoyan's representative, who handled the details of our talks, asked for a higher price at every meeting. This meant that they were asking for more iron and steel. Our capacity was limited, and we needed iron and steel for our own production. We also had trade treaty obligations to other states. Thus the demands of Mikoyan's deputy could inflict immeasurable economic damage.

This is to mention merely the most important points; our ideas even differed on the basis for accounting. We had agreed to use world market prices as the basis; but transport costs remained a bone of contention. The Soviets demanded world market prices plus transport charges. That was to our disadvantage. Low-priced Soviet agricultural produce would add up to huge quantities, while the volume of ours would be small in relation to their value and thus they would incur smaller transport costs. Further, the world price of wheat was F.O.B. Manitoba and transport from the U.S. or Canada to us would amount to about 15 percent of the price. For that reason I demanded that only half the freight should be added to the price. There was a great deal of money involved.

As a result of my report and my recommendation that under these circumstances we should not conclude a treaty at all, our Minister of Foreign Trade came to Moscow. I went to Brest-Litovsk to meet him and on the way to Moscow filled in the picture for him. I again recommended that we ought not to conclude any treaty. Mikoyan met us at the Moscow station. He had prepared a reception for Ripka and to our astonishment said how pleased he was that there were no longer any differences between us and that the treaty would be signed within the next few days. Neither Ripka nor I had any idea what he was talking about; it was only after he had left us that we learned that Stalin and Gottwald had spoken to each other in the meantime. Gottwald had drawn Stalin's attention to the political implications of failure to conclude a treaty and Stalin had not only promised to meet the demands I had been trying to get accepted, but also to raise the quantity of corn and foodstuffs to be delivered by (if I remember correctly) 200,000 tons.

Talks were now held in an entirely different atmosphere. The "timetable" had been dropped and the Soviet Union even granted us an additional credit of 700 million crowns [$14 million]. However, we did not have enough goods to offset the increased deliveries from the Soviet Union in exchange for what they wanted. We proposed to ship them what we happened to have—for example, lead pencils. The Soviet Union had never before imported pencils so there was no organization with a quota for pencils. As a result Sovietskaia Kniga, the Soviet book organization, was told to import our pencils. We even agreed on the price to be paid for wheat. Here I was able to point out that our view finally had been confirmed by Stalin himself. If the Soviet Union had accepted this at the beginning, we would have been able to conclude the treaty at the price then current in the world market. That price was lower than that used in the agreement. On the quantity involved we would have saved over a billion crowns [$20 million].

Back in Prague I made a complete report to Gottwald and Dolansky. Neither of them regarded my behavior as hostile. To me it was perfectly natural that Mikoyan's representatives defended their interests and that we, likewise, defended ours.

Before these negotiations were concluded I met Dr. Antonin Rasla, our attorney, and, in the presence of our attaché, Emil Stefan, told him the story of our trade talks. Rasla's only comment was: "Somebody here is going to end up as a criminal, you'll see." At the time I regarded this as a bad joke.

The Teachers had interpreted my actions in their own way, which Mikoyan accepted. They expected that, as a Communist, I would agree that Soviet interests had absolute priority and that I would subordinate everything to them. The fact that I had not done this was interpreted as a hostile act, that is to say as a betrayal. Above all they accused me of trying, as an agent of the West, to hinder deliveries of uranium to the Soviet Union in order to divert it to the Anglo-American imperialists.

The treaty covering deliveries of uranium was signed by Ripka shortly after liberation. It provided for uranium to be paid for at the cost of mining it plus 10 percent. This was unfavorable as far as we were concerned, but the quantity involved was small and was to offset deliveries of Soviet goods supplied at advantageous prices. Special permission from the Ministry of Foreign Trade was not required for the export of this ore and so this item was dealt with separately and accounted for annually. At the start of negotiations for the exchange of goods between our two states I was not concerned with uranium ore as this did not figure on the list of goods. But then, in November, 1947, the Director-General of our mines came to Moscow bringing written instructions from Gottwald that he and I were to negotiate deliveries of uranium ore to the Soviet Union. I had to familiarize myself with this new set of problems.

The Director-General had been sent to Moscow because of a disagreement on one particular point: In the neighborhood of the Czechoslovak towns of Jachymov and Pribam are large dumps dating from medieval days and these also contain uranium ore. This had been exported to the Soviet Union since the end of the war. Engineer V. Rada, the Director-General, was now asking the same price for this ore as for that which had to be mined. The Soviet representative refused to accept this on the grounds that the agreement was for cost plus 10 percent and the cost of working the dumps was significantly lower than that of mining it underground. I insisted that we should not think in terms of whether the ore was obtained from a dump or a mine. Our talks were with Mikoyan's deputy, Krutikov. I drew his attention to the fact that the old agreement had been provisional and made at a time when our foreign trade relations had not been ratified. Now that we had just concluded a long-term trade treaty based on world market prices, the same must apply to our uranium ore.

Krutikov was prepared to pay more for ore obtained from the dumps, but refused on principle to extend the concept of world market prices to uranium ore. We held half a dozen relatively lengthy meetings in an atmosphere of considerable tension. Never did I suggest that we stop delivery of uranium ore to the Soviet Union, still less that we would prefer to let the Americans have it. There was never any dispute over the question of supplying this ore to the Soviet Union, but only over the price. My argument was that we paid world market prices for wheat and for Soviet iron ore from Krivoi Rog and that I could not see why we should accept other than the world market prices for what was virtually our only natural wealth. After the war uranium was priced very high and considerable sums were involved. Price was all the more important at this juncture as we were expected to increase the amount we mined.

We were unable to conclude negotiations with Krutikov, as he fell ill and went to Karlovy Vary [Karlsbad] for a cure. He was expected back in January, when we would continue negotiations. He told me then that he had referred the matter to his Government and was awaiting a decision. However, Krutikov was suddenly appointed Deputy Prime Minister and the talks were not continued. Then came the events of February, 1948, and the whole uranium question was taken over by Gottwald's Chancellery and put in the hands of Dr. Otto Pohl. Pohl consulted Rada and me on one or two occasions, but after that the subject of uranium ore became taboo and discussion of it the cause for criminal action.

I was surprised not to find Rada in the dock with me. I learned later that he had been interrogated by the police on several occasions and after the last interrogation had gone into the garden of his house and shot himself.

Our "Teachers"

One must not speak ill of the dead. However, in the case of Beria's men in Prague nothing else is possible. Our

Security people called them our "Teachers." After the 20th Congress of the Soviet Communist Party [February, 1956] they were condemned to death and executed. When I became acquainted with them, they were powerful, one might almost say all-powerful. In a way they were the masters of our country.

On one occasion early in December, 1949, I was taken to a large room on the second floor of the prison. Two men were seated behind a desk: one had a bald head and looked about forty-five and spoke Ukrainian; the other, about the same age, spoke Russian. The Ukrainian did the talking. Doubek and Kohoutek were present.

At first, the Teachers tried to persuade me that my sentence had already been passed. If I were to save my life I must at least show positive repentance by revealing the identity of my accomplices and chiefs. When this attempt proved fruitless, they repeated their stereotyped accusations and threatened me. They had plenty of effective means of making me talk, I was told. They then delivered a long tirade against the Jews that would have done honor to any Gestapo man. As time went on, they changed their accusations, but their anti-Semitic abuse continued to pour out.

Originally I was accused of being in contact with Herman Field and of Titoism. Herman Field was an American citizen who after the Munich Agreement in 1938 worked for the British Committee for Czech Refugees and later for the Czech Refugee Trust Fund, an organization that helped people who for political reasons had to escape from Czechoslovakia. Field was very active in helping those of the refugees who were Communists; indeed he gave them preference. For this Herman Field and his brother Noel were both arrested in 1949, one in Poland, the other in Hungary. They were both rehabilitated after the 20th Congress of the Communist Party of the Soviet Union.

The accusation of Titoism was based on the fact that I had conducted the negotiations for a trade agreement with Yugoslavia and had signed the treaty as my country's chief delegate. Not even the Teachers, however, could make any concrete accusation. What they wanted was my admission that I was a spy, a traitor, and a noxious person.

In the second half of December they started calling me a Slovak bourgeois nationalist. According to them I had been one of the leaders of the Slovak bourgeois or non-socialist nationalist group. The group's leader was supposedly Clementis and the others were Laco Novomesky, Gustav Husak,* and I. The trial of the Slovak bourgeois nationalists as Tito's main agents in Czechoslovakia was to take place at the same time as the Lazlo Rajk trial in Hungary.** It is remarkable that at this time the interest of the Teachers was concentrated on the Slovak group. Later on, once they had worked out and amplified the idea of a treasonable Center, they showed less interest in it. After the trial of the Center and especially after Stalin's death and the fall of Beria, the bourgeois-nationalist group became purely a matter of domestic concern.

After Slansky had been "unmasked," Kohoutek told me that the bourgeois-nationalist group was then only of secondary importance and that I would be put in another group—the Center. After we had been given our sentences, Vavro Hajdu *** told me that his interrogators had told him that Clementis, Novomesky, Husak, and I had been executed as leaders of the bourgeois-nationalist group. That, of course, was before the invention of the Center. It was sometime in March, 1950, that I stopped being a Slovak bourgeois nationalist and instead became a cosmo-

* In 1969 Husak became First Secretary of the Czechoslovak Communist Party as successor to Alexander Dubcek. He and Novomesky, a leading Slovak poet, were sentenced to long prison terms in the 1950's as "bourgeois nationalists."

** Rajk, a leading Hungarian Communist, headed the list of defendants in the 1949 Hungarian treason trials, who were executed.

*** A Deputy Foreign Minister and defendant in the Slansky trial.—*Ed.*

politan of Jewish-bourgeois origins and a member of Slansky's treasonable group, which in turn became the "treasonable Center of Conspirators" about a year later.

It is interesting how the concept of the Slovak bourgeois nationalists came into being and also the charges brought against Slansky. They always started with an idea and it then became the task of the interrogators to make the prisoner adjust his testimony to the idea. Let me give an example.

Toward the end of 1947 Slansky sent for me and told me that the Party suspected that Ripka might be an American agent. At this time I was head of a department in Ripka's ministry and so I asked what conclusions I was to draw from this. Slansky replied that he thought I ought to go on working with Ripka as before. He had only told me of their suspicions in order that I be careful. He added that Gottwald, as head of the Government, also intended to continue working with Ripka. In fact they still reckoned with Ripka politically, but no longer trusted him.

The first version of the charge against me was that although Secretary-General Slansky had drawn my attention to the fact that Ripka was an American agent, I had continued to work with him, had informed him of all steps taken by the Party, and thus enabled him to take measures harmful to the Party. Furthermore, on his orders, I had entered into an espionage relationship with the Anglo-American secret service and slanted the Czechoslovak economy in such a way that would make it dependent on the West. Finally, I was preparing for the restoration of capitalism in Czechoslovakia.

When they were preparing to arrest Slansky [apparently in 1951], they altered the accusation against me to the following: Having learned that Ripka had been unmasked, Slansky had sent for me in order to inform me of this. He wished to warn me as his accomplice to be more careful in working with Ripka so that no suspicion should fall on me and thus on him, Slansky.

As I was supposed to be the agent of Field and Tito, I was not allotted to any group. The day I was arrested, they also arrested Vilem Novy * as an agent for Field. I have the impression that, because of the Rajk trial in Hungary, they had to prove that Field's group and the Titoists were at work in Czechoslovakia too. There was talk of this in the Rajk trial. I suppose, too, that they had to make scapegoats of those who were in a position where their relations with Field and Yugoslavia could be twisted to look like activities inimical to the interests of Czechoslovakia.

This was a phase when their accusations were all of anti-Czechoslovak activity. In the second phase they were concerned with imaginary groups and, in their more drastic form, crimes against the Soviet Union. In the third phase, that of the Slansky Center Group, they were solely concerned with the interests of the Soviet Union as seen by Stalin and Beria. The Teachers left me in no doubt that my chief crime was that I had tried to thwart the interests of the Soviet Union, thus implying that the interests of Czechoslovakia were identical in all matters with those of the Soviet Union.

The first phase, according to them: Field, acting for foreign intelligence services, had recruited future agents among the refugees, including me. As a leading official of the wartime and postwar Ministry of Reconstruction and the one in charge of UNRRA** affairs, I had made it possible for UNRRA to open an office in Prague and there build up an espionage network. This organization had simultaneously sought to tie the Czechoslovak economy to the imperialist West. Finally, I was accused of having

* At the time of his arrest Editor-in-Chief of the Communist Party daily newspaper *Rude Právo—Ed.*

**United Nations Relief and Rehabilitation Administration.

made the acquaintance of Ripka, Benes's * closest collaborator, in London, become his friend, and undertaken to do treasonable work for him.

The essence of these accusations was repeated in my indictment at the trial, though only as background material. The prominent members of the Party (and obviously of the Government) were very well aware that the Party had issued instructions that we should co-operate with Field. All members of the Party hierarchy who had been in England maintained contact with Field, especially Nosek and Anezka Hodinova-Spurna. Similarly, both the Party and the Government must have known that the head of UNRRA, Piotr Alexeyev, was a Soviet citizen. Alexeyev had been nominated by the Soviet Government and, as they knew, I had found it difficult to get him accepted as head of the Mission. Another thing that people in those spheres knew was that UNRRA had given us goods in the value of about 15 billion crowns [$300 million]. Nor could these people fail to know that regular political councils had been held in Ripka's apartment in London, in which Jaroslav Stransky, Antonin Uhlir, the Czech National Socialist Deputy. Julius Firt, and sometimes Dr. Ivo Duchacek took part. The Party had delegated Nosek to be in charge of our deliberations, with Hodinova-Spurna, and, if I remember rightly, Josef Valo, Bohuslav Lastovicka, and myself. Thus my relations with Ripka and my collaboration with him had been in accordance with the Party line.

Vladimir Clementis and the Slovak Bourgeois Nationalists

During one nocturnal interrogation in December, 1949, the Teachers told me to tell them about my criminal rela-

*Eduard Benes had been prewar President of Czechoslovakia and resumed his position in 1941 while in exile in England. He retained that title until his resignation in 1948.—*Ed.*

tions with the Anglo-American agent, Vladimir Clementis.

Sometime at the end of September or in early October, 1948, Frejka, who was one of those closest to Gottwald, had sent for me and told me in strict confidence that Andrei Vyshinsky, then Foreign Minister of the Soviet Union, had complained to Gottwald about Clementis's behavior. When I asked what this meant, Frejka told me that he did not know anything concrete and that he had only mentioned the matter because he knew that Clementis and I were friends. A few days later André Simone* told me that the head of the Foreign Section of the Central Committee of the Czechoslovak Communist Party, Bedrich Geminder, had told him that Vyshinsky had raised serious objections to Clementis.

This means that at a time when Clementis was representing his country at the United Nations in his capacity as Foreign Minister of the independent Republic of Czechoslovakia, he was to all intents and purposes being condemned to death in the capital of his own country.

During this and subsequent interrogations the Teachers kept harping on the fact that Clementis had criticized the 1939 Soviet-German Non-Aggression Pact and the Soviet-Finnish war. At this stage there had not yet been any mention of a Slovak nonsocialist nationalist group. Clementis was called a Benes agent who was supposed to have worked with me, the agent of Ripka. Early in January, 1950, or perhaps somewhat later, the idea of the Slovak bourgeois nationalists was thought up. Among other things this concept made it possible to disguise the part played by Vyshinsky and thus the fact that in reality Stalin had never forgiven Clementis for criticizing his policy.

There will be no need to deal further with the case of the Slovak nonsocialist nationalists, or to say how absurd

*The Foreign Editor of the Communist daily *Rude Pravo* and later a defendant in the Slansky Trial—*Ed.*

the accusations leveled at Clementis and the other "Slovak nonsocialist nationalists" were.

I was told to detail all my conversations with Clementis in London. Among others I mentioned one that I had had with him at dinner in a London restaurant. Clementis told me he had heard that the Slovak fascist radio * was exploiting an incident alleged to have taken place in the little town of Mikulas and making a big propaganda campaign out of it. Apparently when the Germans retook Mikulas in 1944 they were told about a respected Slavophile family that had invited some Soviet officers to supper. During the meal the lights were suddenly extinguished and the hostess was raped. Clementis was wondering how to reply to this sort of propaganda. He was afraid that the Slovaks would be touchy and react, and thus took the view that we dare not remain silent.

This conversation, with Clementis's wife the only other person present, could neither have been overheard, nor, if it had been, understood, as we spoke Slovak. Nonetheless, they made an offense of our meeting. Translated into Beria jargon it took this form: In a public place Clementis had repeated and propagated the hostile propaganda of the Slovak fascist government.

I have already said that the Center was a later invention. In this Clementis was made the representative of the Slovak bourgeois nationalists. The Slovak group itself was brought to trial at a time when Beria had already been liquidated in the Soviet Union and the duties of the Beria men in Czechoslovakia had been taken over entirely by their Czechoslovak colleagues.

How I "Unmasked" Slansky

At the beginning of January, 1953, the Ministry of Justice published *The Proceedings of the Trial of the*

*Slovakia had been proclaimed an "independent" Republic under Hitler's personal protection in March, 1939.—*Ed.*

Leaders of the Conspiratorial Center Headed by Slansky. Not everything that was said at the trial appears in the printed *Proceedings.* Many of the things I said have not been included and I take it that this was also the case with the testimony of the other accused. What has been published, however, was said at the trial.

The printed *Proceedings* end with the pronouncement of sentence and do not include any statement of the reasons for passing it. What the President of the court actually said in substantiation of the sentence imposed on me and why it was one of "only" life imprisonment was, above all, because my confession had helped to unmask Slansky. As a result it had been possible to prevent further damage being done to the nation. This is why I feel that I must explain how I unmasked Slansky.

Sometime in March, 1951, when I had already confessed to all the crimes they recounted and these had been duly listed, Kohoutek sent for me and told me that he was unable to accept my confession as I had kept quiet about the most important crime of all: my collaboration with the Party's arch enemy, the imperialist agent Slansky. I had thought that nothing could surprise me any longer, but this bewildered me. Until then, they had never missed an opportunity of emphasizing that I had been arrested with the consent of Gottwald and Slansky. Now, suddenly, Slansky had become not only an imperialist agent, but also my accomplice. Seeing how surprised I was, Kohoutek telephoned the Teachers and they instructed him to take a statement from me about this treasonable collaboration. Kohoutek tipped the receiver in my direction so that I could hear every word the Teachers said. He assured me that the Teachers would never require such a statement from me if Slansky were not already in fact convicted and so I need not be afraid. Slansky would be arrested shortly and my confession concerning him would be to my advantage, as I would then cease to head the list of the accused.

They had lined up a bevy of arrested members of the Politburo, Ministers, and members of the Central Committee; a deputy minister was no longer a major attraction.

I was well aware of the dreadful situation I was in. I knew nothing about Slansky, not even anything that could be twisted to his disadvantage. All matters of the economy had come under Gottwald, and Slansky had never concerned himself with these problems. Only once or twice had I ever reported to him on economic matters. Otherwise I had only met him occasionally at receptions. I had never been in his home and I had no idea with whom he associated. What he did I knew only from the daily press; but I realized that if I did not make a statement I would again be subjected to the old torture of the "harsh regime" and so I asked for a day's time to think it over.

In the cell I debated with myself what I should do. Eventually I had an idea which I thought was a stroke of genius: I felt sure that Gottwald and the other members of the Politburo would see my statement, since it was certainly impossible to arrest the Secretary General of the Party without "proof," and the "proof" surely would be laid before the highest Party official. That meant that Gottwald would read my statement. This was an excellent opportunity to let him see that the confessions were extorted and that a trial was being prepared which would really be an indictment of the policy of the Party and Government, and above all of his own actions. I decided to make a statement in which I would detail conversations I had had with Gottwald. They were important enough for him to remember. However, in the statement I would say that I had had these discussions with Slansky and not with Gottwald.

I drew up a statement on Slansky's crimes and his criminal dealings with me. I stated that on the instructions and with the agreement of Slansky, I had conducted negotiations with the British and later with the American governments on compensation for property that had been nationalized. I brought in the agreement with Yugoslavia, that with the Soviet Union, and so on. In reality these were all discussions I had had with Gottwald, in some of which Dolansky, Kliment, Nosek, and Gregor had also taken part.* As these were problems of exceptional importance and had also needed the approval of a plenary session of the Government, Gottwald would necessarily realize that it was not Slansky but he with whom I had discussed them. This could leave him in no doubt that if there was any crime here it could only be a breach of the law committed by the interrogating body itself. Kohoutek accepted my statement and as the Teachers had nothing to object to, he told me solemnly that a number of statements, including mine, were being laid before Gottwald, along with an application for permission to arrest Slansky.

The next two or three weeks in prison were a "happy" time. Every time a guard approached my cell, I expected to see someone from the Central Committee come to apologize for what had happened and to see that my place in the cell was taken by Kohoutek and his men. Then, in the second half of April, Kohoutek sent for me again. In a voice full of emotion he told me that Gottwald and the Party leaders had taken note of my statement and that Slansky would shortly be arrested. Obviously, such a step required a certain amount of political preparation. However, he now wished to congratulate me on having helped to unmask Slansky. The Party would be grateful to me.

That was toward the end of April. Slansky was still Secretary General of the Party. His first step in the direction of prison was his self-criticism and his nomination as Deputy Premier of the Government. On July 21, 1951, the occasion of a festive celebration of his fiftieth birthday, his collected works were published. Gottwald and Anton

*See above, p. 33.—*Ed.*

Zapotocky* signed the declaration praising the services rendered by Slansky, devoted son of the proletariat and faithful member of the Party. Yet two months *previously* they had signed his death sentence.

It is more than probable that Gottwald must have known before Slansky's arrest that Slansky was not in any way culpable, but that it was rather his own actions, for which he was letting others pay the penalty, that were under indictment.

Harmful Activities

> I allied myself with the American spy and Zionist, Alexander Taub, whose acquaintance I had made in the summer of 1949 at the home of the Director-General of the KOVO,** [Frantisek] Fabinger. I knew from Taub that ever since 1946 he had been working with Fabinger and other harmful persons trying to tie Czechoslovak industry to the American monopolies; and to this end, on Fabinger's instructions, had worked out the so-called Taub Plan. . . . I knew from Taub that he was an official of General Motors in America and later adviser to the Chiang Kai-shek Government. (*Proceedings of the Trial*, p. 389.)

The negotiations with Fabinger were concerned with the erection of a modern automobile factory to export the most successful Czechoslovak private car, the eight-cylinder Tatra. This model was to be modernized and produced on assembly lines. We were planning to produce, if I remember correctly, between 200,000 and 300,000 cars per

*Later to be Gottwald's successor as President of Czechoslovakia 1953–1957. He became Prime Minister in 1948 when Gottwald succeeded to the presidency, and prior to that was head of the trade unions.—*Ed.*

**KOVO was the machine tool industry.

year. Production was to start in 1951. The prospects were excellent. America was to sell us a complete sheet-metal rolling mill. We had an agreement for the supply of a complete factory worth $8 million for making tires. Apart from the home market, there were unlimited possibilities for selling the cars on exceptionally favorable conditions in the European market. We had every chance to become one of the big European car-producing countries, with the automobile industry providing us optimal variants in our production structure.

PROCURATOR: You assisted English capitalists to the detriment of the Czechoslovak economy. How was that?

LOEBL: This occurred when a credit was arranged with the owner of a banking house and director of the Bank of England, Sir [Charles] Hambro. . . . I then allied myself with Hambro and its director, and we agreed on the granting of a credit of £ 1,000,000. . . . This was to make it possible for the City [London's financial center] to control and influence Czechoslovak trade and thus tie the Czechoslovak economy to Great Britain. This credit was disadvantageous not only because of the high rate of interest, but also because it enabled Hambro to keep a check on and influence the foreign trade of Czechoslovakia. For that reason the National Bank had protested against our taking the credit, but I succeeded in pushing it through. (*Proceedings of the Trial*, p. 392.)

What really happened was this: the Czechoslovak Government had concluded arrangements with the British Government for a £ 15,000,000 loan. Despite this agreement, the British Government reacted to our nationalization by reducing the credit to £ 5,000,000. However, we needed the credit and at the same time we were concerned with putting an end to the wave of discrimination and cancellation of business both by governments and private concerns. I discussed the situation with Gottwald and suggested trying to arrange a credit with a City banking house. He thought this was an excellent idea as it would not only demonstrate that this important center of international finance was interested in having trade relations with Czechoslovakia, but also that even after nationalization the Czechoslovak economy was to be trusted.

The Supreme Court referred to this point of the indictment in its reasoned argument for annulling my sentence:*

> The experts are of the opinion that this issue cannot be considered in isolation but only as part of the whole economic situation of the day. This was the period after 1945, when the reconstruction of our economy called for considerably more pounds than the [British] Government credit of five million that had been granted us. For this credit of one million pounds given by the firm in question it was possible to import [iron] pyrites and other important raw materials that our economy needed. Quite apart from this, the credit in question was approved by high Government quarters. In the opinion of the experts the interest on this loan was not higher than what is usual for bank credits.
>
> Thus the accused Loebl was not guilty of a culpable act in this instance either. The accused's defense is that this credit was of great importance for our economy and that he himself had no influence on the conditions on which the agreement was made, and negotiations on this aspect being conducted by members of the Ministry of Finance, the Zivnostenska Bank, and the National Bank, is also confirmed.

Even the export of artificial flowers to the U.S., based on an agreement made by representatives of Centrotex and

*See pp. 295–318 for the text of the Court's "Rehabilitation Statement."

the New York firm of Tirax, was blamed on me as a detrimental act. The Supreme Court has this to say about it:

> The mere fact that this was an agreement between States and was concluded on March 20, 1950, while the accused, Loebl, had been arrested on November 24, 1949, shows that the accused could not have had a hand in anything but the preliminaries to it.
>
> Centrotex's agency in the U.S. was short-lived. It was to have sold artificial flowers, a very advantageous export article. The transaction was part of the so-called dollar offensive. On the evidence available the experts are of the opinion that the idea of selling artificial flowers to the U.S. was good, but that there were deficiencies in the personnel chosen to do it. Questions of personnel, however, were the concern of Centrotex, which had full responsibility for concluding and carrying out the agreement.
>
> Thus no criminal responsibility for contingent damage incurred when the agreement was reached in March, 1950, that is after the arrest of the accused, Loebl, can be attributed to him.

Another accusation was the export to Great Britain of television tubes, something that I had initiated. Of this the Supreme Court said:

> The experts have stated that the export of TV tubes was in no way harmful, but on the contrary advantageous because they were produced from domestic raw materials. There was no need to refuse it on strategic grounds as is proved by the fact that the first refusal of permission for their export made by the Ministry of Defense was gone into thoroughly and, on November 3, 1950, withdrawn. This, then, is another case where no damage was inflicted on our economy.

On Zionism

> In trade negotiations with capitalist states I concluded commercial agreements that were favorable to capitalist, above all Jewish merchants, but disadvantageous to the Republic. (*Proceedings of the Trial*, p. 373.)

It was common knowledge that trade agreements with capitalist countries in those days had the character of so-called quota agreements, that is to say, they fixed quotas for the goods involved. For example, if the arrangement was for the export of shoes to a value of 100 million crowns [$2 million], the capitalist state with which the agreement was being made undertook to grant importers licenses for this amount. Similarly, if we were importing cotton in the value of 100 million crowns, the country concerned undertook to grant its exporters export licenses in this amount. In these agreements nn mention was made of the prices or of the names of exporters and importers. Still less was there any question of the national "origins" of importers and exporters.

The indictment accused me of other Zionist sins, for example one which was known as operation Ueberall.

> In order to assist imperialism in the State of Israel, I tried to further the Ueberall Plan [Ehud Avriel Ueberall was Israeli ambassador in Prague]. With the help of Zionist organizations I tried to obtain credit from American Zionists which was to be used to increase production for and export to the West and so to channel the fruits of the labors of Czechoslovak industry to Israeli capitalism. (*Proceedings of the Trial*, p. 373.)

This also was clearly connected with the so-called "dollar offensive" aimed at increasing exports of the products of our light industries to the U.S. By doing this I was supposed to be trying to "tie the Czechoslovak economy to the West." (*Proceedings*, p. 373.) The facts are as follows:

The Soviet Union was the first major power to recognize the newly formed State of Israel and the U.N. actively advocated that other countries do the same. In harmony with the Soviet policy, Czechoslovakia recognized the State of Israel and granted it comprehensive aid, including munitions. I remember that in 1945 the head of the export department of Zbrojovka [arms factory] came to see me in the Ministry of Foreign Trade and suggested that we should export a whole arms factory to Egypt. Such an action required the approval of three ministries: the Foreign Ministry, the Defense Ministry, and the Ministry of Foreign Trade. Zbrojovka's director recommended that it be approved as the price was good and Egypt was ready to pay in dollars. The Defense Ministry had no objections to the plan, and I asked Clementis about the attitude of the Foreign Ministry. Clementis replied that Andrei Vyshinsky, the Soviet Foreign Minister, was stopping at Prague on his way back to Moscow and that he was going to meet him at the airport to ask him the position of the Soviet Union. After his talk with Vyshinsky, Clementis told me that Vyshinsky had refused to hear anything about it. Thus the Foreign Ministry would not give such a project its approval.

The Soviet Union's policy toward Israel earned it the sympathy of American Jewry, which also appeared inclined to support trade relations with Czechoslovakia. Our concern was to use their sympathy to aid the export of glass, jewelry, porcelain, and other consumer goods. It appeared there was a possibility of obtaining a credit for the expansion and modernization of the production of these items.

This was a favorable opportunity to obtain a footing in the American market. It meant exporting articles made from the raw materials kaolin, coal, and salt which we had in our own country. The conditions were all there for taking advantage of the opportunity. The Japanese and Germans were unable to compete and Czechoslovakia had almost a monopoly position in the American market. We were in a position to select the best of the representatives. In the same year, 1949, we arranged a big exhibition of Sklo-Export, the export branch of the glass industry, and we were anticipating an annual export of $100 million in glass and jewelry alone.

After this effort had been "unmasked" as a Zionist attempt to tie the Republic's economy to the imperialist West, the Ministry of Foreign Trade canceled the contracts and as a result had to pay tens of thousands of dollars in compensation. It goes without saying that we thereby lost the American market for our country's traditional and most profitable export.

The Supreme Court referred to the dollar offensive in my rehabilitation as follows:

> The experts examined this case in detail and commented on its wider implications. They showed that fundamentally there were three possibilities of overcoming the difficult situation caused by a shortage of dollars which were needed for buying in foreign markets. However, they came to the conclusion that the procedure that was chosen at the time was the only one possible and economically the right one.

A further case of Zionism was my detrimental action in arranging for the Koh-i-noor factory to export a complete pencil-manufacturing plant to Israel, where a special company was to be set up to run it. The plant was not to be paid for in foreign exchange, but in shares of this company. The charge was that the plant was needed for producing pencils in Czechoslovakia:

PROCURATOR: I have here a report dealing with your being concerned in the construction of a pencil factory in Israel. The report concludes by saying: "Eight Czechoslovak citizens who intended to emigrate to Israel were trained for three months . . . in the national undertaking Koh-i-noor. They were to be trained in the manufacture of spare, refill leads in which our pencil factories have exceptionally valuable experience. The diligence of the workers prevented this. Ten pencil-making machines had been readied to be sent to Israel and it was only the intervention of the workers and thanks to their vigilance, that the machines were prevented from being sent off, despite all the efforts of the evil men." (*Proceedings*, p. 391.)

The Supreme Court's reversal of my conviction was based on the following summary:

The erection of a pencil factory in Israel was indeed planned. Negotiations took place between 1947 and 1949 and the Party's Economic Commission and the National Bank gave their provisional approval of the project. In March, 1949, however, the Ministry of Industry refused to grant an export license. Minutes of a conference held in the Ministry of Industry on May 13, 1949, show that final approval was refused on the intervention of the accused Loebl, who would not permit the export of the machinery in question from the Czechoslovak Republic. This confirms the defense of the accused Loebl of April 17, 1963, in which he stated that his provisional approval of the project was given in the belief that the machines concerned were surplus and that, when he learned that this was not the case, he refused to allow the deal to go through.

Another pro-Zionist action on my part was the agreement with Israel:

I conferred with Ueberall on how we could misuse the agreement then being prepared with the State of Israel to the advantage of the Zionist organization. The essence of our plan was that only part of the goods exported from Czechoslovakia to Israel should be paid for in foreign exchange, the rest being paid out of the assets of Czechoslovak Zionist emigrants . . . still in Czechoslovakia. . . . To the extent that the National Bank, instead of receiving everything in foreign exchange, with which the Czechoslovak Republic could have imported various products it needed, received payment for a certain proportion of the amount due from the State of Israel out of the assets of Czechoslovak citizens who had emigrated to Israel; in this way the foreign exchange resources of Czechoslovakia suffered damage to the extent of the quota. (*Proceedings*, p. 390.)

I was arrested in November, 1949. The agreement with Israel was concluded in March, 1950, and I only heard of its existence in 1951 when I was in prison. The Supreme Court referred to the matter as follows:

The very fact that the Treaty between the two states was concluded on March 20, 1950, and the accused Loebl was arrested on November 24, 1949, show that Loebl could not have been concerned with more than the preliminaries.

It was in fact four months after my arrest that the Minister of Foreign Trade, Antonin Gregor, concluded the agreement and put it before the Government, which ratified it.

Preparations for the Trial

Paradoxical as it may sound, completion of the final set of questions and answers was an occasion for relief for the prisoner, for it meant that his detention for interrogation, with its "harsh treatment," was almost over. It also meant the end of solitary confinement. After three years of interrogation and solitary confinement any change was welcome.

It was the job of the interrogators to assemble all one's admissions and organize them into the material for the final set of questions and answers. The Teachers worked out the entire draft of the trial and designated the parts to be played in it by the various "actors." Kohoutek informed me about the structure of the trial and the part I was to play. As the intellectual level of the interrogators was such that they were unlikely to produce even a half-serviceable final draft of questions and answers, Kohoutek asked me to prepare it myself. He told me this was what the other accused were doing. In the peculiar state of mind I was in, I did not feel irritated by the ridiculous, degrading role I thereby assumed, as their method had one great advantage for me.

Kohoutek and the Teachers were content with general admissions of guilt. They were quite satisfied if, for example, I stated that I had betrayed information that was secret. They were not interested in details. Thus I was able to say that I had given *The Times* (London) correspondent, Godfrey Lias, information "about the negotiations and conclusion of trade agreements with Sweden and Poland, about how much iron ore we imported from the Soviet Union, and about the various problems of the Two- and Five-Year Plans. (*Proceedings*, p. 382.)

Naturally, there had been nothing secret about the negotiations with the Swedish Government and reports about them had been published regularly in the Swedish press. I conducted negotiations with Poland in 1947 and the result was published both in Poland and in Czechoslovakia. The amounts of iron ore imported by us from the Soviet Union were discussed in a series of articles that appeared in the Czechoslovak press on the subject of the Czechoslovak-Soviet Agreement. In the same way, the Two- and Five-Year Plans were subjects which the press discussed regularly. Thus it was possible to confess and at the same time make nonsense of the confession.

The Supreme Court, in its 1963 judgment reversing the verdicts of the 1952 trial, criticized the Court responsible for being content to accept general declarations:

> In most cases they are statements full of phrases (the accused speak of themselves solely as hardened enemies, spies, and saboteurs of our system); any information that was to be passed to anyone termed a spy thus became an intelligence report, without any attempt being made to examine its contents; any concrete economic measure in the implementation of which the accused were concerned and which was regarded as a mistake was presented as a deliberately damaging act and thus these cases were not examined in their context.

This statement applies to the testimony of all the accused. In prison we thought it probable that this was something that anyone would recognize and that would make people see the trial in its true light. Also, I had hoped that by confessing more I would make top Government and Party officials see how baseless the accusations were. Thus, for example, I admitted having espionage dealings with a Labor member of the British Parliament, Konni Zilliacus, whom I had never seen. Zilliacus reacted as I had hoped, denying this both in the press and on the British radio.

When our sets of questions and answers came to be co-ordinated, all statements about each fact were compared to make sure there were no discrepancies as to time, etc., and that one statement properly supplemented the other. If anything in my answers was in any way contradictory, I was presented with the testimony of all the others. The greater the lie in the first place, the more scrupulous they were about its form. After co-ordination the questions and answers were all translated into Russian and submitted to the Teachers, and I saw them myself. Any comments by the Teachers had to be accepted. In my case this meant working through my testimony an additional four times. The Teachers wanted something left out, or something put differently, or an amplification. No set of questions and answers could lack anything the Teachers considered necessary, just as they could not contain anything which they did not approve.

When the final version had been fixed, we had to learn our questions and answers by heart. Having written them myself, I found this easy. When I had done so, I was tested twice a day, before and after dinner. The interrogator read out the question while I stood as if in the dock and gave my answers. As I have already mentioned, the interrogator was at pains to see that my delivery was what was wanted. Kohoutek, too, observed almost every day, for he was the "producer" and had to be sure of the quality of the performance.

Another sign that solitary confinement was almost over and the trial in the offing was the change in our treatment. I was now taken for exercise twice a day for nearly an hour each time. Our food now came from the Security Service people's own canteen. We now had a salami sandwich in the mid-morning and afternoon, and our two main meals consisted of three ample courses. A few of the prisoners who looked especially ill were given milk, and some of them were even put on a special diet to gain weight. Dr. Somer now actually became solicitous, checking our blood pressure at regular intervals, prescribing sleeping pills, and, at the least suggestion of indisposition, plying one with medicine. In this way, the traces of detention under hard treatment were partially removed. The day sentence was passed on us, we were off the special diets and back on the old regime.

Before the trial, the president of the Court, Jaroslav Novak, came to see me in Ruzyne Prison. He presented me with the state attorney's application for me to be placed under detention for interrogation, adding that I had twenty-four hours in which to appeal. That was when I had already been under arrest for three years.

Dr. Novak also asked me whom I would like to suggest to defend me. I replied that this was quite pointless. I did not want counsel. He told me that the law required me to be defended and that he was appointing a Dr. Vojtech Posmura, whom I met a few days later in the prison office. Our talk took place in the presence of my interrogators. Dr. Posmura had my "questions and answers" lying in front of him on the table and asked me if I had signed the document, and if that meant that I approved it. Did I wish to adduce any mitigating circumstances? The whole thing lasted ten minutes.

A few days before the trial, I was taken to the Governor's office in the prison. As Lieutenant Drozd removed the blindfold from my eyes, I saw that Karel Bacilek, Minister of State Security, was sitting behind the desk. He was wearing the uniform of a general. He told me that he had read my "statement" and then added: "You must realize that this is a political trial and that everything depends on what you say to the Court in agreement with this document."

Such a threat was completely unnecessary. I had no intention of altering anything. However, I wanted him to realize that this was not my testimony, but that of his

Service. That was quite unnecessary as he must have been fully aware of the fact. Anyway, I said to him: "That I have given this testimony is thanks to your interrogation system." His expression gave no clue as to whether or not this had hit home or how he took it. Later, our press reported him as having said, in his capacity as Minister of State Security, that most of the credit for unmasking Slansky and his band was due to Antonin Novotny.*

The Court

The trial began on November 20, 1952. I was awakened at 4 A.M. and dressed in civilian clothes. Then, one by one, we defendants were taken out to a bus in such a way that we could not see one another and had no opportunity of communicating. The bus had a passage down the middle with cells on either side in which we were enclosed. The cells were small and you could only sit in them. In the prison yard, where the bus was standing, there were on duty several dozen armed men of the Security Corps. Three armed Security people traveled in the bus itself. Even so, they thought it necessary to handcuff us. When we got to the yard of Pankrac Prison we were led one by one out of the bus and into cells. The great prison yard swarmed with armed men and armored cars. We each had a cell and here the armed guards were on duty not in the corridor, but in the cell itself—even at night.

Adjacent to the large room in which the trial was held was a long corridor in which each of the accused had a

*At the time Secretary of the Prague Communist Party and shortly afterward Slansky's successor as Secretary-General of the Communist Party. Novotny became Prime Minister and on Zapotocky's death President of Czechoslovakia. He held his party post until his removal on January 5, 1968, and the Presidency a few weeks longer.—*Ed.*

"cell," made of two plank partitions. In each "cell" were two chairs, one for the accused and the other for his interrogator, who never left his charge's side. In the corridor itself were Kohoutek and Doubek and a number of high officials including Dr. Somer and a nurse. What went on in this corridor was even more fantastic than the trial itself.

When he began his final address the Chief Prosecutor said: "Never yet have our people's democratic courts had to try such criminals as these who sit here in the dock today and on whom you are to pass judgment." (*Proceedings*, p. 598.) That really was saying something! Our Courts had already tried cases involving Gestapo men, traitors, denouncers, and collaborators. Yet, even though we were worse than these, the moment we left the Court and were back in the corridor we were treated as if we were national heroes. We were given black coffee and at 10 A.M. they gave us sausage, ham, and salami, brought us lemonade, offered us cigarettes; and the touchingly solicitous Dr. Somer checked our blood pressure. Kohoutek and Doubek went from cell to cell chatting with the accused as if we were about to be rehabilitated.

After each interrogation of one of the accused, the quality of his performance was the subject of lively discussion in the corridor. An interrogator whose charge had acquitted himself well regarded this as his own achievement and there was animated discussion as to which of the accused had said his piece best. On the whole the interrogators were satisfied; the only exception being Otto Sling's.* Sling had had a slight mishap. We prisoners were not allowed either belts or suspenders and although we had been fattened up none of us had achieved the waist measurements we used to have; thus while Sling was making his rueful confession in the dock his trousers slid down,

*Otto Sling was formerly Regional Secretary of the Communist Party in Brno.—*Ed.*

leaving him standing in his white underpants. The proceedings had to be interrupted and they now suspected Sling of purposely allowing it to happen to make the Court appear ridiculous. That, of course, was a bad mark against his interrogator.

The trial had other unusual elements. The judge and prosecutor had our written questions and answers in front of them. They asked each question in the exact wording of the document. They at least had the advantage of not having to learn them by heart as the accused had to, but were able to read them. Judge and prosecutor had decided beforehand which questions each was going to ask, so they all knew exactly where they were. The defending counsel also had a copy of this document in front of him, and could check that both prosecutor and judge stuck to the questions worked out by the Security Service and that his "client's" testimony agreed with that in the written answers.

As the questions and answers had in fact been composed by the accused themselves, you had a situation in which the accused in fact had told the judges and prosecutors what to ask them. The trial was perfectly prepared; even before it began, all the questions, the answers, and even the judgment had been settled.

The Defense Counsel

My defense counsel could not have known enough to be able to point out that the great majority of accusations against me were actions taken on the instructions of the Government. As a trained lawyer, however, he must have been able to see that the proceedings violated a number of laws. Apart from what the Supreme Court had to say in my later rehabilitation trial, from which I have already quoted, there were basic, primitive violations of the law. To quote the Supreme Court:

The Court should not have overlooked the fact that although the accused Loebl had been under detention for three years prior to the trial there was only one statement in the record of his examination, namely that of November 7, 1952, that is to say two weeks before the trial; and this being of 57 pages could not possibly have been obtained in the course of one day.

Elsewhere it states that the Court was in error in calling my actions criminal treason, espionage, and sabotage under §1, §5, and §36 of Law 231/48, since this law only came into force on October 14, 1948, while the actions complained of had, according to the Court, been committed from 1945 on, that is to say, before the law came into force.

Further, according to the laws under which the charges were made, the maximum sentence the Court should have inflicted on me for the crimes of which I was accused was ten years.

Dr. Posmura's defense is scarcely distinguishable from the prosecution's accusation. This is what he said:

> The accused, Loebl, began preparations for his hostile endeavors against the popular democratic regime during the war in London, where he received the direct support of the [Party's] Economic Commission of which Frejka and others were members. The accused has stated that he let himself be guided by his bourgeois-nationalist attitude and dislike of anything that could be called progress. With these aims and views it was natural for Loebl to ally himself with other conspirators like Frejka and, above all, with the head of the conspiracy, Slansky.
>
> Loebl admits knowing that Slansky was as great an enemy of the Communist Party of Czechoslovakia and of the popular-democratic system as he was. He has admitted his guilt frankly and spontaneously and has

never tried to hush it up or to excuse it. His testimony shows that he too subordinated himself to Slansky's guidance.

The 20th Soviet Party Congress and Beyond

About September, 1955, and thus still before the 20th Soviet Party Congress, two officers visited me in the hospital of Pankrac Prison. They introduced themselves as assistants of the Procurator-General and explained that they had come to discover the truth about the interrogatory methods used and also whether I really felt myself to be guilty. At last! My hopes were to be fulfilled after all. The truth was to come out!

With my knowledge of prison matters and methods of interrogation acquired over the years, I realized that the investigation must be very well advanced indeed and that in fact the Procurator-General must already know everything. The two men inquired if I had been interrogated by foreigners, whether they had spoken Ukrainian or Russian, what the Russian-speaking one had looked like, what he had said in Russian. They even repeated one or two remarks that I had made to Kohoutek and from this and other indications I concluded that Kohoutek and Doubek must already have confessed to the use of illegal interrogation methods.

I was given a typewriter and wrote a statement of eighty pages detailing all the methods of interrogation and comparing what I had confessed to with what had actually taken place. (Three years after my rehabilitation I asked the Procurator-General for a copy of my statement, but never got it.)

We had several talks. The two men were very friendly and spirited and seemed convinced of what they were saying. They gave the impression that they were happy to be able to uncover injustice and correct it. They told me that this was a big affair that called for a great deal of "burrowing" and so I would have to remain patient. Meanwhile, they would have me sent to a sort of "superprison," where I could await the solution of the whole affair while convalescing.

On the last occasion on which I saw them, which must have been toward the end of October, 1955, they were utterly despondent. There was no more talk of any superprison, nor of convalescence. They questioned me on a few details in my statement, during which one of them stressed his loyalty to the Party, remarking: "Whatever happens now, whatever they accuse me of, even if it means the grave, I shall remain loyal to the Party."

I only understood what the man had meant by this when I got to the camp near Pribam, where 1,500 political prisoners were kept behind barbed wire. He had meant that there was to be no superprison, no burrowing, no rehabilitation. That, however, does not alter the fact that months before the 20th Party Congress [February, 1956] the Procurator-General was already in possession of proof that there had never been a Center of conspirators.

At the time of the 20th Party Congress I was in the Vojna Camp in the district of Pribam. Here we mined uranium ore—which figured in one of the points in my indictment! The majority of the prisoners were intellectuals. Some of us worked the day shift and so had contact with civilians and thus were well informed about how people who were free reacted to the news about the 20th Party Congress. We received newspapers regularly and the 7 P.M. news was broadcast over loudspeakers every day. We were thus quite well informed and our hopes had begun to rise.

Having heard Novotny's first speech after the 20th Party Congress, we all expected that there would be fundamental changes and a rectification of political distortions, but our hopes were soon dashed. In April or May Viliam

Siroky * was interviewed by foreign journalists and the broadcast was relayed throughout the camp. In this interview Siroky said that Hajdu and London would be rehabilitated. When the Reuters correspondent asked if they were going to rehabilitate me, Siroky did not reply. When asked what was to happen to the political prisoners he said that there weren't any in Czechoslovakia, only lawbreakers.

The inmates of Vojna Camp reacted in a unique way: they failed to turn up for the night shift. When the overseer demanded an explanation, they told him that they did not exist; they had just heard the Prime Minister himself say so.

It was obvious that the changes resulting from the 20th Party Congress were being sabotaged all along the line and events confirmed this. It is quite false to say that the uprising in Hungary [October, 1956] halted the process of rehabilitation. For the prisoners—above all to the Communists—it was clear after only a few weeks of relatively liberal action that things became stricter than ever and we were subjected to the severe concentration camp regime. Things were made even stricter for us following the outbreak of resistance in Hungary. However, the events in Hungary caused a rapprochement between the bulk of the guards and the conservative prisoners. Their attitude toward the Communist prisoners was very unpleasant, to say the least. They studiously put a distance between themselves and the Communist prisoners as though trying to establish a last-minute alibi. Some of us were removed to the Ilava Prison on the grounds that we constituted a "dangerous element." You could now see the true political and moral quality of these small Sejnas ** in the Security

*Prime Minister at the time.—*Ed.*

**General Jan Sejna was head of the Communist Party cell in the Ministry of Defense. After the criticism of Novotny began to mount in the fall of 1967, he actively sought Soviet aid against

Service uniform. There was no doubt which direction they would have taken if the same thing had happened in Czechoslovakia as in Hungary.

From Ilava Prison my odyssey took me to Bory near Pilsen and from there, one day at the beginning of May, I was taken in a bus to Bratislava, handcuffed and crouching in a little cell. Three days later the Security Service took me to my apartment and handed me over to my wife, in the literal sense of the word.

That play was over. I was free and allowed to exercise my skill as warehouseman, handing out pencils, packing paper, string, and such for the modest wage of 1040 crowns [about $21] a month. This I did until the 13th Party Congress of the Czechoslovak Communist Party, which took place in 1963, seven years after the Russian Party's 20th Party Congress.

I suppose you could call it a mini-rehabilitation. Most of us, however, remained in some form of detention. It was not until May, 1963, that the Supreme Court in Prague reversed the lower court's conviction and pronounced me innocent of the charges:

> The testimony of B.D. [Doubek], who between 1949 and 1953 was one of the heads of the Security Service, given to officers of the Procurator-General during the proceedings against him, convinced the Court that in reality no such hostile Center ever existed, that it was a fiction worked out by the Security Service for which they used testimony extorted by illegal means from persons already under arrest. According to B.D.'s testimony these illegal methods took the form of exerting mental and physical pressure on those who would not admit offenses until they gave in and were prepared to admit whatever their interrogators wanted them to say;

---

the liberal elements in the Communist Party. He later fled to West Germany and then to the U.S.—*Ed.*

the interrogators drew up the record of the examination of an arrested person in advance, the statements the accused made in Court were prepared by their interrogators prior to the trial, and the accused, including the accused Loebl, signed these and had to learn them by heart and repeat them in Court. Measures were taken to ensure that there should be no attempt to deviate from this testimony on any essential point. The accused Loebl, who in the early stages of his examination denied having committed any offense, had pressure put on him by means of a threat to illegally arrest his wife.

This is all confirmed by the testimony given by V.K. [Kohoutek] in the proceedings brought against him (and later in the joint proceedings brought against him and B.D.). V.K., a former official of the Security Service, was head of the group that examined a number of persons, including the accused Loebl, in connection with the so-called treasonable Center of conspiracy. He himself repeatedly interrogated Loebl, and he confirmed that illegal means were used in the examination of Loebl in order to obtain the testimony that was needed.

This testimony, given by former members of the Security Service, confirms the defense of the accused Loebl, especially the evidence produced subsequently in his appeal in 1961 for the case to be reopened, showing that the Security Service had extorted his testimony admitting treason, sabotage, and espionage by unlawful means. In view of this important evidence, the testimony of Loebl given during his examination and in Court cannot be considered trustworthy. It is not permissible as evidence in a court of law.

The same applies to the testimony of the other accused: Rudolf Slansky, Ludvik Frejka, and Rudolf Margolius,* which was produced as evidence in the case against

*Prior to his arrest also a Deputy Foreign Trade Minister.—*Ed.*

Loebl. The members of the Security Service we have mentioned stated that in these cases too the same or similar methods of interrogation had been employed, so that their testimony is also inadmissible as evidence.

The testimony of B.D. has also made it clear to the Supreme Court that the opinion of the so-called Commission of Experts which was also produced as evidence for the prosecution against Loebl, was not objective. The reports by the experts were so composed that they could be used to bolster the fiction of a treasonable center of conspiracy and of the harm the accused were supposed to have inflicted on our State. They were so formulated as to avoid any possible contradiction between the experts' reports and the statements of either the accused or other witnesses. The falsity and lack of objectivity of these reports is also proven by the fact that they were not composed until after the conclusion of the examination, immediately prior to the trial. Had they wanted to get an objective picture of the state of affairs, once there was reason to suspect malpractices in the conduct of our foreign trade, in which the accused Loebl might be involved, they ought to have had each concrete case investigated by competent experts. Only then, on the basis of this expert opinion, were they entitled to draw conclusions as to the responsibility of Loebl. Here, of course, the accused, Loebl, ought to have been given the possibility to comment on the findings and inferences of such an appraisal and to put forward a defense.

Although it had been shown even before the 20th Party Congress that the entire trial was fraudulent, I and many others who had been sentenced to life imprisonment were not released until more than four years later and then only by reason of a general, conditional amnesty. Rehabilitation, modest as it was, did not come until 1963, that is seven years after it had been proved that the case against me was constructed on violations of the law. There is a piquant side to the picture: Doubek and Kohoutek were sentenced to eight years each, but were released after serving two years. Their victims had to wait two years longer before they were released.

It may be remembered that between 1956 and 1958, Novotny, the First Secretary of the Czechoslovak Communist Party and President of the Republic, repeatedly affirmed that the trial was conducted properly. He even put forward the theory that Slansky himself started to turn the wheels between which he eventually fell. In other words: the fault was not the murderer's, but that of the person murdered. There is a strange logic here.

Novotny must have known better than anyone that there was more to the trial than just violation of legality, that these violations had their definite causes: such courts, such a Security Service, such defense counsel, such prosecutors and expert witnesses, such a press and the political climate itself did not just suddenly happen and were not the fruit of any sort of cult. They reflected an entire system.

Anyone who had fought in the Spanish Civil War was a potential enemy, because he was a person who had demonstrated that he was prepared to risk his life for his ideals. The same was true for those who had fought in the Slovak National Rising during the occupation and also for all the Czech Resistance fighters. All who had lived in England were enemies, because they had there breathed the air of democracy. Any thinking intellectual was an enemy, especially one with guts. Suspect, too, were all who had belonged to the Party before the war, because the Party ideals were more important to them than propaganda phrases. As in all retrograde movements, anti-Semitism was made to play its part of "diverting the attention of the masses." If you were an old member of the Party and a Spanish Civil War man as well, or had taken part in the

Slovak Uprising, or were a "Londoner" and also of Jewish "origins," in all probability your sentence would already be in your file. There were many exceptions to this, it is true, but if Stalin had not died and Beria not been overthrown, how many trials would there have been? Several other trials were in preparation.

Once in 1951 while defending myself I said that I had done something or other in agreement with Siroky. Kohoutek remarked: "Who is Siroky anyway; do you think he's a lesser rogue than you?" To Kohoutek, Dolansky was a saboteur and my interrogator told me after the trial that Dolansky was going to be arrested in 1953. They already had statements dealing with the criminal activities of Zapotocky and Alexei Cepicka.* Artur London told me that he was questioned about Novotny, particularly about the latter's behavior in the Nazi concentration camp during the war. His interrogator had a substantial dossier in front of him. Not all these persons were to be arrested, it is true, but were held in check by means of the material. Judging by what London told me of Novotny's behavior, I imagine that this was the case with him.

Everyone who was to appear in the dock was put into a group: there was the group of the Spanish Civil War fighters, of the Slovak bourgeois nationalists, of the Londoners, of the prewar Communists, of the Jews.

All that was wrong cannot possibly be attributed solely to the judges, prosecutors, false testimony and opinion, because it has been shown that even they were manipulated.

The trial has not been honestly and unreservedly condemned; nor have we been fully rehabilitated. For this to happen it would inevitably have been necessary to disclose the true and primary reasons for all the things that were done. If the interests of a people are subordinated to foreign interests, it leads to an avalanche of tragedy, the extent and form of which is unpredictable.

*Minister of Justice and Gottwald's son-in-law.—*Ed.*

The entire trial was stage-managed by Beria's organization, which decided which members of our Government, of our prominent Party men, or Central Committee members were to be liquidated. The leading officials of our Party and State subordinated the interests of our Republic, the interests of our People, to the interests and wishes not even of the Soviet Union, but of Stalin, Beria, and their clique.

I suppose that honest friends of the Soviet Union may fear that to discuss these things openly now might adversely affect our attitude toward the USSR, but I believe that in thinking this they are underestimating the judgment and perspicacity of the Czechoslovak people.* When we began being critical of Soviet films and novels, etc., many of us felt that we might be harming the prestige of Soviet art. But the opposite was the case. Uncritical praise of what is of no artistic value has led to uncritical suspicion and even rejection of work that does have artistic value. In the same way the professional, uncritical apologists of the Soviet Union have made possible an equally uncritical acceptance of any calumny.

You cannot have human relationships without conflict. The same is true of relations between peoples and states. We would be badly underestimating the importance and enduring strength of our ties to the Soviet Union were we to fear a frank discussion that would clear the air and improve the atmosphere.

Stalin's antidemocratic policy affected the Soviet Union's international relations. It transferred its domestic methods to the relations between the USSR and Czechoslovakia. The liquidation of Stalinism, begun at the 20th Party Congress, had logically to be extended to the relations between our two states. Both in the interests of honest friendship and of our mutual struggle for peace and

*It must be remembered that this book was written prior to the Soviet invasion of Czechoslovakia on August 20–21, 1968. —*Ed.*

the humanistic ideals of socialism, Stalinism must be entirely removed from our mutual relations. We can no more allow the period of the fifties to be identified with socialism than international socialist relations can accept Stalin's concept of the hegemony of the Soviet Union.

This thesis is specifically stated in the declaration made by the Soviet Union on October 30, 1956, on the foundation, development, and consolidation of friendship and collaboration between the USSR and the other socialist countries. One of the points this document makes is:

> In the process of the rise of the new system and the deep revolutionary changes in social relations, there have been many difficulties, unresolved problems, and downright mistakes including mistakes in the mutual relations among the socialist countries—violations and errors which demeaned the principles of equality in relations among the socialist states.
>
> . . . The 20th Congress of the Communist Party of the Soviet Union quite resolutely condemned these violations and mistakes, and set the task of consistent application by the Soviet Union of Leninist principles of equality of peoples in its relations with the other socialist countries. It proclaimed the need for taking full account of the historical past and peculiarities of each country that has taken the path of building a new life. [*Pravda* (Moscow), October 31, 1956, translated by the *Current Digest of the Soviet Press*, VII, No. 40 (November 14, 1956), pp. 10–11, and reproduced in Paul E. Zinner, Ed., *National Communism and Popular Revolt in Eastern Europe* (New York: Columbia University Press, 1956), p. 486.]

There is one other aspect that we frequently neglect. However tragic a paradox and however intolerably painful it may be that under a socialist regime Communists could be executed, imprisoned, tortured, and persecuted, we must not see only the injustice inflicted on us. We have brothers among all who have been treated unjustly, who have been victims of arbitrariness and dictatorship. Let us not be content with rehabilitating only the deserving Party members.

While I was still in prison I read the proceedings of the trial of Milada Horakova and Zavis Kalandra.* I could recognize the style. The whole production, even the interrogators, were the same. I can remember seeing the dossier on Kohoutek's desk labeled "Milada Horakova."

Socialist Czechoslovakia must become a genuinely free home for all Czechs and Slovaks whatever their opinions and feelings. The same laws, the same justice, the same obligations must apply to one and all. The only permissible difference between Communists and non-Communists must be that the Communists assume *greater obligations.* That is how it once was; that is not how it is today, but that is how it should be in the future.

Socialism is man's creation. With his yearning for freedom and self-realization man must be the center of all political and economic discussion. Man has become a social being because he has been too dependent on Nature. One whole epoch of human history is characterized by the fact that a minority was able to make itself independent of Nature by exploiting a majority.

The mission of socialism is to end this epoch and to bring about a new one. My hope is that this testimony will demonstrate how far we have moved away from the ideals that live in the hearts of decent people.

Let us hope that this trial will serve as a warning that socialism is not decided by the form of ownership, but that we chose this form of socialist ownership in the conviction that by doing so we were creating the prerequisites for true humanity. The task of our new society is to

*Both executed in 1950 for holding divergent views.—*Ed.*

serve people and not the reverse. Otherwise, we will inevitably return to a period when a people, a class, and finally the majority of the people will be manipulated by usurpers who try to identify their own power position with the supposed interests of a socialist order.

This book appears in print * at a time when the people of Czechoslovakia are endeavoring to change their pattern of life and thereby giving a new, firm foundation for our socialist future. It is essential that we forge the most trustworthy weapon that man has yet devised—*the Truth.*

*First published in Slovak in April, 1968.—*Ed.*

Part II

The Trial Proceedings*

The Opening of the Trial

The trial of Rudolf Slansky and his associates opened in Prague on November 20, 1952. The five-member Senate was under the presidency of Dr. Jaroslav Novak. Dr. Josef Urvalek was Chief Prosecutor. In addition, there were the following prosecutors: Vaclav Ales, Miroslav Kolaja, and František Antl. The following accused stood before the Senate of the State Court:

Rudolf Slansky, former Vice-Premier and former Secretary-General of the Central Committee of the Communist Party of Czechoslovakia;

Bedrich Geminder, formerly in charge of the International Department of the Secretariat of the Central Committee of the Communist Party of Czechoslovakia;

Ludvik Frejka, former head of the Economic Department of the Chancellery of the President of the Republic;

Josef Frank, former Deputy Secretary-General of the Central Committee of the Communist Party of Czechoslovakia;

*This section is excerpted from a transcript of the trial proceedings recorded by the BBC Monitoring Service from Radio Prague; the complete transcript is more than 400 pages.—*Ed.*

Vladimir Clementis, former Minister of Foreign Affairs;

Bedrich Reicin, former Deputy Minister of National Defense;

Karel Svab, former Deputy Minister of National Security;

Artur London, former Deputy Minister of Foreign Affairs;

Vavro Hajdu, former Deputy Minister of Foreign Affairs;

Eugen Loebl, former Deputy Minister of Foreign Trade;

Rudolf Margolius, former Deputy Minister of Foreign Trade;

Otto Fischl, former Deputy Minister of Finance;

Otto Sling, former Secretary of the Regional Committee of the Communist Party of Czechoslovakia in Brno;

André Simone, former member of the editorial staff of *Rude Pravo*.

After reading out the names of the accused, the Presiding Judge also announced the names of defending counsel, who had been officially appointed. They were as follows: Dr. Vladimir Bartos to defend Slansky and Margolius; Dr. Vojtech Posmura for Geminder, Svab, and Loebl; Dr. Jiri Stastny for Frank, Clementis, and Reicin; Dr. Vaclav Synek for Fischl, Hajdu, and Sling; Dr. Jaromir Ruzicka for Frejka, London, and Simone.

The Presiding Judge said: "I draw the attention of the accused to the fact that it is in their own interest to follow the contents of the indictments as well as the proceedings of the trial. They also have the right to make a statement about each item of the evidence. Then it is necessary to point out to them that one of the most important extenuating circumstances to be considered when sentence is passed, in case they are found guilty, is a full penitent confession. For the rest, the accused can naturally conduct their defense as they think fit. I will now ask the Chief Prosecutor to read the indictment."

The Indictment

Dr. Josef Urvalek then read out the indictment. The indictment said that the accused, as Trotskyite, Titoite, Zionist, and bourgeois-nationalist traitors created, in the service of the U.S. imperialists and under the direction of Western espionage agencies, an anti-State conspiratorial Center, undermined the people's democratic regime, frustrated the building of socialism, damaged national economy, carried out espionage activities, and weakened the unity of the Czechoslovak people and the Republic's defensive capacity in order to tear the country away from its close alliance and friendship with the Soviet Union, to liquidate the people's regime in Czechoslovakia, to restore capitalism, and to drag the Republic into the imperialist camp once again and destroy its national sovereignty and independence.

Through investigations carried out by the Ministry of National Security, it was confirmed that the U.S. imperialists, trying with all their forces and by all means to attain world domination, organized after the Second World War a new military and political conspiracy directed against peace and the security of nations, just as the fascist pretenders to world domination had done in the Second World War. They ordered their espionage agencies to organize in Czechoslovakia, as in all the people's democracies, political bands recruited from the most reactionary nationalist and fascist elements to carry out counter-revolutionary coups aimed at separating the people's democracies from the Soviet Union and the socialist camp and returning them to the camp of imperialism. In this way the U.S. imperialists wanted to secure for themselves a base for a third world war which was being prepared by the imperialist warmongers. The U.S., British, and French espionage services had, even before Munich,* spread their network in Czechoslovakia in the interest of the imperialist domination and exploitation of Czechoslovakia, and had strengthened their agency during the German occupation from the ranks of émigrés, in order to create conditions after the defeat of Hitlerite Germany, for a new domination and exploitation of Czechoslovakia.

After the liberation of Czechoslovakia by the Soviet Army in 1945, the main representative of this imperialist agency became the clique of traitors led by the old agents of the West, Eduard Benes, Peter Zenkl,** Hubert Ripka, Bohumil Lausman, Jan Sramek,*** and Josef Lettrich.† In addition to this obvious agency, the imperialists created and placed in the Communist Party another agency recruited from the working class. The imperialists, well aware of the strength of the Communist Party, began to prepare this agency in the period of the pre-Munich Republic and, giving it a special importance in their plans for the post-war period, reinforced it on the eve of the war. From the end of 1938, in London and afterward in Kracow, under the pretext of helping Czechoslovak and other refugees, the so-called "British Committee," later known as the "Trust Fund," was an important Anglo-U.S. espionage agency and acted under the cover of the British Ministry of Home Affairs. Here the agency was selected and trained from the ranks of the refugees and afterward was, with the help of the "Trust Fund," sent from Kracow to London.

*The reference is to the 1938 pact between Nazi Germany, fascist Italy, Britain, and France agreeing to the German demands for the Sudeten territories of Czechoslovakia.—*Ed.*

**Before 1948, along with Ripka, a leading member of the Czech National Socialist Party and minister in the coalition government.—*Ed.*

***Before 1948 leader of the Catholic People's Party.—*Ed.*

† Before 1948 leader of the Slovak Democratic Party.—*Ed.*

This activity was directed by Herman Field and later by his brother Noel Field, both the closest co-operators of Allen Dulles, chief of the U.S. espionage organization OSS [Office of Strategic Services], carrying on espionage activities in Central and Eastern Europe.

In this manner the imperialist espionage agencies gained for hostile activity against the Czechoslovak people such individuals as Eugen Loebl, Otto Sling, Ludvik Frejka, Vavro Hajdu, André Simone, and other Trotskyites, Zionists, and traitors to the Czechoslovak people, who penetrated the Communist Party. At the head of this gang of criminals, whose task was to destroy the Czechoslovak people's democratic Republic in the event of Benes's failure, the U.S. imperialists placed Rudolf Slansky, an old agent of the bourgeoisie and a base traitor to the Czechoslovak people. In the agricultural sector, Josef Smrkovsky,* Gestapo agent, was appointed with Frank's approval as general manager of the Czechoslovak State farms and Deputy Minister of Agriculture. Slansky thus created an anti-State conspiratorial Center which began to develop wide diversionary activities aimed at the destruction of the people's democratic order, at tearing Czechoslovakia from the camp of peace, at restoring capitalism, at the transformation of Czechoslovakia into a colony of the U.S. imperialists, and at destroying her sovereignty and independence.

Early in the 1930's Slansky became an agent of the U.S. espionage agency and co-operated with the notorious U.S. spy Granville, representative of international Zionism. During the war Slansky entered into espionage contact with Gen. [Heliodor] Pika, a notorious agent of the Anglo-U.S. imperialists. Slansky said this about it: "Gen. Pika, who acted officially as chief of the Czechoslovak Military Mission in Moscow, was the agent of the British intelli-

*One of the leaders of the liberalization movement in 1968.—*Ed.*

gence service." Fulfilling imperialist instructions to strengthen his own personal position in the Czechoslovak Communist Party and to take over the leading post, Slansky, during the Slovak national rising,* criminally created conditions leading to the death of Jan Sverma, the national hero of the Czechoslovak people.**

After the liberation of Czechoslovakia by the Soviet Army, when Slansky became Secretary-General of the Czechoslovak Communist Party, he increased his activity, giving key positions in the Party and State apparatus to enemies of the Czechoslovak people who had been schooled by Dulles and the Fields. Abusing his position of Secretary-General of the Party and skillfully camouflaging his subversive plans, Slansky surrounded himself with fascists, war criminals, and adventurers of all kinds, such as Josef Frank, Karel Svab, Bedrich Reicin, Otto Fischl, and others who misrepresented themselves before the Party in a similar way. In this way Slansky gradually created an espionage Center against the Republic.

Before February, 1948,*** when the imperialists legally maintained their open agency headed by Benes, Slansky directed the activity of the anti-State Center in support of the Benes clique. In Slansky's own words: "I co-operated with some representatives of the pre-February forces grouped around Benes, such as Bohumil Lausman, etc. By my attitude and activity I assisted these prominent elements of the reactionary wing inside the Social-Democratic Party. The other members of the anti-State Center co-operated in the same way with different representatives of these reactionary pre-February forces. Thus, for example, Vladimir Clementis co-operated directly with Eduard

*In 1944.—*Ed.*

**One of the leading prewar Communist leaders, who died after the Slovak uprising.—*Ed.*

***When the Communists seized power.—*Ed.*

Benes, Eugen Loebl, Hubert Ripka, Marie Svermova,* [Milada] Horakova, etc. There was no substantial difference between the political platform of Benes and his reactionary supporters and the platform of our anti-State Center. The aim for which this anti-State Center headed by myself worked was identical with the objective of Benes and his people. We were both interested in the abolition of the people's democratic regime and in separating Czechoslovakia from the Soviet Union and the peoples' democracies, that is, in the revival of the capitalist order and the subordination of Czechoslovakia to the domination of the Western imperialist powers. In view of the correlation of class forces in Czechoslovakia and especially in view of the strength of the Communist Party and the working class, I knew that the plans of the reactionary representatives of the pre-February reactionary parties led by Benes and aiming at the overthrow by a reactionary coup of the people's democratic regime could no longer have any prospects of success. That is why I directed my hostile activity, together with the anti-State Center, toward the realization of the hostile plans in another, so-called Tito manner. This means that we used the enemies hidden in the Czechoslovak Communist Party, and placed in the Party's important positions and the State apparatus hostile elements, to try to change the revolutionary character of the workers' party. In this way the anti-State Center set up a hostile agency inside the Communist Party. The activities of this agency were directed by us toward the preparation of the overthrow of the people's democratic regime and the restoration of capitalism."

After the defeat of the counter-revolutionary coup in February, 1948, and the routing of the reactionary parties, the U.S. imperialists charged their Czechoslovak lackeys, headed by Slansky, with the task of destroying the people's

*Wife of Jan Sverma and herself a leading Communist Party official.—*Ed.*

democratic Republic through a counter-revolutionary conspiracy inside the Communist Party and by the physical removal of the leader of the Czechoslovak people, Klement Gottwald. In this connection Geminder stated: "Simultaneously with the preparation of the liquidation of the people's democratic regime, we pursued a policy aiming at the isolation and then the removal of President Gottwald. Slansky gradually placed in key positions in the Party and State apparatus his most devoted people from among the Western émigrés, Zionists, Trotskyites, bourgeois nationalists, spies, and other enemies of the Czechoslovak people, concealing from responsible authorities the dark past of these people, keeping silent about them, and covering up in all possible ways their dirty activities."

With the help of Slansky, Josef Frank became Deputy to the Secretary-General of the Central Committee for the specialized field of industry, banking, and trade; later on Frank was unmasked as an adventurer and war criminal, and as such he should have been tried by a war tribunal on charges of torturing Soviet and French prisoners in German concentration camps. At Slansky's instigation the Trotskyite and Jewish bourgeois nationalist, Bedrich Geminder, one of his best friends, was appointed to head the International Department of the Communist Party's Central Committee. André Simone, whose real name is Otto Katz and who was an international spy, a Zionist, and a Trotskyite, was appointed one of the editors of *Rude Pravo*. In Brno, one of the biggest and most important Communist Party regions, the millionaire Otto Sling, who later proved to be an old Anglo-U.S. agent, held undisputed sway. On the recommendation of Slansky and Marie Svermova, Zionists and adventurers were appointed leading secretaries and officials of the Party machinery in many important industrial regions.

Planning, and therefore the national economy, were left in the criminal hands of Ludvik Frejka, Chairman of the

Economic Commission of the Communist Party's Central Committee, an old cosmopolitan and, as was later proved, an agent of the U.S. spy Herman Field and of the intelligence service. In the Ministry of Finance Otto Fischl, one of the organizers of Zionist undermining activities in Czechoslovakia and the most important agent of the Israeli espionage service, an adventurer who, in the service of the Gestapo, helped in the liquidation of Jews and their property, was appointed Deputy Minister and, in effect, representative of Slansky. Vladimir Clementis, one of Benes's closest friends and—as was found out later—an old agent of the American, British, and French espionage services and a stubborn bourgeois nationalist, became Minister of Foreign Affairs. As his deputies, Slansky appointed Hajdu, the son of a millionaire, an old intelligence service agent and Zionist, as well as Artur London, an important U.S. agent and Trotskyite; both were to assist Clementis and at the same time to watch him. In the Ministry of Foreign Trade the posts of Deputy Ministers were given to Eugen Loebl, a prewar agent of Fields' and an intelligence service agent, and to Rudolf Margolius, a cosmopolitan and an agent of the British espionage service. The post of Deputy Minister of National Defense in charge of cadres went to Bedrich Reicin, who was later unmasked as an old Gestapo agent who had handed over and caused the death of members of the illegal Communist Party Central Committee and of the editors of *Rude Pravo*, including the national hero, Julius Fucik. By reason of these very crimes Reicin, after the defeat of the Nazis, became a valuable assistant to Slansky and an important agent of the U.S., British, and Yugoslav espionage services. Karel Svab, a war criminal who tortured prisoners in German concentration camps, became the real head of the Security Services.

Frank said in evidence: "With my approval Josef Smrkovsky, a Gestapo agent, was appointed Director-General of the Czechoslovak State Farms and Deputy

Minister of Agriculture. In the leather and rubber industry we supported the appointment as Director-General, and later as Deputy Minister of Industry, of Dr. Ivan Holy, an old disciple of the Bata * capitalist system and a Gestapo agent. To the office of Director-General of heavy engineering we appointed [Frantisek] Fabinger, an old servant of capitalism and enemy of the Soviet Union." For the preparation of the plot and the gathering of espionage reports from Czechoslovakia the Anglo-American espionage services used their well-tried spies, the Ambassador, the Military Attaché, and foreign correspondents.

Clementis, who had been under contract to the French espionage service since 1939, established espionage connections with [Laurence] Steinhardt, the U.S. Ambassador in Prague, and handed him various secret documents. Moreover, in the interest of imperialist espionage services, Clementis built up an espionage net for the gathering of information in other people's democratic States. Clementis handed espionage information gained in this way over to Steinhardt. The U.S. agent Noel Field, who was unmasked in the Rajk trial in Hungary,** maintained espionage connections with Artur London and met him for this purpose in Switzerland and in Czechoslovakia. Noel Field's brother, Herman Field, had been connected with Eugen Loebl since 1939. Loebl continued to co-operate with Field after 1939 and handed over to him extensive and important espionage information. Frejka, who had been engaged by the British espionage service during the Second World War, also handed Herman Field espionage information. In addition to Ambassador Steinhardt, espionage activities in Czechoslovakia were conducted by the U.S. Military Attachés Col. Woldike and Col. Koenig, with whom the old

*Before World War II, the world-renowned Bata shoe manufacturing company was one of Czechoslovakia's largest privately owned firms.—*Ed.*

**In 1949.—*Ed.*

Gestapo agent, Bedrich Reicin, co-operated. The U.S. press correspondents Maurice Hindus and David Schoenbrun, using their Press cards, were also engaged in espionage activities. The British Ambassadors Nichols and Dixon received espionage information from Clementis and Hajdu. Reicin and Hajdu, who had already been engaged by the British espionage service in 1941, maintained espionage contacts with the British Military Attaché, Col. Mullens, and established in 1946, at the time of the meeting of the Council of Foreign Ministers in Paris, espionage contacts with the British spy Gladwyn Jebb, who later became permanent British delegate to the U.N. Security Council. Active espionage work was also done in Czechoslovakia by the correspondent of the paper *The Times*, [Godfrey] Lias, with whom espionage contacts were maintained by Eugen Loebl and by Slansky's brother, Richard Slansky. André Simone handed over espionage information to the intelligence agents Schoenbrun and Howard Smith,* the correspondents Alexander Werth** and Paul Willert. The French espionage service operated through its important agents in Prague, the Ambassador Maurice Dejean, with whom contacts were maintained by Clementis and Hajdu, and the Military Attaché, Gen. Flippo, who was in contact with Reicin.

In addition to this, the U.S. espionage service, anxious to gather additional intelligence, made use of its subordinated espionage agencies, the Israelis and Yugoslavs. U.S. spies, their identity hidden by Israeli diplomatic passports, the former Israeli Minister in Czechoslovakia, Ehud Avriel Ueberall, and the Legation employees Felix and Ben Schalom maintained espionage contacts with Bedrich Geminder and Otto Fischl. The Yugoslav spy and former Ambassador in Czechoslovakia, Darko Cernaj, received espionage information from Clementis, and the so-called Attaché,

*American correspondent in Europe.—*Ed.*

**World-renowned journalist of Russian origin.—*Ed.*

Novosel, an official member of the Yugoslav espionage service, obtained information from Geminder. Loebl compiled a special report for him about the Czechoslovak-Soviet trade negotiations in Moscow in the autumn of 1947, and Okali, the Commissioner of the Interior, supplied him with secret information about Slovakia. Reicin maintained close espionage contacts with the Yugoslav Military Attachés, Col. Ianovic and Col. Ristic—who was known as a spy from the Kostov trial in Bulgaria. Reicin's evidence, confirming that these activities had already started in 1946, showed how extensive the plans of this subhuman gang were.

Under the leadership of Slansky and by order of their imperialist masters the plotters sought by every means at their disposal to foil the establishment of socialism in Czechoslovakia. In order to be able to influence criminally all branches of Czechoslovak economic life, the plotters set up in the Party center a special so-called Economic Commission, head by Frejka, which was composed of selected hostile capitalist elements. Frejka deliberately omitted from the Two-Year Plan all preparatory work for the development of heavy industry. They made use of various sabotage methods in order to foil the Party's and the people's endeavors to create socialism in Czechoslovakia. By these activities the plotters caused damage amounting to billions to the Czechoslovak national economy. Imbued by a fanatical hatred of the USSR, they sabotaged our relations with the USSR and endeavored to weaken the USSR's international position and to influence Czechoslovakia's political, economic, and cultural life in the direction of an orientation toward the imperialist countries.

Under the influence of [Maurice] Dejean, Clementis, in his endeavor to tie Czechoslovakia to the West, attempted in his foreign policy to implement the so-called theory of the Third Force, under which—as they had agreed—Czechoslovakia was to become a "bridge" between the

West and the East, that is a toy in the hands of the imperialist adventurers. Slansky, Clementis, and their associates, fulfilling the wishes of the imperialists, did their utmost to popularize Western culture and the so-called American way of life.

Slansky, Clementis, Geminder, and their associates, in order to compromise the Czechoslovak regime and to implement the imperialist policy of linking Czechoslovakia to the West, deliberately appointed to high diplomatic offices in the Western States well-known enemies of the Czechoslovak people, who betrayed Czechoslovakia and deserted to the enemy. Among them were [Vladimir] Houdek and [Jan] Papanek, former Czechoslovak representatives in the U.N., [Bohuslav] Kratochvil, the former Ambassador in London, [Jan] Korbel, the former Czechoslovak Ambassador in Yugoslavia, [Richard] Slansky, the former Czechoslovak Chargé d'Affaires in Tehran, and others.

The plotters enforced a number of trade agreements with capitalist countries which were unfavorable for Czechoslovakia, and enabled the capitalists to enrich themselves at the expense of the Czechoslovak people. They also appointed to diplomatic offices in people's democratic States enemies of the peace camp and agents of imperialism. The plotter Otto Fischl was sent to the German Democratic Republic. The bourgeois nationalist Ivan Horvath, who conducted espionage against Hungary, was made a Minister in Budapest. Slansky's brother-in-law [Jaroslav] Hasek, was sent as Consul-General to China, whence he had to be recalled at the request of the Chinese Government because of espionage activities against people's party and in the service of the U.S. Rudolf Slansky's brother, the spy Richard Slansky, was given a diplomatic post in Poland.

Slansky's associates supported and protected capitalist and kulak elements at home and among the émigrés. On the occasion of nationalization, capitalists were illegally highly compensated and tremendous amounts in cash were left to them. For a number of years the families of capitalists received various cash payments. In the hands of the enemy of the people, Otto Fischl, who was Deputy Minister of Finance, and at the instigation of Slansky, the Restitution Act became an instrument of cynical robbery of the Czechoslovak State in the interest of capitalism.

It was proved in the course of the investigations that Slansky, as Chairman of the Parliamentary Defense Committee, and Reicin, as Deputy Minister of National Defense, in their endeavor to liquidate the people's democratic regime in Czechoslovakia and to destroy the Republic's independence, sabotaged the development of the Army at the directives of their masters so that it should not be able to defend the freedom and independence of the country. The anti-State and subversive Center headed by Slansky was able for some time to continue its undermining activities, because Slansky had also succeeded in assuming the direction of the security machinery, which he used for the protection of the plotters and their associates. It was his intention to wipe out all traces in the event of danger and to create favorable conditions for the plotting activities of the agencies of imperialist espionage services and for the protection of various hostile elements.

Slansky, Geminder, and the other plotters gave particular support and protection to the undermining activities of the Zionists, the reliable agents of U.S. imperialism. The U.S. spy Orenstein stated in his evidence on the direction of Zionist undermining activities in co-operation with U.S. monopolists that in Washington in 1947 Truman, Acheson, and the Israeli Premier Ben Gurion had agreed at a conspiratorial meeting with [Henry] Morgenthau, the former U.S. Minister of Finance, and [Moshe] Sharet, later the Israeli Minister of Foreign Affairs, on the so-called Morgenthau plan, laying down the conditions under which the U.S. would support the State of Israel. It was part of this plan that Zionist organizations should be widely used for espionage and other undermining activities in peoples' democratic States in the interest of U.S. imperialism and world domination. The implementation of these criminal aims in Czechoslovakia was entrusted to the important agent of U.S. espionage and former Israeli Minister in Czechoslovakia, Ehud Avriel Ueberall. Various Zionist organizations of the "Betar" type were allowed to engage with impunity in subversive activities. They published anti-State leaflets, trained terrorists, and organized illegal escapes abroad of capitalist hostile elements.

The plotters and their imperialist masters, preparing a counter-revolutionary plot against Czechoslovakia, realized that the main obstacle to the implementation of their criminal aims was the leader of the people, President Gottwald. Although the plotters had succeeded in occupying important positions in the Party and the State, they realized that so long as Gottwald, beloved by the entire nation, was at the head of the Party and the State, it was completely out of the question for them, following Tito's example, to assume power in the Party and in the State, to fulfill the imperialists' hope for a re-establishment of capitalism in Czechoslovakia, and to divide Czechoslovakia from the Soviet Union. Hence Slansky, the cunning criminal, did not cease to think about Gottwald's forcible removal, and he made preparations to this end. With this in mind he selected a personal doctor for Gottwald, coming from a hostile environment and with a murky past. With this doctor the plotters established close contact, hoping that they would make use of him in their hostile plans. Slansky maintained the closest contacts with Dr. [Vladimir] Haskover, who attended Gottwald from 1945 to 1948 and systematically reported to Slansky on Gottwald's state of health and received instructions from Slansky.

The imperialists, in their warmongering plans, ascribed particular weight to the liquidation of the people's democratic regime in Czechoslovakia. Hence they entrusted with a special mission their well-tried henchman, a master of deceit and provocation, the British MP Konni Zilliacus, one of the most experienced agents of the British intelligence service. After having established direct contacts with the leader of the plot, he supported and directed the subversive activities of the plotters and at the same time collected various espionage reports from Slansky and his associates. Mordecai Oren,* the well-known Zionist imposter arrested in Czechoslovakia for subversive activities, stated in his evidence what great hopes the imperialists reposed in Zilliacus. He had been convinced of this fact by his talks with the well-known warmonger, the former British Foreign Minister Herbert Morrison.

The U.S. imperialists also used for their preparations of a counter-revolutionary plot in Czechoslovakia the Titoite fascist clique, the agents of the warmongers, the cunning and sworn enemies of peace and democracy. In spring, 1946, the executioner of the Yugoslav people, the imperialist lackey Tito, visited Czechoslovakia. He was greatly interested in the inner political situation of Czechoslovakia. Clementis was at his side all the time and had long talks with him. In May, 1948, Tito sent his henchman Moshe Pijade** with the special task of giving Slansky Titoite experiences, advice, and directives for the strengthening of counter-revolutionary activities in Czechoslovakia.

When the plot was uncovered and most of the plotters arrested, the U.S. imperialists realized that Rudolf Slansky, the head of the plot, was in danger of being arrested. It has been established during the investigations that the Americans attempted, with the help of their espionage service in Frankfurt, to organize Rudolf Slansky's escape from Czechoslovakia. This plan was entrusted to Kauders,

*Oren, also known as Orenstein, was later compensated financially by Czechoslovakia for his unjust imprisonment.—*Ed.*

**The Yugoslav Party's chief ideologist.—*Ed.*

a member of the U.S. espionage service, and to the U.S. woman agent in Czechoslovakia, Daniele Kankovska. For the purpose of transmitting identification signals, the "Free Europe" transmitter was used. Thanks to the vigilance and preparedness of the security organs, this attempt of the U.S. imperialists was foiled.

The Chief Prosecutor said, in conclusion: "Thus it is irrefutably proved that the accused, headed by Slansky, were committing the most serious crimes against the State and the people. There is no worse crime than treason against the Fatherland and the nation, whoever commits it. The treachery of attacking the freedom, sovereignty, and independence of the Fatherland planned by these criminals is all the greater because they abused their membership in the Czechoslovak Communist Party, misused the trust of our working people's Party, misused their high official positions, and joined hands with our bitterest enemies—the U.S. imperialists and their lackeys—in order that our Fatherland might be thrown into the shackles of capitalism. They could only carry out their criminal activities by pretending their approval of the program and policy of the Communist Party, and by cleverly masking themselves so that they should not be found out. Even when the first members of the anti-State conspiratorial Center were unmasked and imprisoned, that crafty double-dealer Rudolf Slansky tried to divert attention from himself as head of the conspiracy by pretending that he himself was the victim of the subversive activities of Sling, Svermova, and others.

But, although the conspirators, headed by Slansky, succeeded in occupying important posts in the organs of the Party and the State, from which they could dangerously threaten the Republic, the people's democratic regime, and socialist reconstruction, they did not succeed, as had Tito in Yugoslavia, in mastering the highest organs of the Party and the State, usurping power, and realizing their criminal intentions . . ."

Examination of Slansky

Guilt on All Counts Admitted

The afternoon session began with the examination of Slansky.

PRESIDING JUDGE: "Accused Slansky, step before the microphone. Are you guilty of the four criminal acts of which you are accused?"

SLANSKY: "Yes."

PRESIDING JUDGE: "The first crime is espionage."

SLANSKY: "Yes."

PRESIDING JUDGE: "High treason."

SLANSKY: "Yes."

PRESIDING JUDGE: "Sabotage."

SLANSKY: "Yes."

PRESIDING JUDGE: "Military treason."

SLANSKY: "Yes."

PRESIDING JUDGE: "Will you please tell us in what respect you admit your guilt?"

SLANSKY (speaking slowly and haltingly, with a deep voice): "I fully admit my guilt and I wish to describe in detail and truthfully everything I have done. I have done serious wrong so far as the interests of the Czechoslovak people are concerned. It is by right that I am judged by this court, by the people's democratic court, by right I am forced to answer to charges today before all the Czechoslovak people and also before all democratic peoples of the world. I shall therefore, in my testimony, spare neither myself nor my partners. Above all, I shall not spare myself, because I, as one of the most important officials of the Communist Party, misused this great trust vested in me by the Communist Party and the Czechoslovak people, whose great achievements gained since 1945 I have threatened through my activities. First of all I wish to confess my guilt in that, as an enemy of the Communist Party and the people's democratic regime, I formed the anti-State conspiratorial Center at the head of which I stood for several years—this Center of ours, in which I concentrated a number of varied capitalist and bourgeois nationalist collaborators.

"My collaborators became agents of imperialist espionage services, i.e. of the French, British, and, in particular, the U.S. services; and carried out hostile activities serving the interests of the Anglo-U.S. imperialists which aimed at liquidating the people's democratic order, restoring capitalism, and effecting a reorientation of Czechoslovak foreign policy in favor of the Western capitalist powers. I carried out hostile activities within the Czechoslovak Communist Party, in the economic, foreign, and security sectors, etc. We worked for a complete seizure of power in the Party and State to enable us to restore capitalism and to liquidate the people's democratic order. I admit that I established contact and relations with Konni Zilliacus, a representative of the Anglo-U.S. imperialists and of their espionage service, who interfered in the internal affairs of Czechoslovakia. I also admit that at the time of the Slovak Rising, when I was sent to Slovakia by the Moscow leadership of the Party, I engaged in hostile activities, supported the interests of the Anglo-U.S. imperialists and of the Benes Government in London, and betrayed the interests of the Czechoslovak people. Finally, I admit my responsibility for the death of Jan Sverma."

Slansky's Bourgeois Background and Early Deviation

PRESIDING JUDGE: "How is it that you, who have been a member of the Czechoslovak Communist Party for thirty years, could become a servant of the imperialists and the organizer and leader of a conspiracy against the Czechoslovak people's democratic Republic?"

Slansky replied that he had come from the bourgeois family of a rich merchant and this had influenced his personal traits and character. In 1921 he had joined the Party, burdened with "petty bourgeois opinions, which I never abandoned. This prevented me from becoming a real Communist. Therefore I did not act as a Communist and I did not fulfill honorably the duties arising from my membership in the Communist Party. At the very beginning of my activities in the Communist Party, I became guilty of small and gradually more serious opportunist deviations to the right and left, I moved away from the Party line, I wavered and behaved like an opportunist. I behaved as an opportunist when I faced the police and courts of the first bourgeois Republic. In 1927, when I was Regional Party Secretary in Moravska Ostrava, I expressed Trotskyite opinions and took up a Trotskyite point of view. The reason why I avoided exposure for so long was because I masked my hostile activities and acted politically in a two-faced manner. In public I played the part of a supporter of the Party's Bolshevik line, while in reality I had abandoned the Bolshevik position. This is how I became an enemy of the Communist Party, an agent of the bourgeoisie, and that is why I did not really fight against capitalism in the defense of working-class interests. This explained why in the end I came to fight actively against the Communist Party and the people's democratic order."

PRESIDING JUDGE: "I put it to you that you never became and never were a real Communist."

SLANSKY: "Yes."

The Judge then asked Slansky when he had taken up the active struggle against the Communist Party.

SLANSKY: "In 1944, when the Moscow Party leadership sent me to the Ukrainian Partisan staff as Czechoslovak political representative to organize the partisan movement in Czechoslovakia. At that time I made contact with the Anglo-U.S. agent, the former Gen. Pika, and I followed his policy of the betrayal of the Czechoslovak people, the Western imperialists' line supported by the Benes émigré Government, which aimed at using the Slovak Rising in the interests of the bourgeoisie." Slansky admitted to "cowardly and opportunist" behavior on occasions when he faced the police and courts of prewar Czechoslovakia. The Judge then read out a number of documents to support this accusation . . . "a protocol signed by you on July 8, 1924, on the occasion of a search of your flat, in which you offered information about a Communist student organization to the police commissioner instead of protesting against the search. Is this the sort of case you had in mind?"

SLANSKY: "Yes."

PRESIDING JUDGE: "I also have another protocol, from which it appears that on January 12, 1925, before the examining magistrate of the Prague Provincial Court, you abandoned your Communist ideas. Is this a similar case?"

SLANSKY: "Yes."

The Judge then read out parts of a letter written by Slansky in humble language to the "bourgeois court" to postpone his sentence.

PRESIDING JUDGE: "All this means that at the beginning of your political activity you behaved like a coward and an opportunist, and not like a Communist?"

SLANSKY: "Yes."

"I Leaned toward Trotskyite Opinions"

Slansky then explained the origin of his Trotskyite views, which had been prompted by the actions of Zinoviev and other Trotskyites. "At the time I expressed doubts about the policy of the Comintern with regard to the Chinese question, and I leaned toward Trotskyite opinions." The Judge then told Slansky that "the notorious Trotskyite Eugen Klinger says in his deposition that he knew you as a Trotskyite in 1927." Slansky admitted that Klinger had been in a position to know his views, as he had co-operated with him and had helped him to an important position in the Ministry of Foreign Affairs. He had done this in full knowledge of Klinger's Trotskyite views. The Judge then read from Slansky's prewar police record, where the fact of his Trotskyite connections had been noted in 1928, and Slansky admitted that he had shouted "Long Live Trotsky!" in public in October, 1927.

Collaboration with Benes

Describing his opportunistic activities Slansky said that in 1935 he had tried to "influence the Party to co-operate with reformist leaders and with Benes, who were agents of the bourgeoisie. I did not follow the correct Party line of mobilizing the working class . . . because I wanted to gain the reformist leaders for common action, at least in some questions."

PRESIDING JUDGE: "What happened on the occasion of Benes's election to the Presidency?"

SLANSKY: "Here too I failed to direct the Party toward the mobilization of the working population so that a number of partial claims should be staked."

PRESIDING JUDGE: "What happened about the Czechoslovak-Soviet Treaty?"

SLANSKY: "At the time when this Treaty was concluded I propagated the illusion that Benes was an honest friend of the Soviet Union, although he was an imperialist agent. By this activity I made the Party's fight against reaction and fascism more difficult, I undermined the Party's mobility, and I aided the reformist leaders and the reactionary bourgeoisie which was already thinking in terms of the Munich betrayal."

PRESIDING JUDGE. "This means that in fact you also assisted the imperialist agent Benes?"

SLANSKY: "Yes, I personally assisted the imperialist agent Benes."

PRESIDING JUDGE: "Your work as agent of the bourgeoisie inside the Communist Party was fully acknowledged by Benes and by his closest co-operators. His agent and collaborator, Hubert Ripka, on the day of Czechoslovakia's occupation by Germany, included you in a list of Benes's followers for whom, in agreement with Benes, he had organized escape to the West. We have this list here, found in Ripka's archives, where your name appears together with those of a number of well-known reactionaries."

SLANSKY: "Yes, I know this list, and it proves that Benes and his associates wanted me to join the émigrés in the West so that they could make use of me for their plans."

PRESIDING JUDGE: "The letter accompanying the list of names states that Ripka had taken steps to save the lives of certain people. It also shows that Ripka had made arrangements, with the help of the British agents Eade and Miss [Marie] Grant-Duff, a relative of Winston Churchill, so that the British Legation in Prague had instructions to assist you. All this shows that Ripka's and Benes's interests coincided with the interests of the British ruling circles, who had obviously been well informed about you by Benes and Ripka."

SLANSKY: "Yes, all this is proved by the documents mentioned by you."

This intended help from the British Legation, however, had come too late, continued the Judge. Slansky had already gone to the Soviet Union, where he had gone as an "agent of the bourgeoisie and enemy of the Party." The Judge then asked Slansky about his methods in the fight against the Party and against the Czechoslovak people during his stay in the USSR.

Slansky's Attitude to the Partisans

Slansky described how in 1944 the Moscow leadership of the Party had sent him to the Partisan's General Staff to organize groups of partisans to be sent to Czechoslovakia. Before Slansky left for Slovakia, Gen. Pika had asked him to arrange that the partisan units should come under the then Czechoslovak military command in Banska Bystrica, headed by Gen. Golian. Slansky admitted that he had promised Pika to make arrangements accordingly. "By this action I sabotaged the directives given to me by the Party." Pika had intended to bring the partisan units under Golian's reactionary command, thus enabling it to control and direct the activities of the partisans. "Pika wanted, in the interest of the Anglo-U.S. imperialists and of Benes's London Government, to reduce as much as possible the influence of the partisans upon the Slovak National Rising so that the bourgeoisie could make use of the Rising to strengthen its own position and influence."

Here the Presiding Judge remarked that Slansky's co-operation with Pika was proved by a letter which Pika had sent on September 28, 1944, to the former Minister in the Emigré Government, the "traitor Gen. [Sergei] Ingr," in London. In this letter Pika had confirmed that his co-operation with Slansky was very good and that Slansky had promised to implement all Pika's directives. Slansky then stated that his co-operation with Pika represented "a complete betrayal of the interests of the people of Czechoslovakia." He then described how, in Slovakia, where he arrived at the end of September, 1944, he had co-operated with various "unreliable, hostile, bourgeois-nationalist elements."

He had established contact with Bohumil Lausman, an agent of the Anglo-U.S. imperialists, whom he had aided in performing his political work. He had also abetted the reactionary work of the Golian command, which had failed to supply the partisans with adequate equipment. He had also kept silent in the face of a "slander campaign" conducted by reactionary army officers against the partisans.

Responsibility for Sverma's Death

PRESIDING JUDGE: "You have not yet mentioned another very serious crime which you committed at the time of the Slovak Rising."

SLANSKY: "I have already stated that I committed a grave crime in connection with the death of Jan Sverma."

PRESIDING JUDGE: "Whom did Sverma represent in Slovakia and what were your relations with him?"

SLANSKY: "Sverma arrived in Slovakia with me as the political representative of the Moscow leadership of the Communist Party. He was one of the leading workers in the Communist Party and a close associate of the Party Chairman, Gottwald. In Slovakia he helped to safeguard the progressive and democratic interests of the Rising, he assisted the Slovak people in their struggle against the Hitlerite invaders. After the suppression of the Rising he withdrew with the partisans to the mountains in order to continue the fight. While Sverma firmly stood by the principles of the Party, I had adopted a hostile attitude, having joined the other camp, where I acted as Sverma's political opponent . . ."

The Judge then asked Slansky to describe Sverma's death.

SLANSKY: "It happened on November 10, 1944, during a march from Chabenec Mountain in the Low Tatras. On that day I failed to do all I could have done to save Sverma's life. Before the beginning of the march I had not given Sverma, whose constitution was weak, sufficient cover. I had failed to make arrangements to help him. At the beginning of the snowstorm Sverma walked slowly and was frequently forced to rest. This was also due to the fact that his boots were too small. He had been forced to put on these boots after he had lost his own pair. When the snowstorm rose Sverma fell behind and I did not arrange for assistance for him. I feel, therefore, that I am responsible for Sverma's death and I admit this responsibility." Slansky admitted that it would have been his duty to send a party of partisans to help Sverma. Sverma's death had considerably weakened the position of the Slovaks and was a great loss to the Party and to the nation's fight for liberation. It was also a great loss to the present national reconstruction effort. "Since I was in the hostile camp, Sverma's death assisted these hostile interests, and after his death my own hostile activities could no longer be so closely watched as could have been done by Sverma. Thus his death made it easier for me to continue in my hostile work."

The Judge then produced a pocket watch which had been stolen from Sverma's body by one Sebesta, who had been present when Sverma died. This man and other participants of that particular march in the mountains had confirmed Slansky's responsibility for Sverma's death. Slansky agreed that these witnesses were correct in making him responsible for Sverma's death. Slansky was then asked what he had done to cover up his hostile activities in Slovakia in his capacity as Secretary-General of the Party. Slansky said that he had pretended to the Party that he had fulfilled the tasks entrusted to him, and he had also claimed various services he had allegedly rendered to the Slovak Rising. He had seen to it that he was given publicity among the partisans and he had concealed his hostile work in order to be able to continue it.

Placing of Hostile Elements in Key Posts

After the liberation of Czechoslovakia, Slansky had misused his position as Secretary-General to place various hostile elements in important positions in the political and economic administration and in the Party, thus forming a Center of conspiracy. These people had included many who had spent the war in exile, especially in Britain, and who were mostly of bourgeois origin. Western intelligence services had recruited their agents from among that group and had used them after their return to Czechoslovakia. The imperialists had used various methods for recruiting the agents: in Britain, for instance, they had formed a cover organization, the "Trust Fund," financing émigrés and thereby enlisting them as agents. "I, myself, found myself on the same platform with these enemies and placed them in various important posts in the State administration and in the Party. Holding myself a high position in the Communist Party, I came to assume the leadership of this anti-State Center of conspiracy."

Asked for whom he had procured such important posts Slansky enumerated the following: Geminder, "a Jewish bourgeois nationalist"; Marie Svermova, "a Czech bourgeois nationalist"; Frank; Frejka, who had co-operated with British imperialist circles during the war; Svab and Josef Pavel, who had become heads of the Security Department of the Party Secretariat; Sling, "an agent of the Anglo-U.S. imperialists"; and others. All these had been given positions within the Party apparatus, whereas others had been found posts in the State and economic administration; in this Slansky had been most effectively supported by Frank and Frejka, the latter combining a number of functions in the General Secretariat with others in the State administration, and thereby finding it easier to place numerous enemies within the economic organization. Among those placed in the Economic Ministries Slansky named Fischl, who had co-operated with the Nazis during the occupation; Margolius and Loebl, "imperialist agents"; [Eduard] Outrata, Director of the Brno Zbrojovka Works during the first Republic, Minister in the exile Government of Dr. Benes in London, later Secretary-General of the State Economic Council of the Prague Government, and finally Deputy Chairman of the State Planning Office; [Josef] Goldman, who had become an agent of the British imperialists during the war and later Deputy Chairman of the State Planning Office; as well as others.

Slansky also admitted to having placed other enemies in different Ministries, such as Svab and [Josef] Pavel in the Ministry of the Interior; Clementis, who had assumed an anti-Soviet attitude as early as 1939, and later collaborated with Dr. Benes and with the French and other intelligence services; Reicin, an agent of the Gestapo and of the Anglo-U.S. intelligence service, as well as of Tito; with Slansky's help he had become Deputy Minister of Defense and collaborated with various enemies, such as Gen. [Antonin] Bocek and others. Slansky further mentioned Simone, "a typical cosmopolitan and agent of the French intelligence service." "These people were the leaders of the conspiracy." Slansky was then asked how he had bound these people in loyalty to his conspiratorial activities. He replied that they all realized that they owed their positions to him, that he knew their "shady past" but had nevertheless promoted them to their posts.

Slansky was then confronted with a variety of documents in possession of the court which were produced to illustrate his "methods of recruitment." The first incriminated Svab of criminal activities in a concentration camp and was shelved at Slansky's instructions. Slansky admitted this. The second listed Frank as a war criminal, wanted for collaboration with the Nazis in concentration camps. Frank had testified that he was bound in gratitude to

Slansky for having covered up these activities. The document in which Frank was named was an international list of war criminals, written in English, and containing his name as No. 148. Slansky admitted this. The third document proved the hostile activities of Fischl. The fourth proved Slansky's agreement to Fischl's receiving an important post. Slansky admitted that during the pretrial investigations the documents had been shown to him. The fifth paper proved the hostile work of Simone and the sixth was a letter by Slansky to the Titoite Minister, [Milovan] Djilas, asking him to afford every possible help to Simone on his trip to Yugoslavia. Slansky pleaded guilty to having known Simone as an enemy and yet having secured an important official post for him.

The seventh paper showed that the Party Screening Commission had described Sling as a "superficial idler and shirker in Party work, as well as a dictator"; Slansky had nevertheless written to the Brno Party Secretariat that that was not an official judgment of the General Secretariat. Slansky pleaded guilty to this also.

Links with Western Powers

The Prosecutor then asked Slansky to explain how his Center of conspiracy "was linked with the Western imperialist powers or imperialist circles and in what manner these circles directed the activities of the Center." Slansky said that one link had been people who had become agents of the imperialist intelligence services of Britain, the U.S., France, and Yugoslavia; another link had been diverse organizations such as Zionists and Freemasons, all interconnected, and controlled by the Anglo-U.S. imperialists. With the help of these links the imperialists had been able to influence and direct the work of the Center of conspiracy.

Numerous members of the Center had maintained contact with the imperialists. Slansky named Clementis, a collaborator with the Anglo-U.S. imperialists and an agent of the French intelligence service; Geminder, serving the British intelligence and co-operating with Israel diplomatists who "were in fact U.S. agents"; Fischl, also a collaborator of the Israeli diplomatists; Reicin, an agent of the Gestapo and of the Anglo-U.S. imperialists; Loebl and Margolius, both Anglo-U.S. agents; London, a U.S. intelligence agent; Simone, working for the French and Anglo-U.S. intelligence. There were also others. Slansky admitted to having himself maintained contact with Zilliacus, "who in fact was a representative of the Anglo-U.S., but primarily U.S., ruling circles."

Slansky's Contacts with Zilliacus

Slansky then answered numerous questions about his contacts with Zilliacus, and the following picture emerged: Slansky described Zilliacus as primarily a representative of the U.S. imperialists because "Britain today serves the predatory interests of the U.S. imperialists, who in their lust for world domination have subjugated Britain. In effect, the British intelligence service is today a branch of the Washington intelligence." Slansky had met Zilliacus for the first time toward the end of 1946, when they were introduced by Pavel Kavan, an official of the Czechoslovak Foreign Ministry. On that occasion he gave Zilliacus "espionage information." The second meeting took place some time in the autumn of 1947, when Zilliacus was received by Slansky at the General Secretariat. At that time Slansky knew of Zilliacus's anti-Soviet attitude and his "hostile activities in Czechoslovakia and other democracies." In the summer of 1947 Frejka had come to Slansky to convey a suggestion from Zilliacus that he, Frejka, should attend an economic conference in Britain. Although Slansky knew the anti-Soviet tendency of the conference he agreed to Frejka's going there. Frejka was present at the meeting with Zilliacus. Slansky could not remember details of the conversation but he recalled that Zilliacus had asked him various questions concerning Czechoslovakia's foreign policy, internal situation, and economic problems. "I answered his questions and gave him espionage information in doing so." Frejka also answered questions and gave similar information. "From these answers Zilliacus was able to conclude that I held views differing from the Communist Party line and that I was maintaining an anti-Soviet attitude."

Illustrating this point Slansky said that Zilliacus had emphasized the need for economic relations between Czechoslovakia and the capitalist countries and Slansky had agreed with this view. "I was in favor of extending economic links with the capitalist West." Zilliacus was also able to infer Slansky's subversive views on the reactionaries, on the situation within the National Front, and on the relationship between the Communists and the Social Democrats. "I remember Zilliacus asking me about my views as regards a people's democracy and the dictatorship of the proletariat. I stated that I thought the system of the people's democracy to be fundamentally different from that of the dictatorship of the proletariat, thereby intimating to Zilliacus that I supported the counterrevolutionary concept of a specific Czechoslovak road to socialism."

Espionage Information Obtained by Zilliacus

Slansky's "harmony of views" with this representative of the Anglo-U.S. imperialists led to their agreement to co-operate in the future. Slansky instructed Frejka to place any information of economic interest at the disposal of Zilliacus, whenever he asked for it. He also telephoned Clementis to give Zilliacus information on foreign policy.

Asked about the aims of Zilliacus, Slansky stated that Zilliacus aimed at the goal of the Anglo-U.S. imperialists—separating Czechoslovakia from the USSR and the peace camp. As Slansky had worked for those aims before meeting Zilliacus the Prosecutor suggested that the agreement with Zilliacus merely specified the methods and aims of subversive activities. Slansky agreed that the conspiracy Center had been operative since 1945 and that it had maintained contact with Western imperialist powers and intelligence services before the meeting with Zilliacus. But the contacts became even stronger as a result of this personal link, through which Slansky had received "support and a clear target." In essence the agreement amounted to aiding the Anglo-U.S. imperialists in their plan to restore capitalism in Czechoslovakia, liquidate the peoples' democracy, and modify Czechoslovak foreign policy.

The methods to be used "were similar to those employed by the Tito clique for the restoration of capitalism in Yugoslavia, i.e. the use of hostile elements inside the Communist Party." Zilliacus was interested in the disintegration of the Party. The imperialists used similar methods in other people's democracies, which Zilliacus frequently visited. Slansky had maintained written contact with him through Dr. [Eduard] Goldstuecker,* of the Czechoslovak Embassy in London, and through Geminder, of the International Department of the General Secretariat of the Party. He also personally had another meeting with Zilliacus. Through Goldstuecker he received various items of information from Zilliacus. He also enabled Zilliacus to publish, in *Svetove Rozhledy*, various articles propagating counter-revolutionary opinions. A later meeting with Zilliacus took place in June, 1948, when Zilliacus again visited

*Scholar and diplomat jailed in connection with the Slansky trial, one of the leaders of the 1968 liberalization movement, head of the Writers' Union and Vice-Rector of Charles University, Prague, and a principal target of Soviet attacks.—*Ed.*

Slansky at the General Secretariat. Geminder was present when problems of foreign policy, economy, domestic affairs, etc., were discussed. Again Slansky had passed on "espionage information" to Zilliacus. At that meeting, which took place after the February revolution, Zilliacus had wanted to satisfy himself as to whether he, Slansky, was still adhering to the same anti-State concept as before and to find out what subversive activities were being carried out.

"We Were Working for the Aims of the Imperialists"

Asked about the aims which the subversive group had pursued in collaboration with Zilliacus, Slansky said: "We were working for the aims of the Anglo-U.S. imperialists, the aims of the aggressive bloc of the U.S. and British imperialists, these aims being the restoration of capitalism and the preparation of a new world war, which is today being prepared by the imperialists. The aim was to get Czechoslovakia, which emancipated itself from the imperialist sphere in 1945, back into that sphere, to make the country dependent on the imperialists, as under the First Republic, to enable it to be exploited by the imperialists, to foil the building of socialism in Czechoslovakia, and to enslave the Czechoslovak people once again, so that industrialists, bankers, and landed gentry could exploit them once again and so that foreign imperialism should profit from the toil of the people. The aim was to draw Czechoslovakia into the preparations for a new world war which the imperialists were preparing—principally the U.S. imperialists—a war against the USSR, the people's democracies, and hence also against Czechoslovakia. By my hostile work I aided these barbarous plans of the Western imperialists, these contemporary heirs of Hitler. It was the aim of the imperialists to draw Czechoslovakia into the preparations for a third world war because they attached great importance to Czechoslovakia; for one thing Czechoslovakia is an economically powerful country, highly developed industrially, for another she occupies an important strategic position in Central Europe; and lastly, as a neighbor of the USSR, she would serve the imperialists as a springboard for their attack on the USSR.

"The imperialists pursued similar aims in the other people's democracies. There too they used Zilliacus. He specialized in the people's democracies, traveled about the people's democracies, made contacts in these under the mask of a Left-wing Social Democrat, a mask he assumed in order the better to conceal his hostile activity and to be better able to interfere in the internal affairs of the popular democratic countries, just as the imperialists used to interfere in Czechoslovakia during the bourgeois First Republic. Zilliacus would travel about these countries, make contacts with Right-wing elements in the Social Democratic Parties and with hostile elements in the Communist Parties—as he did with me in the Czechoslovak Communist Party, with Gomulka in Poland, with Tito's fascist clique in Yugoslavia, with Kostov in Bulgaria, with Rajk in Hungary—and these hostile elements he then made into his agents."

Contacts with Pijade

Slansky was then asked about his contacts with Pijade. He stated that when Pijade came to Prague with a Yugoslav delegation early in 1948, he had been called to the Yugoslav Embassy under a pretext, and there Pijade had mentioned conflicts between the Soviet Communist Party and the Tito clique and had sounded him on his attitude. Slansky had made it clear to Pijade that he himself stood on the same hostile platform as Tito's clique. Pijade must have known of Slansky's attitude from Zilliacus; there had been nothing accidental about the interview.

A deposition by Mordecai Oren was then read out in court to the effect that Pijade had told him that Slansky supported Tito's policy. Slansky agreed that this evidence confirmed his own statement.

In reply to the Prosecutor, Slansky agreed that he had been in indirect contact with Tito via Zilliacus and the Western imperialists and in direct contact with Tito through Pijade. Three letters produced in evidence—one from Goldstuecker to Slansky, enclosing a letter from Zilliacus, another from Slansky to Geminder, enclosing a translation of Zilliacus's letter, and the third from Frejka to Goldstuecker, with information to be passed on to Zilliacus—were accepted by Slansky as genuine and as proof of his contacts with Zilliacus.

Co-operation with Tito

Asked to describe the way in which he and his conspiratorial group had worked on Titoite lines, Slansky explained that a widespread network of Titoite agents had been permitted to establish itself in Czechoslovakia. He had furthermore guided the Party toward the application of Titoite-Yugoslav experience at the expense of Soviet experience. Delegations had been sent to Yugoslavia and had made propaganda for Tito's regime on their return. Long-term trade agreements had been concluded with Yugoslavia and although Yugoslavia had soon failed to supply the stipulated raw materials he had repeatedly advocated an indulgent policy and the delivery to Yugoslavia of Czechoslovak industrial manufactures despite Yugoslavia's failure to honor her part of the bargain. Economic relations with Yugoslavia had been more extensive than with any other country and had been at the expense of relations with the USSR. They had damaged Czechoslovakia and economically buttressed Tito's regime.

Even after the Cominform Resolution,* Slansky said, he had continued co-operation with Tito. Yugoslav spies had been allowed to operate in Czechoslovakia to the detriment of Czechoslovakia's interests and Titoite agents had been allowed to infiltrate into the Army to undermine its fighting efficiency and loosen its alliance with the Soviet Army. When anti-Tito émigrés began to organize themselves in Czechoslovakia Slansky, with Geminder's help, had introduced Trotskyite and criminal elements into their ranks. His co-operation with Tito had "served chiefly the interests of the Anglo-U.S. imperialists—in particular the U.S. imperialists—because the Tito clique was an agency mainly of the U.S. imperialists."

Slansky's Work with Zionists

The Prosecutor then asked Slansky to elaborate his admission that he had placed Zionists in important posts. Slansky explained that he had done so "because the Zionists were conducting hostile activity aimed at the liquidation of the popular democratic regime in Czechoslovakia. I collaborated with them and I placed various Zionist elements in important posts in the administrative, economic, and Party apparatus. In the Party apparatus I placed such Zionists as Bedrich Geminder, Ludvik Frejka, Otto Sling, and others; in the administrative apparatus I introduced Zionists such as Loebl, Margolius, Hajdu, London, Goldstuecker, and a number of others. These Zionists in turn placed other Zionists in various posts in the administration and economic offices and through them I was linked with the Zionist organizations."

The significance of this lay in the fact that Zionist organizations in Czechoslavakia were in turn connected with similar Zionist organizations in the capitalist coun-

*In June, 1948, the Cominform denounced the Yugoslav Communist Party and expelled it from its ranks.—*Ed.*

tries. "The whole worldwide Zionist movement was in fact led and ruled by the imperialists, in particular the U.S. imperialists, by means of U.S. Zionists. For U.S. Zionists, who are the financially most powerful and politically most influential Zionists, form part of the ruling imperialist circles of the U.S.A." The Zionist organizations had moreover been a channel through which the imperialists carried out extensive espionage and subversive work in Czechoslovakia. The "Joint" * organization in Prague was "a branch of the American Zionists" and had played an important part in various hostile machinations. One of these had been "the abuse of the emigration scheme under which Jewish citizens left for the capitalist countries, thereby removing from Czechoslovakia property of an unjustifiably large value and causing grave economic damage to Czechoslovakia."

Hostile Activities of Zionists

Slansky admitted that he had ensured the legal existence in Czechoslovakia, both before and after February, 1948, of these bourgeois-nationalist Zionist organizations. Though his attention had been drawn to the hostile work conducted by them, he had protected them. "I deliberately shielded them by abusing the campaign against so-called anti-Semitism. By proposing that a big campaign be waged against anti-Semitism, by magnifying the danger of anti-Semitism, and by proposing various measures against anti-Semitism—such as the writing of articles, the publication of pamphlets, the holding of lectures, etc.—I criminally prevented the waging of a campaign against Zionism and the revelation of the hostile character of Zionists and Zionist organizations."

Slansky said he had discussed these matters with Ge-

*Joint Distribution Committee, a postwar, American-sponsored Jewish relief organization.—*Ed.*

minder, Svermova, Frank, and others. In addition to the campaign against anti-Semitism there had also been a "press publicity drive for the State of Israel without it being pointed out that Israel was a bourgeois State and in fact represented the most advanced outpost of the U.S. imperialists in the Near East. I deliberately shielded Zionism by publicly speaking out against the people who pointed to the hostile activities of Zionists and by describing these people as anti-Semites—just as did my collaborators—so that these people were in the end prosecuted and persecuted and sometimes even excluded from the Party, as happened to certain members of the Central Secretariat. I thus created an atmosphere in which people were afraid—even prominent officials in the State apparatus—to oppose Zionism and Zionist organizations."

Co-operation with Israeli Diplomats

With regard to the emigration scheme—in which Geminder and Fischl had played important parts—he had condoned the export from Czechoslovakia of excessive quantities of valuable property. In this he and his group had collaborated with members of the Israeli Legation, such as the Israeli Minister Ueberall, "who is in fact an agent of the U.S. imperialists." Another field in which his conspiratorial group had worked through the Zionists was foreign trade. Here Loebl and Margolius had played important parts. Czechoslovak foreign trade had been misused to the advantage of Zionist organizations at home and abroad, thereby supporting the bourgeois State of Israel. Czechoslovakia had suffered economic damage as a result of her goods being sold at unfavorable prices, lower than in the capitalist market, while manufactures from capitalist countries had been imported at high prices. Huge profits had gone to Zionist organizations and had benefited Israel. These transactions had been justified under the pretext of an "export offensive" in the U.S. with the alleged purpose of gaining dollar and sterling currency.

The State Prosecutor then submitted documentary evidence pointing to these criminal activities. Slansky, when asked whether he knew of these documents, said he did not, but admitted that from all that had already been said it was obvious that his associates, Loebl and Margolius, had been co-operating with the Israeli diplomats, who had acted as agents of the U.S. imperialists, and with the U.S. Ambassador, Steinhardt. The State Prosecutor drew the conclusion that Slansky and his group were actually co-operating directly with U.S. official circles through the representatives of the Zionist organizations and Israeli diplomatists. Asked by the Prosecutor which of his associates had been co-operating in this direction, Slansky mentioned Geminder, Loebl, Frejka, and Fischl.

Slansky and Freemasonry

STATE PROSECUTOR: "In your subversive activities have you also made use of other organizations?"

SLANSKY: "Yes."

STATE PROSECUTOR: "Which were they?"

SLANSKY: "Freemasons. The anti-State conspiratorial Center made use of Zionist organizations in their activities as well as of Freemasons and their lodges. I myself had connections with Freemasons—for example, with Ing. Machon and Dr. Vancura, who were outstanding officials of Freemason lodges."

Slansky continued by saying that Vancura had had important connections with Freemasons abroad, particularly in Britain. Slansky had known that Vancura had maintained these connections and he had also known that these connections had served anti-State and espionage purposes. "I wish to stress," said Slansky, "that the inimical character of Freemason lodges was emphasized by the fact that Dr. Benes, the imperialist agent, was also a member."

The court was then handed a letter written by Dr. Vancura in which he had informed Slansky about his journey to Britain in May, 1948. Vancura had mentioned in his letter that he had succeeded in meeting leading members of the British Grand Lodge, who had received his information with great interest. Slansky had written his reply on that letter, thanking Vancura. Slansky, referring to the letter, reiterated that he had learned that Vancura had been engaged in anti-State activities because of his connections abroad.

The next exhibit submitted to the court was a letter written by Ing. Machon, in which he had stated that when founding new Freemason lodges after 1945 he had always sought Slansky's advice. Asked what this letter meant, Slansky replied that it was relevant to his co-operation with Machon. In Machon's notes, which had been found, it had been stated that Slansky's attitude toward Freemasons was favorable and Machon had stated elsewhere in his notes that before making a decision it was necessary to contact Slansky, who would furnish explanations. Asked what this meant, Slansky said that against the advice of the Communist Party Chairman he had maintained contacts with Freemasons with whom he had collaborated and whose activities he had facilitated.

Disruptive Activities within Communist Party

PRESIDING JUDGE: "We are now coming to a new phase of your anti-State activities. How and in which sectors did you and your associates carry on anti-State, that is, disrupting activities, framed in the preparations for the liquidation of our people's democratic regime?"

SLANSKY: "I carried on these activities together with my associates in various sectors, particularly within the Communist Party, in national economy, the Army, the Foreign Service, and in the security forces."

PRESIDING JUDGE: "Describe now how you and your associates carried on hostile activities within the Communist Party."

Slansky then described his activities, which had consisted in infiltrating hostile elements into various sections of the Party apparatus, particularly the Central Committee. Many hostile elements had been posted to important positions, and with his help such enemies as Svermova, Geminder, Svab, Frejka, and Frank had been put in charge of various important sections of the Central Committee. These people had worked inside the Party. By appointing these hostile elements within the Party, Slansky had tried to usurp power over the Party in order to restore capitalism. Slansky and his associates had also tried to change the revolutionary character of the Party by using bourgeois and petty bourgeois elements. This had been done by concentrating on the recruitment of bourgeois property owners. Attempts had thus been made to change the social structure of the Party. At the end of 1947 Slansky had addressed a letter to Communist members of all National Committees asking them to recruit new members for the Party from the bourgeois and petty bourgeois ranks. After February, 1948, Slansky had facilitated the infiltration of careerist elements, who had been joining the Party for personal ends. In this way Slansky and his associates had tried to break up the Party. "In doing so we by-passed and deceived the Chairman of the Party, Gottwald, and isolated him in his leadership of the Party."

Sabotage within the Party

Slansky admitted that he had introduced "wrong, anti-Party methods" in the Party apparatus; he had particularly failed to use "the method of persuasion." He had thus led the Party away from its primary task of political work among the masses, and the links between working class and Party had been weakened in this manner. "Under my leadership the administrative machinery of the Party assumed powers exceeding its function, and I and my associates interfered with State authorities and economic bodies without authority and without the knowledge of the Ministers concerned. We interfered in matters concerning cadres; I myself supported the appointment of various hostile elements, transferring and promoting them at will, and we issued hostile directives to the workers of these bureaus. In this way I distorted the leading role of the Party. I by-passed Party authorities; I solved many important political and organizational matters on my own, without presenting them to the Party Chairman and the Party Presidium. In this way I isolated the Chairman and the Presidium from the rest of the Party. I sabotaged the application of the experiences of the All-Union [Soviet] Communist Party."

Asked to give examples of his subversive activities in the Party, Slansky said that on many occasions the Economic Department under Frejka and Jancik had interfered in the work of various Ministries and industries; and the International Department, under Geminder, and the Security Department, under Svab and Pavel, had meddled with the Ministries of Foreign Affairs, the Interior, and National Security. "We decided many important matters concerning cadres without consulting the Party Presidium," and in other instances important information with regard to hostile appointments had been withheld from the Party Presidium. Slansky recalled that on one occasion he had suppressed a report on Party recruitment in the Louny District (Central Bohemia), which had recorded the fact that bourgeois and petty bourgeois elements, particularly kulaks, were joining the Party in considerable numbers. "This also went on in other regions and districts; it was in fact general." But Slansky withheld this information from the Party Chairman, Gottwald.

The introduction of bourgeois elements had been directed at changing the revolutionary character of the Party, and "we would be able to rely on these elements in our anti-State activities." "Like Tito in Yugoslavia, we tried to transform the Communist Party into an instrument for the restoration of capitalism."

The Prosecutor then presented to the court a circular directive sent by Slansky to Party officials in 1947, asking them to recruit bourgeois and petty bourgeois elements as Party members. Slansky recognized this document.

In the economic sector Slansky and his associates had aimed at "damaging Czechoslovak economy, preventing full utilization of industrial resources, hindering the development of socialism in industry, and linking Czechoslovak economy with capitalist States." This policy has been carried out by placing in important positions hostile elements such as Loebl, Margolius, Fischl, Ivan Holy, the former Deputy Minister of Industry and Director-General of the Leather Industry, and Frantisek Fabinger, a former Director-General of the Metal Industry. A wide network of various economic commissions containing numerous bourgeois elements had influenced economic policy and had tried to replace State economic authorities. The Party had been diverted from its main task of mobilizing the workers for plan fulfillment.

Sabotage of Five-Year Plan

Slansky stated that he and his associates had conducted hostile activities in all sectors of economic life. In the field of planning, his associates Frejka, Goldman, and Outrata had drawn up plans in which final targets were set down at low figures. It was their aim to hold up the development of heavy industry and the exploitation of indigenous

Czechoslovak raw material. This had caused great damage to Czechoslovak national economy. Full use was not made of industry's productive capacity, and no provisions were made for the fulfillment of production tasks. Slansky said that he had discussed the draft of the Five-Year Plan with his associate Frejka toward the end of 1947 at his villa in Prague. His hostile activities were designed to hold up the development of heavy industry and to expand light industries, although these already had a productive capacity far beyond the needs of the country. This applied particularly to the textile and ready-made clothing industry, in which new factories were set up. This made it necessary to import wool, cotton, and leather from capitalist countries. At that time the prices of these imports were rising, while the prices of manufactured goods were falling. This caused great financial losses and made Czechoslovak industry dependent on the capitalist markets. The holdup in the development of heavy industry resulted in a shortage of machinery, e.g. equipment for power stations, which was needed not only by Czechoslovakia but also by the other peoples' democracies; and thus the economic development of other peoples' democratic countries was also hampered. Moreover, numerous new factory buildings were erected, although the productive capacity of existing buildings could have been increased by the introduction of second shifts. These activities absorbed a considerable labor force and caused shortages of building material.

Slansky went on to describe his sabotage activities in the field of iron ore production. Although there were considerable deposits of iron ore in Czechoslovakia, ores were imported from capitalist countries while the development of indigenous deposits was held up. The same applied to nonferrous metals and to the production of substitute materials. All this was designed to tie Czechoslovakia closer to capitalist economy.

The Prosecutor produced a letter from Dr. [Jan] Pelnar, a

mining expert, who had written to Slansky recommending the mining of basic industrial raw materials in Czechoslovakia, particularly coal, iron ore, and nonferrous metals. Slansky admitted that he had received this letter and said that he had simply filed it.

Other sabotage committed by Slansky and his associates consisted, according to his own evidence, in the refusal to adopt Soviet experiences for the reorganization of industries. Hence industry labored under the disadvantage of large administrative staffs, and this put up production costs and deprived factories of considerable manpower reserves. These activities were mainly in the hands of his associates Frank and Frejka.

In the field of foreign trade Slansky and his associates had also done their utmost to organize sabotage and to cause damage. This applied particularly to trade relations with the USSR and the peoples' democracies. In this sector Loebl and Margolius had been particularly active. Owing to their Zionist convictions, these associates had co-operated with various U.S. agents and had endeavored to link Czechoslovak economy to the capitalist West. Machinery was bought in the capitalist West, although it could have been supplied at more favorable prices by the USSR. On the other hand, deliveries to the Soviet Union were sabotaged by charging exorbitant prices or by delaying delivery dates. Orders from the Soviet Union had been rejected under the pretext that Czechoslovak productive capacity was insufficient, although these goods could have been manufactured.

The Prosecutor produced a letter to Slansky from Comrade [Josef] Blazek, the Czechoslovak trade representative in Moscow, in which he cited concrete examples of high prices charged by Czechoslovakia to the Soviet Union. Blazek asked in this letter to be recalled from his post, since as a Communist he felt he could not continue under such conditions. Once again Slansky admitted that he had received this letter and had simply filed it. He and his associates had made it possible for foreign trade to remain in the hands of bourgeois capitalist elements, former wholesale merchants who were selling Czechoslovak goods at low prices yet amassing huge profits. Out of these profits, the treacherous émigrés abroad and their fight against the people's democratic regime were financed.

Sabotage in Agriculture

Slansky admitted having committed hostile acts in the field of agricultural production. He and his associates had sabotaged the establishment of socialism in the sector of agriculture and had strengthened the position of class enemies among the farmers. They had deliberately caused dissatisfaction inside agricultural co-operatives, endeavoring to undermine the Government's agricultural policy. Together with Frank and Sling he had supported hostile elements in agriculture. Implementing this policy, he had issued a circular letter addressed to National Committees, asking them to accept into the Party various bourgeois elements, including kulaks. This policy also had enabled kulaks to infiltrate into agricultural co-operatives.

Together with Frank, Slansky had made it possible for hostile elements to worm their way into the administration of State farms and State forests. These elements included especially former estate owners and hostile people who were expelled from the Party after February, 1948. Sling had also undermined the cadre policy, placing former estate owners in important positions in the Ministry of Agriculture or other administrative posts. Such elements were able to find their way into the Ministry of Agriculture as a result of Slansky's own subversive policy.

Slansky was then questioned specifically about the activities of Smrkovsky, former Director-General of State Forests and State Farms, who had, according to the defendant, "carried out widespread sabotage," appointing and protecting hostile elements within his sector. Slansky admitted to having known of this, and that he had refrained from taking action because it all "served the interests of the central conspiracy. We carried out such hostile activities in various sectors of agriculture, we interfered with agricultural production, etc." The expected results, however, had not been obtained, mainly because that nefarious work "was foiled by the correct policy laid down by Gottwald."

Sabotage in Foreign Policy

Asked by the Prosecutor to describe his sabotage activities in the field of foreign policy, Slansky said: "Our hostile activities consisted above all in appointments of cadres hostile to the regime. Proposals in this respect were prepared by my associates Clementis, London, and Geminder. In making proposals for appointments the positive qualities of the persons concerned were underlined, and their hostile character was not mentioned. By this method we managed to appoint many hostile elements to important positions in the foreign service.

"This was done by my associates Geminder, Hajek, and London, who formed a commission for the appointment of hostile personalities in diplomatic services. Through my associates Clementis and Geminder, I also influenced appointments inside the Foreign Ministry, such as that of Eugen Klinger; and I supported the Trotskyite group inside the Ministry which was headed by [Frantisek] Dufek and Hajdu, which undermined the Ministry. We also made it possible for hostile elements to be appointed to the diplomatic service abroad, so that they could, after February, 1948, join the émigrés in the capitalist countries and fight against the people's democratic regime. By this we helped foreign espionage services to recruit agents from the ranks of these émigrés. By this method I assisted the treacherous Czechoslovak émigrés abroad in their activities on behalf of the imperialist powers against the Czechoslovak people's democratic regime. All this was designed to influence our foreign policy toward co-operation with the Western capitalist powers and toward a separation of Czechoslovakia from the Soviet Union and the people's democracies. My associate Clementis and others used their position for co-operation with Western capitalist diplomatists. They went out of their way to help them, even beyond their official duties. These hostile activities made possible the existence of various so-called cultural institutes, such as the U.S., British, and French institutes, which were set up on the strength of unilateral cultural agreements concluded with capitalist countries. On the other hand, my associates held up negotiations with people's democratic countries, such as those with Hungary concerning the position of Hungarians in Slovakia and of Slovaks in Hungary."

Sabotage in the Army

"My anti-State group also conducted anti-State activities inside the Army. These activities threatened the development of the Army as a popular and democratic force and undermined its fighting fitness. Our activities consisted above all in sabotaging the implementation of the Kosice Government program.* This program laid down that the Army should be purged of reactionary officers and that the new officers' corps should consist of reliable and democratic elements. My associates in the Army, Reicin and others, sabotaged the purge of the Army. The purge commissions which were set up after 1945 were composed

*The program of the Czechoslovak postwar coalition government, established in the city of Kosice in Slovakia as the Soviet Army moved westward in the later stages of the Seeond World War.—*Ed.*

mainly of reactionary officers, which made it possible for old reactionary officers to take over the new Czechoslovak Army. My anti-State group made it possible for the Army Command to remain in the hands of a number of high-ranking reactionary officers. Even after February, 1948, I did nothing to remove them; on the contrary, I co-operated with them and made their hostile activities possible."

Sling had co-operated with leading reactionary officers in Moravia, such as Gen. Novak, Commander of the Brno Military District. Slansky himself had taken part in a meeting between Sling and Novak. Reicin had been Slansky's main confederate in the Army, particularly in the cadres questions. Reicin had presented to the Supreme Defense Council proposals for appointments to high commands, and had withheld information about hostile elements whom the conspirators wished to see in important positions. Reicin and Slansky had also been members of the Party's Military Cadres Commission. Slansky admitted that he had sabotaged the Government program with regard to the Army, although he had known that the Army was to be built up in accordance with Soviet precepts. "Party organizations in Army units were not directed to fight against reactionary officers; on the contrary we made it possible for hostile elements to enter these organizations.

"I and my confederates tried to prevent the Army's reconstruction in accordance with the Kosice Government program and in a democratic spirit. We also tried to prevent the purge of reactionary officers. We were interested in maintaining old traditions in the new army. This came to the fore in a talk between Reicin and Benes, when Benes expressed his opposition to the purge of reactionary officers and to the prosecution of imperialist agents by Military Intelligence. Our subversive activities in the Army were part of our preparations for the restoration of capitalism and for the liquidation of the people's democratic order, since they weakened the fighting potential of the Czechoslovak Army and threatened its development as a people's democratic force."

Sabotage of National Security

"In the sector of national security our anti-State Center held relatively strong positions. I interfered with the security sector mainly through Karel Svab." Again, Slansky and his confederates had placed hostile elements in important positions in the Security Service. "My confederates worked for the inclusion of old police and constabulary cadres in the new Security Service, cadres which had served the bougeoisie in its struggle against the working class. Newly recruited members of the Security Service included many unreliable elements, and reliable men of working-class origin were left in unimportant positions, were not promoted, and were subordinated to the old unreliable elements. The Security Service's ability to act was thus undermined. My confederates relied on the old unreliable elements, and thus protected the activities of the conspiratorial Center. For example, Svab concentrated in his hands all the material about the U.S. agent Noel Field, who was exposed in the Rajk trial in Budapest and who also interfered in Czechoslovakia, where he had connections with some members of the anti-State Center. Thus Karel Svab was able to protect those members of the anti-State sector. After the Rajk trial I myself tried to spread the view that the Czechoslovak Community Party—which had been legal * whereas the Hungarian Party had been illegal—could not have been penetrated by imperialist agents, and I thus tried to divert the attention of the Security authorities from checking and prosecuting hostile elements. Some of my associates showed police reports

*In the interwar years.—*Ed.*

on members of the anti-State Center to the persons concerned in order to warn them." As in the Army, Party units in the Security Service had been permitted to recruit hostile members.

Further Anti-State Activities

In reply to the Prosecutor's questions about his anti-State activities other than those mentioned in his evidence on that day, Slansky said: "In my hostile activities I relied on the support of various hostile organizations such as the Zionists and Freemasons, and on hostile elements among partisans and false trade unionists, etc. I made the existence of false partisan units possible. Like Tito in Yugoslavia, I relied on demoralized members of the International Brigade in Spain. I also co-operated with various false trade union elements such as the "Boj" group, which was in reality directed by Trotskyites, and I became Honary Chairman of this group.

"In view of the class conditions of Czecholsovakia and of the strength of the Communist Party and of the working class, I knew that the plans of the pre-February reactionaries, centered around Benes and directed by him, and aimed at destroying the people's democratic order by means of an open coup, had little prospect of success. I therefore directed the work of the anti-State Center in another way—in Tito's way—by trying to make use of hostile forces within the Party. We therefore hid these hostile forces in important positions in the Party. Even though I knew that their plans had little chance of success, our anti-State Center helped the pre-February reactionaries led by Benes. I co-operated with Bohumil Lausman and Blazej Vilim, who were leading representatives of the Right-wing Social Democrats. Clementis collaborated with Benes, Loebl with Ripka, Svermova with Horakova. I want to stress that there was no substantial difference between our program and Benes's platform, that we served the same interests of the Western imperialists. In February, 1948, the Western imperialists hoped for the destruction of the people's democratic order by the reactionary forces grouped round Benes, while the anti-State Center represented a sort of reserve."

Self-Magnification

Continuing his evidence, Slansky said that after February, 1948, the anti-State Center had become the main power which had been preparing the liquidation of the people's democratic regime. The Center's activities had grown in scope and its positions had been strengthened within the State economic apparatus. The chief object had been the usurping of power in the Party and State. "I was isolating the President; I cheated him, I was pushing his leading officials into the background, while I was strengthening my own position."

PROSECUTOR: "And popularized yourself?"

SLANSKY: "Yes."

PROSECUTOR: "How did you strengthen your own position?"

SLANSKY: "In addition to what I have already told, I claimed merit, for instance, for the February events, by falsifying their history and by claiming merit which belonged to Klement Gottwald. I did so in various publications and in the press, and my associates acted in a similar way. For instance, in a publication entitled *The Victorious February in Photography* I had authorized a caption under my own picture to the effect that I directed all the February events, and did not show the really leading part played by Klement Gottwald. In a similar way I ordered a film about the February events in which I played the leading part, and did not show the actual leading part played by the Chairman of the Party; this film, which was made after the February events, could also serve later for the purpose of strengthening my own position. On many occasions I acted in a similar way, when I claimed merit for various Party successes."

Hostile Doctor Appointed to Attend Gottwald

PROSECUTOR: "How did you intend to effect a complete usurpation of power?"

SLANSKY: "I worked toward the usurpation of power through the anti-State Center, so that the highest positions in the Party and State would fall in the hands of the anti-State group. I counted on the possibility of gaining the leading place in the State and Party. I knew that the obstacle to the realization of our final plans was Klement Gottwald, who would never consent to the restoration of capitalism; and I was aware that if I came into power it would be necessary to get rid of Klement Gottwald. I admit that I arranged for Dr. Haskover to attend the President of the Republic. Haskover was a Freemason, and therefore an enemy, a fact which I hid from the President of the Republic. Dr. Haskover, being an enemy, did not provide proper medical care for the President, and thus caused the shortening of the President's life. I could have used Haskover for the liquidation of the President for the purpose of my full usurpation of power."

PROSECUTOR: "So you counted on the liquidation of the President of the Republic if you should usurp power?"

SLANSKY: "Yes."

Answering the Prosecutor's questions as to how he and his group had planned to restore capitalism in Czechslovakia, Slansky said that it had been intended to do so gradually, because in that way the working people could have been more easily deceived. Slansky and his group could have pretended, in order to achieve their ends, that they had not given up the building of socialism. "Today I see that we built our plans on sand, that the working people would not have allowed us to realize our plans." Slansky said that he had intended using Titoite methods in achieving his plans.

PROSECUTOR: "That means putting imperialist agents in the Government, honest Communists in jail, and the country in servitude?"

SLANSKY: "Yes."

CIC Proposal of Escape to the West

The State Prosecutor then mentioned a letter addressed to Slansky by the [U.S.] Counter Intelligence Corps [in Germany], from which he quoted a passage warning Slansky of the pending legal proceedings against him, in the same way as in the Gomulka * case [in Poland], and offering to arrange Slansky's escape to the West. Slansky added that this letter was a proof that the imperialist circles in the West had known that his position after his recall from the post of Secretary-General of the Communist Party had been shaken. They had been interested in his escape to the West because of his hostile attitude toward the people's democratic regime.

The State Prosecutor then read a passage from another letter by the U.S. intelligence service, informing Slansky that a password would be broadcast by the "Free Europe" transmitter on 408.9 m. on November 10, 17, and 24 and December 1, 1951, always at 19.53 hours [7:53 P.M.]. The password read: "Bad things are coming to light

*Wladyslaw Gomulka had been removed as Communist Party leader in Poland and jailed as a Titoite, or national communist. He again became Secretary-General of the Polish Communist Party in 1956—after the death of Stalin and the denunciation by Khrushchev.—*Ed.*

says Ceston." Asked by the Prosecutor to explain this, Slansky said that the U.S. intelligence service had been seriously preparing his escape. The Prosecutor added that this password had been actually broadcast, as was evident from the report by the Ministry of National Security.

End of Slansky's Evidence

PROSECUTOR: "One can thus make these main conclusions: First, that as an old bourgeois agent and an enemy of the people's democratic Czechoslovakia you organized an anti-State conspiratorial Center against the Republic. Is this so?"

SLANSKY: "I have admitted this in my evidence."

PROSECUTOR: "Further it is apparent from your evidence that the purpose of your anti-State group was the liquidation of the people's democratic regime and the restoration of capitalism in Czechoslovakia. Is this so?"

SLANSKY: "I admit this."

PROSECUTOR: "Further, that your anti-State conspiratorial Center carried out espionage on behalf of the Western imperialists and did everything to foil the building of socialism in Czechoslovakia, whereby you caused Czechoslovakia immense political and material damage. Is this so?"

SLANSKY: "Yes, it is so."

PROSECUTOR: "Further, that you directed your hostile activities for the purpose of usurping power in the State and for the removal of Klement Gottwald, which was your ultimate aim?"

SLANSKY: "That is so."

PROSECUTOR: "Further, it is clear from the evidence you have given that you formed an anti-State conspiratorial Center which was preparing the overthrow of the people's democratic regime and the restoration of capitalism, and that you carried on these activities in the service of the

Western imperialists, and primarily in the service of the U.S. aspirants to world domination . . ."

SLANSKY: "I admit this."

PROSECUTOR: ". . . in order to become a Czechoslovak Tito. Is this so?"

SLANSKY: "Yes."

Evidence of Witnesses

Dr. Goldstuecker's Evidence

Dr. Eduard Goldstuecker described his role of intermediary between Slansky and "the agent of the British intelligence service Konni Zilliacus." His relations with Slansky, he explained, went back to 1946 when Slansky's attention had been drawn to Goldstuecker's "Jewish-bourgeois origin" and his "connections with various enemy elements in the West." Slansky had then advised him to change his name to Zlatisty in which case Goldstuecker's past would easily be forgotten. Before taking up his post at the Czechoslovak Embassy in London, Goldstuecker had called on Slansky in February, 1947, and asked him for instructions for his work in England. Slansky had asked him to co-operate with Kratochvil, who had just been appointed Ambassador to London, and to support him.

Asked whether Slansky had given him any instructions about working with Zilliacus, Goldstuecker replied that in December, 1947, when he had been in Prague on an official visit, he had twice called on Geminder, who had told him that, together with Kratochvil, he should maintain contact with Zilliacus. On the occasion of a third visit to Geminder, Goldstuecker had been told that Slansky wished to see him. Slansky had told him that he knew what Geminder had said to him about Zilliacus, but he had nevertheless repeated his instruction that he—Goldstuecker—should maintain contacts with Zilliacus beyond the scope of his official duties. Slansky had said that he had known Zilliacus personally for some time and wished to keep in touch with him. Asked to give details of how he had maintained contact between Slansky and Zilliacus, Goldstuecker said he had met Zilliacus several times after his return to Britain and had given him political information "which ought to have been kept secret in the interests of the Republic." He had also received sealed letters and packages from Zilliacus which he had forwarded to Slansky by diplomatic pouch, sometimes via Geminder, and he had similarly passed on the Zilliacus letters which had arrived by diplomatic pouch from Prague. He knew that the man through whom this was done at the Prague Foreign Ministry was Artur London. Goldstuecker had also enabled Ludvik Frejka to use the diplomatic bag for contacts with the West; Kratochvil had done the same. In the summer of 1948 Kratochvil had told Goldstuecker that he had sent a letter from Zilliacus to Clementis; in this letter Zilliacus had given Clementis his views about matters concerning the United Nations. Otherwise Goldstuecker knew nothing about the contents of the correspondence.

Speaking about his appointment as Minister to Israel, Goldstuecker said that Slansky had told him that he had been given this post because "I had proved myself in England and because I had worked well in accordance with his instructions." On his arrival in Israel at the beginning of 1950, Goldstuecker had made contact with leading Zionists and had sent reports to Slansky through Geminder about his relations with them. In the summer of 1949 he had contacted Ueberall, the then Israeli Minister in Prague, and "later this relationship culminated in an espionage link under the influence of Slansky."

Goldstuecker then told of the help he had given to

Jewish nationalists like himself, whom he had helped to return from Israel to Czechoslovakia to enable them to hold responsible positions in Czech economic affairs. This he had done on Slansky's instructions.

Evidence of Pavel Kavan

The next witness was Dr. Pavel Kavan, former press attaché in London and Embassy Counsellor from May, 1949, until his recall in November, 1950. According to Kavan, he himself had "acted as intermediary between the agent of the British intelligence service, Zilliacus" and Slansky. He had become acquainted with Zilliacus in August, 1946, during the latter's visit to Prague, when he had been instructed to act as his guide and interpreter. At that time Zilliacus had visited Slansky in Kavan's company. "Zilliacus interrupted his stay in Czechoslovakia and went to Yugoslavia for a few days. On his return from Yugoslavia, where he had had talks with Tito, he asked me to arrange a meeting with Slansky, whom he wanted to see urgently. This meeting took place at the beginning of September, 1946.

"Zilliacus himself told me that he had met Slansky in September, 1947, shortly before the visit of a group of Labor MP's who toured Czechoslovakia, Yugoslavia, the USSR, and Poland at that time. At the beginning of 1948, when I was working in the Czechoslovak Embassy in London, Zilliacus called me on the phone and asked me to come and see him at the House of Commons. There he gave me a letter which he asked me to send to Slansky through safe channels." Kavan had sent another letter for Zilliacus in July, 1948. Other persons concerned in the exchanges between Zilliacus and Slansky were the Czechoslovak Ambassador in London, Dr. Bohuslav Kratochvil, Dr. Goldstuecker, and the defendant London. Kavan had also handed "espionage reports" from Margolius to Zilliacus in 1949. These reports "dealt with negotiations about an Anglo-Czechoslovak trade agreement and with the Czechoslovak attitude toward this agreement."

Evidence of Mordecai Oren

Mordecai Oren, also known as Orenstein, an Israeli citizen of Polish extraction, was a member of the Central Committee of the Palestine Jewish Trade Unions and of the Mapam Party. He was arrested in Czechoslovakia at the beginning of 1952. Speaking in broken Czech, Oren said that he had specialized in the affairs of the peoples' democracies, "where I traveled to carry out my Zionist and espionage tasks. I linked my Zionist and espionage activities because I was a member of the British intelligence service and from 1945 till my arrest I carried out my espionage activities in the peoples' democracies, i.e. in Poland, Hungary, Bulgaria, in the German Democratic Republic, and in Czechoslovakia." He had also tried to win leading personalities for co-operation with the Zionists in order to gain "the maximum possible aid in the organization and strengthening of the capitalist State of Israel." In order to fulfill this task he had posed as a friend of the USSR and of peace.

Oren had visited Titoite Yugoslavia several times in the interests of Zionism and of the British intelligence service. "From Titoite representative I learned about the collaboration between the General Secretary of the Czechoslovak Communist Party and the Titoite fascist clique and that he was carrying out a policy similar to the Tito line in his own country." In the second half of 1948 he had discussed the Cominform resolution with Pijade, when the latter had told him that the Titoites "have supporters in the peoples' democracies." Pijade had named Slansky in Czechoslovakia and Gomulka in Poland. According to Pijade the support given to the Cominform resolution by Slansky and Gomulka was not in accord with their real opinions. Pijade had been in touch with Slansky through Ueberall, who himself had confirmed this to Oren in 1948.

"I also know that Slansky was in contact with the Israeli Foreign Minister Sharett through Ueberall, who told me so himself in 1948. I also know that Sharett met Slansky personally. I was told this by Sharett himself in the plane from Belgrade to Prague in 1947, when we went to the European Zionist Conference in Karlovy Vary [Karlsbad]."

Oren's Acquaintance with Herbert Morrison

The Prosecutor asked the witness whether on his wide travels across Europe he had also visited England. Oren stated that in 1946 he had met Herbert Morrison, later Foreign Minister, in London, "with whom I got more closely acquainted." Morrison "was a great supporter of Zionism." Numerous representatives of Zionism had also discussed Zionist problems and the Palestine question with Morrison. Morrison had been in touch with Ben Gurion, Sharett, and others. The witness, who had been in Britain both in 1946 and 1947, had informed Morrison in 1947 about the peoples' democracies, in which the British Minister had shown great interest. Morrison had asked him various questions about the situation in those countries, including matters relevant to the influence of the Communist Parties, members of Governments, etc. In 1947, "Morrison told me that in the peoples' democracies there remained some people who would fight the new popular democratic regime and that they would receive support from the Western imperialists in that struggle." Mr. Morrison had not, however, named anyone in particular.

Asked about the conclusions the witness had drawn from these conversations, Oren said: "It is clear to me that the

Anglo-U.S. imperialists are preparing a new world war. This was further confirmed by Mr. Morrison in a later conversation when he spoke of a plan to destroy the Soviet Union. In that connection he mentioned Mr. [Neville] Chamberlain,* who, he said, had tried to destroy the USSR by using foreign forces, i.e. Hitler and the fascists. That, according to Mr. Morrison, had been the wrong way. Now the task of destroying the USSR rested upon the shoulders of the Western imperialist powers. On this occasion Morrison grossly abused the Soviet Union and disparaged her peace policy."

The Prosecutor then wanted to know what Morrison had told witness about Zilliacus. Oren answered that Morrison had told him about Zilliacus's visits to various countries, and that "Zilliacus is a staunch champion of British imperialism and a veteran agent for British reactionary governments as well as a die-hard enemy of the USSR and the peoples' democracies." In addition Morrison had informed the witness that Zilliacus "played a direct part in preparing the Tito clique's betrayal of Yugoslavia to the war camp." Pressed for more details of Morrison's disclosure about Zilliacus's activities, Oren quoted Morrison as saying: "Zilliacus told me in confidence in 1947 that great political changes were afoot in Yugoslavia and that Tito already had one foot in the U.S. camp." Morrison had emphasized that Tito would soon go over to that camp entirely, for which Zilliacus deserved great credit. In further conversation Morrison had let Oren know that thanks to Zilliacus's visits to Hungary, Czechoslovakia, and Bulgaria "influential friends" had been placed in important Government and Party posts.

The witness was then asked how he had come into possession of papers concerning Slansky's views, which were

*Before, and in the first months of the war, British Prime Minister and chief exponent of appeasement of Germany; organized Munich Pact.—*Ed.*

found on Oren when he was arrested. Oren explained that he had secured those papers in Prague when, apart from working for the British intelligence service, he had been working also for the Israeli espionage service. He had got these papers at the express orders of the Israeli Foreign Minister through the Israeli Minister in Prague. Evidently the Israeli Government was perturbed at the arrest of Slansky. The witness had been happy to accept these instructions, but he had failed to complete his task, as he had been arrested.

Examination of Bedrich Geminder

The court resumed its hearing on Friday morning, November 21. Evidence was taken from Bedrich Geminder, who spoke with a strong German accent * and was at times difficult to understand. The Presiding Judge had to ask him several times to speak into the microphone.

Asked to tell the court about his association with Slansky, Geminder began by speaking of his "cosmopolitan, bourgeois, Zionist background," his "family connections with the West," and his early education, which had fostered in him "petty bourgeois and cosmopolitan views." His parents had been merchants, his youth had been carefree, and there had been nothing in his personal experience that would have provided any ties with the revolutionary working class. While still at school he had joined the "Blau-Weiss" Zionist youth organization. All this Slansky had known. He had also known that he had a brother in Chile.

Although the interests of the working class had been alien to him, he had, like many other careerist elements,

*Geminder, like a number of other Czech Communist leaders, was a Czech-German by origin, his native tongue being German. —*Ed.*

joined the Communist Party for selfish reasons. In 1925 he had been closely linked with Alois Neurath, who had later been unmasked and expelled from the Party as a Trotskyite. In 1927 he had been in touch with Desider Fried, who had been expelled from the Party for grave political errors and hostile views; in 1930 he had become friendly with Josef Gutmann, who was unmasked as a Trotskyite and expelled in 1933. Between 1926 and 1935 he had been in touch with various Jewish nationalist and cosmopolitan elements such as Reicin, Polac, Frejka, London, and others. With them he had masqueraded as a loyal Communist, while in fact they were working against the Party.

Geminder then told the court how he had met Slansky in 1930. Their friendship had grown quickly and he had soon become his unqualified admirer and willing tool. Slansky had soon confided in him and told him of his own connections with the Trotskyites. Since 1946 he had co-operated with Slansky and other members of the conspiracy in filling key positions in the Party and State with their own followers. Frejka and Frank had been placed in the economic administration; London, Dufek, and others in the Ministry of Foreign Affairs; the Zionist Goldstuecker and the adventurer Richard Slansky in diplomatic posts in the West.

Links with the Past

Geminder explained that for their conspiracy they had relied largely on people who had spent the war in Britain and who had come back after the liberation as supporters of British imperialist policy and often as out-and-out agents of Western imperialism. In the field of foreign affairs the main agents of the conspiracy had been Clementis, "on whom Slansky relied personally," Dufek, Hajdu, London, "the international spy Simone, who had connections with

Western journalists," Slansky's brother Richard, and Goldstuecker. The court then asked Geminder to describe how he had established connections with imperialist espionage organizations. Late in 1947, Geminder said, Slansky had told him that he was in touch with "the British spy Zilliacus." "I had known from Party circles that Zilliacus was a British spy. When I asked Slansky if he knew that Zilliacus was an old spy he said that of course he knew, but Zilliacus played an important part in Britain and suited his plans." Zilliacus was presented in the periodical *World Outlook* as a progressive Labor man, and this just at the time when he had openly appeared in the role of a Titoite advocate.

Geminder then described how he maintained contact between Slansky and Zilliacus. Slansky had given him sealed letters—six or ten of them, usually with a red-gummed seal on which Slansky had signed his initials. Occasionally Slansky had sealed them in his presence after showing him the contents, which constituted "real espionage." These were sent to Zilliacus through the London Embassy. In reply to a question by the Prosecutor, Geminder admitted that in addition to acting as a link between Slansky and Zilliacus he had also had personal contacts with Zilliacus.

The Prosecution submitted three letters illustrating Slansky's and Goldstuecker's collaboration with "the British spy Zilliacus" for the purpose of "tying Czechoslovakia to the economic policy of the West." Geminder recognized the letters as part of the correspondence that had gone through his hands. In connection with one of them, which dealt with Czechoslovakia's acceptance of the Marshall Plan, Geminder stated that Slansky had told him in 1947 that he favored Czechoslovakia's acceptance. A Czechoslovak delegation had been all ready to leave for Paris. This was one instance of how Slansky had worked to Zilliacus's directives. Asked about his personal contact with Zilliacus, Geminder said that in June, 1948, when Zilliacus was in Prague, he had been present at the tail-end of a conversation between Zilliacus and Slansky. What Slansky had told Zilliacus in his presence "must be described as espionage material." "With Zilliacus's help we brought about the prerequisites for the liquidation of the popular democratic regime in Czechoslovakia."

Zilliacus, Geminder suggested, had been more than a mere link with the Western espionage centers; in carrying out their criminal designs the conspirators had counted on active help from the Western imperialists and had worked in accordance with their plans for the severance of Czechoslovakia from her alliance with the USSR and the people's democracies and for her return to capitalism.

Conspirators Given Important Posts

Geminder next described how he had established a network of conspirators in the Ministry of Foreign Affairs and in the Diplomatic Service in order to be able to pursue the conspiratorial Center's foreign policy. Clementis had been a collaborator of Slansky even before February, 1948. From some remarks made by Slansky, Geminder had gathered that Clementis was a member of the conspiracy. A group of Trotskyites had been formed in the Ministry of Foreign Affairs, in the persons of Hajdu and London, and by putting them in charge of personnel questions the conspiratorial Center had gained control of the whole apparatus of the Foreign Ministry.

Slansky had told the defendant of his closest collaborators. They counted, apart from their prewar collaborators, mainly on those who emigrated to London during the war, and who during their stay in the West had tied themselves to capitalist circles, both personally and through family relationships. Interference with the Czechoslovak economy

Slansky concentrated in the hands of the war criminal, Josef Frank, and the cosmopolitan Frejka. . . . Slansky's accomplice in Brno was the spy and Jewish nationalist Otto Sling. . . . In the sphere of the defense of the Republic, the Army, and State security Slansky directed the hostile activities himself. In the leadership of the Army he joined ranks with the Jewish nationalist Bedrich Reicin, and in the State Security Service with his lackey Karel Svab. The corrupt and demoralized Antonin Svoboda, former member of the International Brigade in Spain, was placed in the Army, and in the field of security were placed the Trotskyite members of the International Brigade, Pavel Zavodsky, Hoffman, and Vales.

Contacts with Titoites and Zionists

When asked about further ways in which the conspirators were connected with the West, Geminder stated that various hostile Zionist organizations enabled Western imperialists to infiltrate into Czechoslovakia. Geminder stated: "On the basis of Slansky's directives, and with his help, we not only maintained direct connection with these agencies and their agents, and agents who worked behind the mask of a diplomatic function in the Yugoslav and Israeli embassies, but we also enabled these hostile agents and organizations, through numerous concrete measures, to carry out anti-State activity in Czechoslovakia." At the Cominform session in Poland in 1947, Slansky made contact with representatives of Titoite Yugoslavia. In the summer of 1948 he had an unofficial meeting with the biggest and most active agent of the imperialists, a close collaborator of Tito, Moshe Pijade. Slansky, and on his instructions Josef Frank, sent various delegations or commissions of experts to Yugoslavia. These delegations, which were usually led by members of the conspiracy, primarily

Frejka and Loebl, had the task of executing instructions to tie Czechoslovakia with Titoite Yugoslavia. During the time when Yugoslavia was no longer fulfilling agreed deliveries, for example of nonferrous metals, Slansky insisted in spite of this that the export of valuable machinery to Yugoslavia be continued. The conspirators enabled the Titoite agents, behind the mask of official activity, to spread propaganda in favor of Titoite Yugoslavia and to carry out anti-State activity in various Titoite propaganda centers, as for example the "Yugoslav bookshop," which the conspirators allowed to remain open even after the Cominform resolution.

In connection with hostile Zionist organizations, there was the emigration of citizens of Jewish origin, contrary to official agreements with the State of Israel. The Israeli Embassy wanted to organize these campaigns itself and therefore asked for the continuation in Czechoslovakia of the activity of Zionist organizations. Slansky ordered Geminder to support these campaigns. Bedrich Reicin was entrusted with the organizational aspect, Otto Fischl with the economic and financial side. The defendant said: "When emigrating, Jewish capitalists were given an opportunity to export various industrial equipment, machinery, objects of great value, silver, gold, and objets d'art. Some of the industrial products exported in this way had been bought earlier for hard currency by Czechoslovakia in the West."

The hostile Zionist organization could work in Czechoslovakia under various pretexts. For example, the U.S. "Joint," which was a camouflage branch of the American intelligence service, could carry on its activity under the guise of charity work. The decision to permit "Joint" to continue its activities was taken by Slansky himself. Also, it was through his intervention that the Hagana and branches of the Stern terrorist organization were enabled to continue their activities.

Examination of Dr. Clementis

The hearing of evidence from Dr. Clementis began at 14.00 [2 P.M.] on November 21. Clementis began: "I plead guilty to having become involved in 1939 with the French intelligence service of the Sûreté Nationale and to thus having become an agent of the Western imperialists. Later, as Under-Secretary of State and afterward Czechoslovak Foreign Minister, I established espionage contacts with Anglo-U.S. spies. I carried out espionage in their interests and against the Czechoslovak Republic." Clementis said that, as a supporter of Benes's pro-imperialist policies, he had established close contact with Slansky after Benes had lost his position. With him he carried out a subversive policy in the organization of the cadres in the Ministry of Foreign Affairs, and thereby began to play his part in the conspiratorial Center. He further pleaded guilty to having carried out subversive activities aiming at the overthrow of the people's democracy and the restoration of capitalism. On Slansky's instructions Clementis had established contact with Zilliacus, to whom he passed on information about Czechoslovakia and whom he enabled to interfere in Czechoslovakia's internal affairs. In 1946 he got in touch with Simone, whose criminal activities he financed and to whom he passed on espionage information. "I also supported the Trotskyite group in the Ministry of Foreign Affairs."

"I Never Was a Genuine Communist"

"To tell the truth, I must say that I never was a genuine Communist." He had grown up in an atmosphere of Slovak nationalism, and described in detail his activities as a student from 1921 to 1925 in Prague when he took part in political activities as a result of which he came into contact with the Communist Party. In Prague he had gathered around him nationalistically minded Slovak students, and as early as 1924 he had taken up a polemical attitude in his paper *Dav* * against the official Communist Party line on the Slovak nation. He had not found the "right attitude" toward the Party and the working class. Clementis admitted to having instilled his bourgeois nationalism into the paper *Dav* and thereby into the Slovak intelligentsia, which had consequently fallen victim to this alien ideology. The attitude of *Dav* was admittedly antidemocratic and antiprogressive.

Clementis was then asked by the Prosecutor how he had established contact with foreign espionage authorities. He said that in 1939 he had been introduced to the Sûreté Nationale in Paris, where he had been in exile, and later in his capacity as Under-Secretary of State and Foreign Minister he had established direct contact with Anglo-U.S. spies. He described in detail the beginning of his contacts in Paris in 1939, first with Hubert Ripka. Ripka was Benes's right-hand man in Paris. Despite his knowledge of that fact, Clementis had openly conveyed to Ripka the views of the Communist Party on topical problems. He also knew that Ripka passed on that information to Dr. Benes. When war broke out he openly took up an anti-Soviet attitude over the question of the Soviet-German Pact and Finland,** whereby he drifted into the reactionary camp and which contributed toward the case with which he "got involved with the Sûreté Nationale."

Work for the Sûreté Nationale

Clementis was then asked to give details of his connections with the Sûreté Nationale. In October, 1939, he

*A publication of leftist Slovak intellectuals, mainly Communists, prior to the Second World War.—*Ed.*

**Clementis had been expelled from the Party for his public opposition in 1939 to the Soviet-German Non-Aggression Pact and the Soviet attack on Finland.—*Ed.*

said, he was arrested by the Sûreté Nationale and examined at the police prefecture in Paris, during which investigation he betrayed various important data concerning the activities of Communist émigrés in Paris such as Sverma and [Viliam] Siroky.* Thereupon he had been asked bluntly whether he was prepared to work with the Sûreté Nationale, to which he had agreed. That important interview had, according to the Prosecutor, been witnessed by an interpreter, who in his deposition had stated: "Clementis did not behave like a member of the Communist Party and willingly answered all questions put to him. He also committed himself in writing to working for the Sûreté Nationale." Clementis admitted that this was all true. Czechoslovak reactionaries as well as numerous French and British personalities had made great efforts to secure his release. Ripka, in particular, had shown the utmost interest in seeing Clementis freed.

Clementis then said that he had remained in London from April, 1941, until his return to Czechoslovakia. In London he had renewed his contact with Ripka, and in 1942 or 1943 he had been told by the latter that [Maurice] Dejean, de Gaulle's representative, was interested in meeting him. Dr. Ripka and Dr. Benes were informed about his connections with the Sûreté Nationale. The Prosecutor then told Clementis that Gen. Bartik, head of the intelligence service in 1945, tried and sentenced for military treason to five years' imprisonment in 1948, had confirmed on examination that he knew of Clementis's betrayal to the French police. To which Clementis added: "Bartik was in a position to know this, being so close to the French authorities and President Benes's expert on French affairs as well as head of the intelligence section of the Czechoslovak General Staff." Asked about his meeting with Dejean, Clementis said that

* Slovak Communist leader, Vice-Premier, and later Prime Minister of Czechoslovakia.—*Ed.*

he realized that the instigator of that meeting had not been Dejean but Benes and Ripka. In 1946, when Dejean handed his credentials to Clementis on his appointment as French Ambassador in Prague "I established direct espionage relations with him as the representative of the French espionage service."

Wartime Relationship with Benes

Speaking about his relationship with Benes during the war, Clementis said that in 1941 Benes had invited him to discuss their future co-operation. "I know that Benes was for the capitalists, against the USSR, and that his policy aimed at depriving the USSR of influence in Czechoslovakia after the war. I told him that I was in agreement with his Western orientation. After this conversation Benes made it possible for me to take part in the Czechoslovak transmissions of the BBC to enable me to propagate his pro-imperialist ideas."

PROSECUTOR: "I present document No. 11, which proves Clementis's close co-operation with the reactionary Slovak politicians [Juraj] Slavik, Lichner, [Jan] Becko, [Jan] Pauliny-Toth. This is a record of negotiations about the appointment of the editor of the Slovak transmissions from London."

PRESIDING JUDGE: "This document has been presented to you during the preliminary investigation. Do you know its contents?"

CLEMENTIS: "Yes, correct."

Clementis continued: "Benes made it clear that he agreed with my appreciation of the international situation and with the tenor of my broadcast talks and that he counted on me for an important post after the war. He wanted to have his man in the Communist Party to enable him to claim that he was playing a progressive role in co-operating with the Communists in the Government."

PROSECUTOR: "I put it to you that you became a traitor to the Czechoslovak people just like your friends who hold these same opinions."

CLEMENTIS: "I admit that."

Slovak Nationalism

Speaking about his activities as a Slovak bourgeois nationalist, Clementis said that on his return to Slovakia in 1945 his activities were "hostile to the people's democratic Republic because I remained a bourgeois nationalist. I must admit that the ideas of the subversive group of Slovak bourgeois nationalists were clearly marked by Titoite influence. Like the Titoites in Yugoslavia, we in Slovakia propagated a foreign and hostile ideology of bourgeois nationalism. I fully admit my guilt in taking part in this subversive group of Slovak bourgeois nationalists, which tried to separate the development of Slovakia from the development of the State as a whole, thus strengthening reaction and hindering the progress of socialism and the development of the people's democratic order."

Espionage for the West

Returning to his collaboration with Benes, Clementis recalled his swearing-in as Secretary of State in the Ministry of Foreign Affairs in 1945. "In April, 1945, in the President's villa, we agreed between ourselves and without the presence of witnesses about fundamental policy in foreign affairs. Benes instructed me to take action immediately after my return to Prague to secure privileges for the U.S. Army which would enable its members to move freely in Czechoslovakia, i.e. in the rear of the allied Soviet Army."

In May, 1945, Clementis had joined with Jina, a creature of Benes, who introduced him to the Anglo-U.S.

agent Arnost Heidrich.* Clementis had entrusted Heidrich with working out the Statute of Organization for the Ministry of Foreign Affairs and had appointed him Head of the Political Section of the Ministry. "In this way I made possible the execution of the Benes policy of linking up with the West and of removing Czechoslovakia from Soviet influence."

PROSECUTOR: "This means that you acted as an agent serving the interests of the Anglo-U.S. imperialists?"

CLEMENTIS: "Yes it does, I do not deny it."

Turning to his own espionage activities Clementis described his relationship with Dejean, who came to Prague in 1946 as French Ambassador and who "immediately, at our first meeting, reminded me of my obligations to the Sûreté Nationale." He had supplied Dejean with information on Czechoslovak foreign and home policy and Dejean "often told me that we must try to limit the growth of Soviet influence in Czechoslovakia." The Prosecutor then placed before the Court a document proving Clementis's connection with Dejean.

"Following the instructions and example of Benes and Masaryk," Clementis went on, "I established espionage links with Nichols ** and [Laurence] Steinhardt *** immediately after my return to Prague in 1945. . . . Nichols and Steinhardt had the task of preventing the people's democratic order from becoming established in Czechoslovakia and to bring the country into the imperialist camp. They worked out a plan of setting up various information and cultural organizations to promote U.S. culture as a bulwark against Soviet influence in the center of Europe. . . . On his first visit Nichols assured me of his confidence and later repeated this when he brought me a personal

*Formerly Secretary-General of the Czechoslovak Foreign Ministry.—*Ed.*

**British Ambassador to Czechoslovakia.—*Ed.*

***U.S. Ambassador to Czechoslovakia.—*Ed.*

letter from [Ernest] Bevin thanking me for a telegram of congratulations which I had sent to him on his appointment as Foreign Secretary. Nichols declared on that occasion that he valued my friendly feelings toward Britain. Both Nichols and Steinhardt had particularly close and intimate relations with Benes and Masaryk, who informed them fully of all Czechoslovak affairs, and I gave them information about the views held by the Party.

"I want to emphasize that while the French and English showed interest in political questions, Steinhardt concerned himself mainly with economic problems and with questions affecting international organizations under U.S. influence such as the ILO [International Labor Organization, a U.N. body], the International Fund, the World Bank, and others. I passed on espionage information to Steinhardt through Loebl. With his aid I strengthened Steinhardt's position in Czechoslovakia. Steinhardt also paid attention to his private affairs in Czechoslovakia as partner of a New York law firm. In 1948 Steinhardt approached me several times on behalf of the notorious warmonger John Foster Dulles * and tried to make me take steps to ensure the payment of compensation for the nationalized property of the well-known Petschek banking family. John Foster Dulles, who became notorious through his advocacy of German bankers during the First World War and who is also known for his dirty bargains with Nazi bankers during the second war, was the lawyer entrusted with representing the Petschek interests.

"I want to state that I also collected intelligence reports from the peoples' democracies. Immediately after the liberation I arranged through the Military Mission in Budapest the establishment of a wide espionage network in Hungary. Gen. [Frantisek] Dastich, who deserted after February, 1948, to become an open U.S. agent, directed

*U.S. Republican foreign affairs specialist and later Secretary of State under President Eisenhower.—*Ed.*

this espionage network and sent me intelligence reports from Hungary by courier. This activity was financed from dollar funds.

"I admit that together with Slansky I carried out a subversive cadres policy in the Ministry of Foreign Affairs." All the candidates proposed by Slansky for posts in the foreign service were taken from the ranks of the London émigrés and of the Jewish bourgeois nationalists. "I knew of them . . . that they had established close relations with reactionary circles in Britain."

Relationship with Zilliacus

About Zilliacus Clementis said: "After the war he came to Czechoslovakia, and on Slansky's orders I received him. It was generally known that he was in the pay of the intelligence service. I know definitely that in 1947 Zilliacus called on Slansky, who then rang me up to tell me to see Zilliacus. . . . In autumn, 1948, when I was head of the Czechoslovak delegation at the U.N. General Assembly in Paris, the then Czechoslovak Ambassador in London Kratochvil brought me memoranda from Zilliacus dealing with questions under discussion at the U.N. General Assembly. As leading Czechoslovak delegate he wanted me to take up the position of an intermediary and this would have in reality represented the first step toward abandoning the camp of peace led by the USSR and toward moving into the imperialist camp." The Prosecutor then showed the Zilliacus memoranda to Clementis, which the latter identified.

PROSECUTOR: "This means that Zilliacus, through the relationship which he established with you, tried to make use of you in the U.N. as a lever for the realization of his imperialist intentions?"

CLEMENTIS: "Yes. That is a fact."

PROSECUTOR: "In this way Zilliacus openly tried to interfere with Czechoslovakia's internal affairs, which belonged exclusively within the sovereignty of the Czechoslovak Republic?"

CLEMENTIS: "Yes, that was like Zilliacus, who wanted to play the role of a young Labor Party member but was in fact a foreign spy."

PROSECUTOR: "From your and Slansky's evidence one must conclude that Zilliacus was in contact with Czechoslovakia's mortal enemies led by Slansky, as the emissary of the Western imperialists."

The Prosecutor then accused Clementis of having established hostile contacts with the agent of Western espionage services, André Simone, of whose close relations with Slansky Clementis had been aware. Asked to describe Simone, Clementis said: "I became personally acquainted with Simone in Paris in 1938. Even at that time, in conversation with him, I learned about his vast connections with the representatives of the world capitalist press and of his connections with the West. After the war his entire orientation can be described as typically cosmopolitan."

PROSECUTOR: "How did you know that Simone was in touch with the British intelligence service?"

CLEMENTIS: "Rudolf Slansky told me so in 1949, when I enquired about Simone's past."

PROSECUTOR: "And what did Slansky know about your relationship with Simone?"

CLEMENTIS: "Simone himself told me that Slansky was interested in this co-operation."

End of Clementis's Examination

Clementis then told the court that he, Slansky, and Simone had lunch together during the Peace Conference in Paris. After Clementis's return from the Peace Conference Simone had visited him at the Ministry of Foreign Affairs. After the February events in 1948 Simone had tried to secure the post of head of the Intelligence and Information Section of the Foreign Ministry. When Clementis had consulted Slansky he had told him that he, Slansky, had other plans for Simone. Asked by the Prosecutor whether he had passed on information to Simone, Clementis said that he had given him reports on Czechoslovak foreign policy and international problems, and in particular confidential information concerning agreements with the Soviet Union, Poland, Romania, Hungary, and Bulgaria, and information relating to Czechoslovakia's participation in important international discussions and meetings, including secret negotiations with regard to the Marshall Plan in Czechoslovakia and a treaty of alliance with France.

PROSECUTOR: "This points to the fact that Simone was a further link between you and the imperialist agents?"

CLEMENTIS: "Yes."

PROSECUTOR: "You have also admitted that you financed Simone's criminal activities?"

CLEMENTIS: "Yes. At the end of 1947 I gave Simone Kcs.60,000 [$1200] from the Ministry's funds and told him that this sum was to cover his expenses in connection with his activities as a publicist."

PROSECUTOR: "To put it correctly that means espionage activities. Do you wish to add anything to your evidence?"

CLEMENTIS: "I have told you everything. I have admitted that I became an agent of the Western imperialists. I have admitted my participation in the subversive activities of the Benes clique and later of Slansky's anti-State espionage Center. All my activities in this Center were directed toward the liquidation of the people's democratic regime and the restoration of capitalism, and to detaching Czechoslovakia from the peace camp and making her subservient to imperialist interests."

Examination of Artur London

The proceedings continued with the examination of Artur London, former Deputy Minister of Foreign Affairs.

London began by pleading "guilty of active participation in the anti-State conspiracy created and directed by Slansky. I carried out my activities from 1948 up to the date of my arrest. This anti-State Center planned the liquidation of the people's democratic order and the restoration of capitalism in Czechoslovakia. Together with Geminder I directed the Trotskyite group in the Ministry of Foreign Affairs. This group seized control of the Party organization in the Ministry in order to create conditions favorable to the placing of hostile cadres in important positions in the Ministry of Foreign Affairs. I also admit my guilt in acting as a link in the espionage relations between Slansky and the old British agent Zilliacus. For this purpose I made use of the diplomatic mail facilities of the Ministry of Foreign Affairs. I myself had espionage relations with the U.S. agent Herman Field, to whom I gave intelligence reports."

Relations with Trotskyites

Speaking about his past, London admitted that he had established contact with a Trotskyite group in France in 1940. This group, consisting of Czechoslovaks who had been members of the International Brigade in the Spanish Civil War, had been centered in Marseilles and later in Paris. The group had included Osvald Zavodsky, Laco Holdos, and Antonin Svoboda, all of whom had been given important positions by Slansky after the war. "Slansky did this because he himself was a Trotskyite, supported the bourgeois view, attracted to himself similar men, and counted on these people in his criminal plans."

Deputy Foreign Minister

From March, 1949, onward, London had carried out Slansky's directives while holding the post of Deputy Minister of Foreign Affairs. "At the same time on Slansky's and Geminder's orders, I misused the diplomatic mail for the espionage purposes of the anti-State Center. I was a link in the chain of espionage connections between Slansky and Geminder on the one hand and the old agent of the intelligence service, Zilliacus, on the other. In March, 1949, Geminder told me to take charge of the Courier Department of the Ministry of Foreign Affairs and he stressed that I was being given this task because they regarded me as reliable and that Slansky himself was greatly interested in this. Geminder added that he would give me letters for forwarding to employees of Czechoslovak diplomatic missions abroad. . . . He emphasized that letters addressed to him from these employees must be delivered immediately."

Espionage Activities

Among Slansky's correspondents were Kratochvil and Goldstuecker in London, who received letters for the "notorious anti-Soviet agent and intelligence service agent Zilliacus." In 1947 London had made contact with the "well-known U.S. agent Noel Field" in Geneva. At that time "Field was a leading representative of the American aid organization, the Unitarian Service Committee. In practice the U.S. espionage service concealed itself under this label and Field himself was under the orders of the U.S. espionage service chief, Allen Dulles, who lived in Switzerland. Under the cover of aid and rehabilitation the U.S. espionage service made use of the Unitarian Service Committee to penetrate the peoples' democracies and to develop treasonable and espionage activities. Field . . . made use of this to establish contact, to create confidential links, and to tie people to himself and thus try to build up a U.S. espionage network. In this manner Field tapped many important sources of espionage directed against the people's democracies, as had been proved by the Rajk trial in Hungary. Field recruited his agents from among those who had succeeded in reaching important positions in Party and State after their return to the people's democracies."

PROSECUTOR: "Some of this information was secret and top secret?"

LONDON: "Yes, that is correct."

Contact with Zionist Circles

London was then asked what he knew about the connections between the members of the conspiratorial Center and Israeli and Zionist organizations. He replied: "Slansky and Geminder maintained contact with Zionist circles and Israel by Goldstuecker through the diplomatic pouch."

PROSECUTOR: "By extending connections with representatives of the West you sabotaged our relations with the USSR and the people's democracies. Tell us about this."

LONDON: "Slansky, Geminder, and myself sent to the people's democracies people with pro-Western and anti-Soviet views, proven hostile elements. In this way the Zionist Otto Fischl was sent to the German Democratic Republic, where he spied. The cosmopolite Richard Slansky was sent to Warsaw, where he behaved in such a way that he compromised Czechoslovakia and weakened relations with the Poles. Jaroslav Hasek was sent to China, where he abused his official position. They all tried to complicate and weaken relations between Czechoslovakia and the other countries and played into the hands of the enemies of democracy."

Examination of Vavro Hajdu

The next accused to be questioned was Vavro Hajdu, the former Deputy Minister of Foreign Affairs.

PRESIDING JUDGE: "Do you plead guilty to the charges in the indictment?"

HAJDU: "I do."

PRESIDING JUDGE: "Explain your guilt."

HAJDU: "I am guilty of having been a member of the anti-State conspiratorial espionage Center in Czechoslovakia. On instructions from Slansky and Geminder I carried out active hostile activities against the Czechoslovak Communist Party and people. This hostile activity was aimed at the overthrow of the people's democratic regime, the restoration of capitalism in Czechoslovakia and the country's breaking away from the camp of peace and democracy led by the USSR. Until my arrest I was a member of the Trotskyite group in the Ministry of Foreign Affairs, created by Geminder. The aim of this group was to get hold of important posts in the Ministry. One of the means to this end was to gain control of the leadership of the Party organization in the Ministry. I also plead guilty to having been a spy in British service from 1941 until my arrest. I supplied the British Secret Service with various espionage reports. As Deputy Minister of Foreign Affairs I betrayed the interests of my State by being an imperialist agent and by betraying important secrets relating to Czechoslovak policy on international affairs."

Enrollment by British Police at Wiveliscombe

PROSECUTOR: "Under what conditions did you begin your plotting activities against democratic Czechoslovakia?"

HAJDU: "In 1939 I returned from Paris with Clementis, who even then openly admitted his anti-Soviet attitude and his hostility regarding the German-Soviet pact and the Finnish-Soviet war."

PROSECUTOR: "During the investigations you said that in 1941 you were enrolled by the British police in Wiveliscombe. Tell us all about this."

HAJDU: "I confirm my earlier statements. In 1941 I was enrolled by the British police in Wiveliscombe and I undertook to supply espionage reports on political and economic matters in Czechoslovakia."

PROSECUTOR: "Now tell us about the circumstances, how you were enrolled by the British for espionage services."

HAJDU: "In 1941 I was called to the police station in Wiveliscombe to give some information about my past. I was led to the chief of police. When he knew that I had been in Slovakia in 1939 he asked me about some industrial undertakings there. I gave him information about some factories in the neighborhood of Bratislava. He was satisfied with my information and asked me to supply similar reports in future."

PROSECUTOR: "Did you agree to this?"

HAJDU: "I promised to supply the British police with reports of interest to them."

PROSECUTOR: "Did you sign an undertaking?"

HAJDU: "The chief of police gave me the text of an agreement and I signed it."

A deposition was then read by Hajdu's wife, Karola Hajdu, confirming the above.

PROSECUTOR: "In what way did you continue to cooperate with the British espionage service?"

HAJDU: "I soon came to the conclusion that the British police were, in fact, not interested in my reports about industry in Slovakia; this was only a pretext to get me to sign the undertaking. Even then their main task was to build up their agency among the émigrés in preparation for the postwar period. The British took up espionage connections with me in 1946 when I worked at the Ministry of Foreign Affairs in Prague. I again worked for them and from 1946 to 1950 I had frequent contacts with various British spies who held responsible positions in the British diplomatic service and to whom I gave important reports about decisions of the Czechoslovak Government on international questions. By so doing I betrayed the interests of the Czechoslovak people."

Return to Czechoslovakia

PROSECUTOR: "From what you have said it is clear that you returned to Czechoslovakia not only as an enemy of the Czechoslovak Republic but also as an enrolled spy of imperialist Britain."

HAJDU: "Yes, because of my past, of my Trotskyite opinions, and my connections in London, I returned to Prague, with a hostile attitude toward the USSR and the peoples' democracies and as an enrolled spy of the British Secret Service."

Hajdu then explained how he noticed that Clementis was pursuing a foreign policy along the conceptions of Benes and placing people with a pro-Western attitude in important posts. Clementis had told him that all important questions had to be decided by Slansky. It had become clear to him as early as 1947 that Slansky, Geminder, and Clementis were carrying on a policy hostile to the people's democratic regime. In discussions with Geminder, they had found out that they held the same hostile opinions and this had become the basis of their friendship. Geminder had then recruited him for the plot.

PROSECUTOR: "What, concretely, was your plotting activity in the Ministry of Foreign Affairs?"

HAJDU: "In 1947 we began to set up Trotskyite groups in the Ministry. At that time Slansky appointed to the Ministry the Trotskyite Dufek, my old friend from London." In 1948 hostile elements were placed in missions abroad. After February, 1948, Geminder had given him and Dufek "hostile instructions to step up their activities in order to capture the most important positions in the Ministry and thus be enabled to carry out their anti-people's democratic aims."

Asked who had been in charge of the Trotskyite group in the Foreign Ministry, Hajdu named Geminder. Hajdu had first met Slansky in person in the autumn of 1947 on the eve of an official journey to Western Germany which he was to undertake with Gen. Pika. Interrupted by the Prosecutor with a request to state who Pika was, Hajdu called him "a reactionary, a Benes agent, the head of the Czechoslovak Military Mission in Moscow during the Second World War, who was eventually unmasked as an enemy of democratic Czechoslovakia." Three days before his departure, continued Hajdu, he had seen Slansky and discussed his trip with him. Slansky had told him on this occasion that he knew Gen. Pika to be a British agent.

Contacts with Gladwyn Jebb

Hajdu then described his contacts with Gladwyn Jebb. "In the summer of 1946 I was sent by Clementis to the Paris Conference of the Council of Foreign Ministers as the Czechoslovak Government's observer. There I called on Gladwyn Jebb, a senior official of the British Foreign Office, at the Hôtel Georges Cinq. I had known him from earlier negotiations in London and Paris."

PROSECUTOR: "What did you call on him for?"

HAJDU: "I wanted to discuss with him, as the senior member of the British delegation, our demands in connection with the peace treaty with Hungary. Jebb invited me to come to the bar with him to have a drink because we should then be able to talk better. In the course of the conversation he told me he knew that I had signed on with the British police at Wiveliscombe and suggested that I should therefore continue my espionage connections with him."

PROSECUTOR: "Did he ask you about any matters constituting State secrets?"

HAJDU: "Jebb asked me a few general questions about the Foreign Ministry, what the real position was between Masaryk, Clementis, and Heidrich, what relations were like among them, how the Ministry was organized, what position I held, and what my prospects were for the future. I informed him in detail about conditions in the Ministry and told him that we were preparing a peace treaty with Germany. In the course of our conversation he then said that we should meet again and reach agreement with one another."

PROSECUTOR: "Agreement about what?"

HAJDU: "Agreement about our future collaboration."

PROSECUTOR: "And did you meet Jebb again?"

HAJDU: "Yes, in October, 1946, when I was in Paris as the Czechoslovak delegate to the Peace Conference. Jebb invited me to dinner. At this dinner I told him, at his request, what the Czechoslovak delegation's views were on the progress of the Peace Conference and what preparations we were making for further negotiations. At the end of our talk Jebb was highly satisfied with my espionage information and told me that Britain counted on my further co-operation."

PROSECUTOR: "Were you aware that this information was a State secret?"

HAJDU: "Yes."

PROSECUTOR: "That it concerned the interests of the Czechoslovak people?"

HAJDU: "Yes."

PROSECUTOR: "And that you should have kept absolutely silent about it?"

HAJDU: "Yes."

PROSECUTOR: "And why did you betray it?"

HAJDU: "Because I had been enlisted."

At this point the Prosecution produced a photograph and asked Hajdu to identify the person shown with Masaryk. Hajdu identified him as Gladwyn Jebb, the man he had supplied with espionage material over several years.

Espionage for France

The Prosecution asked Hajdu to speak of his espionage contacts with the former French Ambassador in Prague, Dejean.

HAJDU: "This is how my contacts with Dejean started. In the spring of 1947, at a reception at the British Embassy, Dejean came to me and told me that he knew of my collaboration with the British. He had not, however, spoken to anybody about it because, as a matter of fact, he would like some information for himself, and nobody need hear about it. Since that time Dejean used to receive various important espionage reports from me, about Czechoslovak policy in international questions, mainly about Czechoslokavia's foreign-political negotiations. In 1949 I informed him about the reorganization of the Foreign Ministry, I told him about my new position and my sphere of competence, about the new conditions in the Ministry, and what personnel and other changes had taken place. Thus Dejean was informed by me about matters which ought to have been kept secret in the interests of the Republic. In 1949 Dejean asked me to intervene in favor of the condemned French woman spy Pospisilova. During the same year he asked me to intervene in the matter of the espionage affair of the former French Military Attaché in Prague, Helliot; he asked that this espionage affair should not be published in Czechoslovakia. He also asked that in connection with the French-Czechoslovak Trade Agreement the question of the payment of interest on the old Austro-Hungarian debt should be discussed. I tried to comply with Dejean's requests by giving twisted or inaccurate information to Vice-Premier Siroky who, at that time, represented Clementis during the latter's absence."

The Prosecution here submitted a number of documents confirming Hajdu's evidence. Hajdu accepted them as authentic and accurate. In conclusion Hajdu said that he had made a full confession of the part he had played in the conspiracy headed by Slansky. He knew that there was no point in denying it since the whole gang of criminals had been unmasked.

Examination of André Simone

Shortly after 14.00 [2 P.M.] hours André Simone, whose real name is Otto Katz, was called to give his evidence. Simone was a former editor of the Communist daily *Rude Pravo.*

PRESIDING JUDGE: "Do you plead guilty to charges as outlined in the indictment?"

SIMONE: "Yes."

PRESIDING JUDGE: "Tell us in which way do you admit your guilt?"

SIMONE: "I admit my guilt in that I was a member of the treacherous anti-State conspiratorial Center led by Slansky. The conspiratorial Center's aim was to overthrow the people's democratic regime in Czechoslovakia, the restoration of capitalism, to transform Czechoslovakia into a colony of Western imperialists. I admit my guilt in that I was in the service of the French, British, and U.S. espionage and that I was engaged in active espionage activities against democratic Czechoslovakia."

PRESIDING JUDGE: "What led you actively to fight the people's democratic regime in Czechoslovakia?"

SIMONE: "I shall tell the truth. I am the son of a manufacturer, educated in the spirit of bourgeois ideology. The working class was alien to me. This was why my surroundings were formed of people spiritually akin to me, from the ranks of traitors against the working people, Trotskyites, Right-wing socialists, and Jewish bourgeois elements. For thirty years I defended bourgeois ideology, disrupted the unity of the working class and the workers' movement in various capitalist countries and I carried on similar activities in Czechoslovakia, as a participant in Slansky's conspiracy."

Simone then went on to tell the court that he had become a Trotskyite in 1926 in Germany. At that time he had gotten in touch with the Trotskyite Erwin Piscator, a theatrical director in Berlin.

Work for French and British Espionage Services

PROSECUTOR: "When and how did you become associated with the French espionage service?"

SIMONE: "In September, 1939, I pledged myself to the French Minister Mandel in Paris, a Jewish nationalist."

Continuing, Simone said that Mandel had maintained his own espionage service with the help of Jewish and some French magnates. In 1939 Mandel had discussed with the accused the Daladier plan and had told him about his belief that a Second World War would break out. Mandel had expected Germany's defeat and had stressed the point that after the war matters would have to be settled with the Soviet Union. The accused had agreed with Mandel's views and had told him that he, Mandel, could always rely on his co-operation. In November, 1939, shortly after the accused had begun to work for the Czechoslovak Information Bureau in Paris, which had been directed by Ripka, Mandel had given the accused the task of finding out whether Benes and Ripka desired an agreement with [Eduard] Daladier.* The accused then reported back to Daladier and at the end of 1939 he had left France for the U.S.A. In the U.S. Simone had collaborated with Louis Fisher,** and since 1939 with the Jewish nationalist, Judge [Felix] Frankfurter of the U.S. Supreme Court. Between 1941 and 1946 he had edited *Tribune Israelita* in Mexico, which spread Jewish nationalist propaganda and ideology hostile to the working class, socialism, and progress.

PROSECUTOR: "In 1939 you pledged your co-operation to the British intelligence service. Tell us about it."

SIMONE: "I pledged my collaboration with the British intelligence service in Paris in 1939 in the office of the agent Paul Willert."

PROSECUTOR: "How were you enlisted for collaboration with the British intelligence service?"

SIMONE: "In April, 1939, I became acquainted in New York with Willert. He was then the director of the New York office of Oxford University Press."

PROSECUTOR: "Who is Willert?"

SIMONE: "He is the son of Sir Arthur Willert, who, after the first war, became the head of the Press Department at the British Foreign Office. Brenda, wife of Paul Willert, is the daughter of a British peer whose family enriched itself through oil business in Mexico."

Noel Coward an Intelligence Chief

PROSECUTOR: "When did you meet Willert?"

SIMONE: "I was invited to a dinner in a restaurant near the Comédie Française. Already during our first meeting Willert told me that he was working for the British intelligence service. He asked me to meet his chief, Noel Cow-

*French Premier before the war and a signatory of the Munich Pact.—*Ed.*

**U.S. journalist and expert on the Soviet Union.—*Ed.*

ard, who at the time held an important position in the British intelligence service. I lunched with Noel Coward in Willert's presence in a private room in a Paris restaurant."

Both Willert and Coward requested from him information on German propaganda in France, on the activities of pro-Hitlerite groups, on the attitude of the French people, on the French Army, the activities of the working class movement and the Communist Party, and on antiwar propaganda. The defendant admitted that he complied with this request.

PROSECUTOR: "Who is this Coward?"

SIMONE: "Coward is a British novelist and playwright whose works are very popular in the Anglo-Saxon world. In France in 1939, during the war, Coward never hid the fact that he was working for the intelligence service. He was full of confidence and vanity."

PROSECUTOR: "What did you discuss at your meeting with Coward?"

SIMONE: "Coward told me at the very beginning that he knew about my collaboration with important French circles and named certain members of these circles but pointed out that this method of collaboration did not meet present-day needs. He appealed to me then to join him. I told him that I would think it over and we agreed on a further meeting at which I pledged myself to work for the British intelligence service."

Return to Czechoslovakia

Simone then told the court that he had left Czechoslovakia in 1922 and returned there in 1946. In New York he had undertaken to co-operate with the Jewish nationalist and U.S. intelligence agent, Schoenbrun,* induced

*Schoenbrun was at the time a correspondent for the Overseas News Agency.—*Ed.*

by Schoenbrun's statement that the U.S. Secret Service was in possession of Simone's undertaking vis-à-vis the French Minister Mandel to co-operate with the latter. Schoenbrun had told him that if the Communist Party learned of that fact it would have serious repercussions for Simone. Witness added that he did not want his hostile activities to be known to the Communist Party, and so in February, 1946, he had met Schoenbrun again, in New York on his return journey from Mexico to Czechoslovakia. They met at a restaurant and Schoenbrun informed him that he was instructed by the U.S. Secret Service to negotiate with him. Schoenbrun emphasized that the U.S. was conducting the same policy as Mandel, who, were he alive, would have wholeheartedly backed Washington. Mandel had rendered splendid service to capitalist Jewry. Schoenbrun had said: "It is the duty of every Jew to support the Americans even if he does not agree with every detail of their policy." Simone's best way of showing his support was by providing "information," which the Prosecutor interpreted as meaning "espionage information."

Simone then explained what he knew of Schoenbrun's background: he was the son of a Jewish capitalist who emigrated to the U.S. before the First World War. In 1946–47 Schoenbrun was in the service of the U.S. Overseas News Agency, which "is an organ of the U.S. Jewish capitalists" financed by Bernard Baruch and others. This Agency was one of the important links among the U.S. Zionists and Jewish nationalists in the U.S. and co-operated closely with the State Department. Through this Agency, the U.S. Board of Psychological Warfare Strategy was spreading "outrageous lies and slander against the peace camp." All this Simone knew when he agreed to work for Schoenbrun.

Simone was then asked to say something more about the U.S. Board of Psychological Warfare Strategy. He said that the section was headed by Gen. [Walter] Bedell-Smith and its members were officials of the State Department, of the War Department, of the Catholic and Protestant Churches, and the Jewish organizations. That Board "organizes murder, sabotage, diversionary activities, etc. in China." It had at its disposal hundreds of millions of dollars under the Mutual Security Act to be used for the same ends in the USSR and the people's democracies as well as for the recruitment of émigrés for the U.S. forces. The correct name for that Board ought to be "U.S. Board for a shooting war and for the liquidation of progressive people, for murderous atomic aggression on the USSR and the peoples' democracies, and for the elimination of anything in the way of the U.S. imperialists."

Simone agreed with the Prosecutor that he had returned to Czechoslovakia in 1946 as a "triple agent of the British, U.S., and French intelligence services." His return had been made possible by Dr. Ripka. In March, 1946, he had approached Slansky to find out whether he was to stay in Czechoslovakia or to go to Germany.* Slansky decided that he should stay and a fortnight later Slansky, in his apartment, had asked him about his life abroad. Simone, realizing that all his Trotskyite activities were well known, had given Slansky a full report about his close connections with Jewish nationalists and Zionist circles in Mexico and of his work as editor of the paper *Tribune Israelita.* Slansky had accepted that news as a matter of course. Slansky had also shown particular interest in the activities of the former General Secretary of the U.S. Communists, [Earl] Browder, "unmasked in 1944 as an enemy of the working people."**

*Czech Communists of German origin, although born in Czechoslovakia, were either assigned to positions in their own country or sent to East Germany after the war. Hostility to Germans was very marked right after the war.—*Ed.*

**Actually, in April, 1945, the French Communist leader Jacques Duclos denounced Browder and his policies. Some months later the U.S. Communist Party denounced Browder's

His interest in details of Browder's technique as a "liquidator" became understandable to Simone only later when he realized that Slansky wanted to "emulate Browder and Tito in usurping power and in liquidating the Marx-Lenin Communist Party of Czechoslovakia" whereby he would have tried to destroy the popular democratic regime.

Appointed to Rude Pravo *by Slansky*

Simone then referred to a later conversation with Slansky at which the offer was made to him to take charge of the international department of the Central Committee of the Czechoslovak Communist Party. In 1946 Slansky had told him of the need to "popularize Tito and Yugoslavia's specific road to socialism." At that time he had not known that Slansky had talked with Tito. Slansky had also shown great interest in co-operating with the Zionists and Jewish nationalists in Mexico.

The Presiding Judge asked Simone why he thought Slansky had confided to him his "hostile intentions." Simone replied: "He wanted to ensnare me in his conspiratorial Center in Czechoslovakia." Owing to Simone's background, Slansky had found it easy to win him over.

With a view to promoting the conspiratorial design, Slansky had obtained an important position for Simone on *Rude Pravo* and substantial financial gain. The Prosecutor wanted to know more details of the way in which Slansky "planted" Simone on *Rude Pravo*. Simone said that in May, 1946, he had discussed in Slansky's study a number of articles he was to write about him. Slansky desired to be portrayed as the chief actor in the Slovak National Rising and wanted the decisive role of the Czechoslovak Communist Party to be suppressed. Slansky showed

---

policies and removed him from office. Duclos's article was reportedly written by Soviet Communist Party leader Andrei Zhdanov.—*Ed.*

himself satisfied with the article written in that spirit and said: "This is the way articles ought to be written."

Describing conditions in *Rude Pravo* Simone said that the paper had been under Slansky's "iron" control and that no article could be published without the consent of Slansky or one of his associates. In the spring of 1946 Slansky tried to suppress one of the important pre-election speeches of the Party Chairman, Gottwald, by moving it from the front page to page two. Slansky also sabotaged the popularization of the peaceful policy of the USSR, and after February, 1948, Slansky instructed Simone to write a short note instead of a leading article on the Soviet Government's proposal to the U.S. Government with regard to the discussion of disputed questions. In the autumn of 1948 after Gottwald had stressed the importance of close links between the press and the masses, Slansky and his gang decided to oppose that. On Simone's appointment as head of the Press Department in the Ministry of Information in May, 1946, Slansky had told him to maintain unofficial relations with capitalist correspondents and "he told me exactly: 'You know how to get on with them.' In the spring of 1947 I informed Slansky in his office about my relations with Western journalist agents."

PROSECUTOR: "That means that you confided in Slansky with respect to your espionage links with America and Britain."

SIMONE: "I spoke about this with him as early as 1946 when he came to Paris for the Peace Conference. During our conversation in May, 1946, I informed Slansky in the following words with regard to the foreign journalists: 'You know that everything I tell them is passed on.' Slansky agreed with this. Before my departure for the Paris Peace Conference in June, 1946, Slansky instructed me to co-operate closely with Clementis. Clementis knew that the reports he gave to me were being used for the information of Western spies, who even visited me in my apartment for this purpose . . . Clementis fully agreed with my activities."

PROSECUTOR: "And for this reason Clementis gave you a reward of Kcs.50,000 [$1,000] * in the autumn of 1947?"

SIMONE: ". . . Clementis told me that he intended to give me Kcs.50,000 in view of the expenses I incurred in my contacts with foreign journalists."

PROSECUTOR: "This means that in effect Clementis financed your espionage activities in connection with Western journalists who in reality were nothing but imperialist spies?"

SIMONE: "Yes, Clementis financed my espionage activities."

In March, 1948, Slansky had instructed Simone to write a book on the February events in a Trotskyite spirit. "Slansky asked me to describe him as the chief personality of the February events. When he described these events to me he always put himself in the foreground, in the Titoite manner." Slansky had told Simone to model his book on [John] Reed's *Ten Days That Shook the World*, which was written in the Trotskyite spirit.** "By falsifying history Slansky wanted to gain popularity among the Czechoslovak people and to suppress the leading and decisive part played by Gottwald." Simone, however, had not written this book because it would have exposed him immediately as a Trotskyite and an enemy of the Czechoslovak people. Slansky's instructions to Simone with regard to relations with foreign journalists had not changed after February, 1948. "He told me that these relations were even more important after February, 1948, and that the hostile policy of our anti-State Center had remained unchanged."

* See p. 161 for conflict with Clementis's testimony.—*Ed.*

**Reed, an American newspaperman and friend of Lenin, is buried in the Kremlin. His book on the Bolshevik Revolution had been warmly received by Soviet Communist leaders.—*Ed.*

Renewed Contacts with British and U.S. Intelligence Services

Simone had renewed his contacts with the intelligence service agent, Willert, in August, 1946, at the Paris Peace Conference, when he had supplied him with a detailed report of his activities in Czechoslovakia and when "I told him that Slansky had his own notions and plans for future development in Czechoslovakia." Willert had asked many questions about Slansky. Simone had also informed Willert of his co-operation with Clementis. Willert had encouraged him "to strengthen relations with Slansky and Clementis and told me to make use of Slansky's instructions with regard to my contacts with foreign journalists to furnish reports to all British agents who might call on me."

Simone stated that information for his espionage reports had been given to him by Slansky, Geminder, Loebl, Frejka, Clementis, and Hajdu. "When I was unable to supply these Western agents with the information they required I put them in touch with other members of the espionage Center, Slansky in particular. In March, 1948, I arranged a meeting between Slansky and two hostile Labor MP's, [Richard] Crossman and [Richard] Wigg. I arranged this meeting by telephone and it was to be held in the Communist Party Secretariat. After his return to Britain Crossman wrote a number of hostile articles against people's democratic Czechoslovakia.

Anti-Semitic Attitude

Simone, asked by the Presiding Judge whether he wished to supplement his evidence by any statement, said: "As a conspirator I am responsible for every action and crime of each Jewish member of the conspiratorial Center.

Which are the countries where fierce anti-Semitism is on the increase? The U.S. and Britain. I have joined the spies of those States. Which country has a law against racialism and anti-Semitism? The USSR. I have joined the U.S., British, and French anti-Semites against the Soviet Union. Therein lies my crime. I am a writer, supposedly an architect of the soul. What sort of architect have I been, I who have poisoned people's souls? Such an architect of the soul belongs to the gallows. The only service I can still render is to warn all who, by origin or character, are in danger of following the same path to hell. The sterner the punishment . . ." (voice falls too low to be intelligible).

Examination of Ludvik Frejka

The next accused to be questioned was "Ludvik Freund, alias Frejka."

PRESIDING JUDGE: "Do you plead guilty in the sense of the indictment?"

FREJKA: "I do."

PRESIDING JUDGE: "Tell us about your guilt."

FREJKA: "I admit that until my arrest I was an active member of the conspiratorial Center led by the accused Slansky. I further admit to having been an agent of the intelligence service since 1941 and to having made contact during the Second World War with Konni Zilliacus and the important U.S. spy Herman Field."

PRESIDING JUDGE: "How did you maintain contact with Zilliacus and Field after the war?"

FREJKA: "After the war I renewed contact with Zilliacus and Field in Czechoslovakia, even then as a member of the anti-State plot. I met them on various occasions in Prague and made available to them important confidential reports, mainly on Czechoslovak economy. By doing so I endangered the country's security. Furthermore, for the purpose of evaluating the espionage material, I recruited other members of the conspiratorial Center, namely Josef Goldman and Eugen Loebl." Slansky had also co-operated. Frejka further pleaded guilty to having "spread among the masses of Czechoslovakia the opportunist theory that 'socialism can be built without the dictatorship of the proletariat' for the purpose of promoting the interests of the Western imperialists." They had also denied "the inevitability of the intensification of the class war and preached co-operation with the exploiter classes and their lackeys." The spreading of these opportunist theories had enabled the plotters to avoid being unmasked for years.

Economic Sabotage

PRESIDING JUDGE: "How, in practice, did you hamper the building of socialism?"

FREJKA: "By wrecking and sabotage in the spheres of planning, industry, commerce, finance, agriculture, etc. We strengthened and extended Czechoslovakia's dependence on the U.S., Britain, and their satellites. We further hampered the utilization of Soviet experience in building socialism. On the other hand, we collaborated closely with the Tito clique, although we were aware of their anti-Soviet attitude even before the Cominform resolution." On Slansky's instructions and on his own initiative he had sabotaged economic planning together with his accomplice Josef Goldman. In the sphere of heavy industry, for instance, they had purposely left out of the plan the utilization of "a whole number of important iron ore-bearing areas." In this way they had safeguarded the dependence of the iron and steel industry on imports, mainly from the West.

PRESIDING JUDGE: "What were your crimes in the sphere of fuel and power?"

Yes, Choose Any 3 of These Remarkable Books FREE

to Introduce You to the New, Monthly Evergreen Review... the Most Exciting, Tuned-in Magazine Published Today

Yes, Evergreen's Editors would like to send you any three of these eight exciting books you choose—with their compliments.

This richly rewarding gift is our way of inviting you to celebrate with us a new phase of the exciting cultural explosion we are living in. We think you will share with Evergreen's more than 200,000 readers (grown from 25,000 just three years ago) a delight in the most adult—the most literate—the most exciting and meaningful writing, theatre and art on today's cultural scene. Every issue is a fresh experience, filled with the work of the most gifted writers, artists, playwrights, and photographers in the world — lavishly illustrated with eye-opening color and stunning photos. You'll enjoy such stimulating, varied reading as these recent features:

- **MARIJUANA AND SEX**—A University Professor reports on astonishing interviews with 200 users.
- **THE BEARD**—the full text of the sensational "funny, fast and authentically outrageous brilliant little monster of a play." (Newsweek);
- **EP (EPIDERMAL) ART**—Six glorious pages of eight fantastic females illustrating the newest, wildest art form ever;
- **THE NEW EROTICISM**—A noted art critic surveys and illustrates the new sexuality in the world of painting, sculpture and dance.
- **ELDRIDGE CLEAVER RAPS**—A no-holds barred interview with the Black Panther Minister of Information.
- **FILM A LA WARHOL**—Behind the scenes with the DeMille of the underground set;

(continued over)

PLUS AN EXTRAORDINARY EXTRA FREE BONUS FOR YOU

- **A FRENCHMAN LOOKS AT EROTICA**—Alain Robbe-Gillet, one of France's most distinguished novelists, expresses his intriguing views on everything sexual from Kinsey to Cardinale;
- **LE ROI JONES VS. "WHITEY"**—Saul Gottlieb's interview with the poet and black militant shortly after the Newark riots—**plus the poem that the judge cited in giving Jones an unprecedentedly savage sentence;**
- **GRIDIRON MAIDENS**—Sensational photographs taken secretly in the girl's locker room of a midwestern high school;
- **CONFESSIONS OF A HIPPIE**—An exclusive interview telling it like it is—exactly like it is—on the hippie scene... sex, drugs, babies, homosexuality, you name it;
- **ROSENCRANTZ & GUILDENSTERN ARE DEAD**—the complete script of this international hit that may well be one of the most important and enduring plays of this century.
- **THE MAGICAL MYSTERY TRIP**—Timothy Leary takes you on a guided visit to turned-on Anglo-India, a hip session of London's Parliament and the Beatle's revelations.
- **I WAS CURIOUS**—Excerpts from the diary of this sensational Swedish film kept by the Director.

AND MORE MORE, MORE!

Exciting? Yes. Provocative? Yes. Fresh and literate? Yes. Why miss out on the Evergreen Review explosion? Take advantage of this introductory subscription at the low rate of only $9 for the next year—12 issues at a saving of $3 from the newsstand price. And at the same time, choose any *three* of the eight books shown here as your FREE BONUS. There never was a better time to see the new monthly *Evergreen Review*.

CHOOSE YOUR 3 FREE BOOKS

#181 A MAN WITH A MAID. A runaway national best seller. This anonymous classic of literature in the Victorian tradition explores with rare candor the various relationships between a gentleman and a woman whom he holds in bondage.

#1028 ROMANCE OF LUST or Early Experiences. Anonymous. An unputdownable 537-page volume, suppressed since the Victorian Era, that describes the most delightful variety of experiences ever put between the covers of one volume. The hero tells how he begins his amorous career at the age of 15, first being taught by a married friend of his mother's, and then initiating a succession of governesses and others in an amazing succession of almost superhuman scenes.

#155 THE PEARL. 3 Volumes Complete in 1 Giant Volume. This giant volume of "Facetiae and voluptuous reading" includes six complete novels that are standards of the black literature of the time ("Lady Pokingham, or They All Do It," "Miss Coote's Confession," "La Rose d'Amour, or The Adventures of a Gentleman in Search of Pleasure," etc.) A remarkable collector's item.

#1032 SUBURBAN SOULS The Erotic Psychology of a Man and a Maid. Anonymous. When this autobiographical work was published in a limited edition in 1901, its outspoken revelations made it as sought after as My Secret Life. It has never been reprinted up to now and G. Legman lists it as one of the three most rare sexual memoirs ever published.

#1026 MEMOIRS OF A RUSSIAN PRINCESS. An extraordinary underground classic, depicting the infamous license of behavior of the royal court in Imperial Russia.

#178 JULIETTE. 6 Volumes Complete in 1 Mammoth Volume. By The Marquis de Sade. One of the most extraordinary works of literature ever written. Juliette is the embodiment of evil—and these 1216 pages detail her monstrous and debauched career.

#127 MY SECRET LIFE. "The anonymous autobiography of a wealthy Victorian who lived for sex alone." (Book Week) Now you can read this famous sexual memoir unexpurgated in one giant volume.

#1025 HARRIET MARWOOD, GOVERNESS. Anonymous. The story of the "education" of a young man by his beautiful depraved Victorian governess.

PLUS FREE CLUB MEMBERSHIP—You also receive full benefits of membership in the Evergreen Club, the only Club of its kind that makes available honest, powerful, adult books which may never show up at your corner bookstore. Members **never** have to buy any book ever, but if they do, they benefit from unusually low Club prices. Your membership is completely free.

FREJKA: "In this sphere we created such a disproportion between supply and demand that the supply of fuel and power suffered continual interruptions. I believe that the liquidation of this sabotage of ours will take a long time."

PRESIDING JUDGE: "What was the effect of your sabotage in industry?"

FREJKA: "I committed a terrific amount of sabotage in industry, together with my accomplices, mainly by distributing investments wrongly, by directing them to unproductive industry." They had also planned for too low a productive capacity. They had sabotaged the chemical, machine-building, leather, and rubber industries. They had also sabotaged foreign trade. In the sphere of food supplies the group had committed "extensive wrecking and sabotage and created a situation that still exists in Czechoslovakia today. . . ."

PRESIDING JUDGE (interrupting): "We shall deal with these concrete facts later."

Frejka said that "in England in 1941 I undertook to cooperate with the intelligence service. In July, 1940, I was arrested by the British as a Communist. I was put into an internment camp. A tribunal decided later that I should be released and in September, 1941, at the time of my release, I was called to the camp authorities to see the intelligence service captain. On his proposal I signed a declaration that I would support the war aims of the British Empire and that I would also work for Britain after the war." Frejka confirmed the Presiding Judge's submission that he had returned to Czechoslovakia "as an agent of the intelligence service and of the Benes clique."

Frejka then described his return immediately after the war with the help of Lausman; that he reported to the Party and was told by Slansky that he need not report to Lausman as he, Slanksy, had a job for him. "From this I gathered that Slansky and Lausman had come to some agreement about me." Slansky had given him the posts of economic adviser to the then Vice-Premier Gottwald and also of Secretary to the Economic Committee of the Central Committee of the Party.* He had been instructed to work on Slansky's directives and "had agreed with Slansky to work together in strengthening economic relations with the capitalist countries." They had also agreed to fill the most important posts with "old capitalist so-called experts." "We also agreed to recall Josef Goldman and Bedrich Lewit from England in order to place them, after their return, in influential positions in the economic sector." He had further agreed with Slansky "to preserve the prewar structure of economy in the way desired by the capitalists." In this way they had aimed at preserving Czechoslovakia's dependence on the capitalist West, and it was through this that he had joined the conspiratorial Center.

Placing "Hostile" People in the Economy

Speaking about the placing of hostile persons in the economic sector, Frejka named "our direct confederates" who had been given important positions. They included the "Jewish bourgeois nationalist and Ripka agent Loebl, and Margolius, who had a Zionist past," both of whom became Deputy Ministers of Foreign Trade. Other confederates were "the old servants of the international financial magnates, the Rothschilds," and Dr. Frantisek Fabinger, who became Director-General of the Metal Industry and later of heavy engineering, who "used his positions to sabotage the building up of the heavy engineering industry"; [Zdenek] Jicinsky, the Director-General of Foundries, and an "old agent of prewar capitalism who systematically undermined the building up of the foundry industry and prevented it from becoming the basis of Czechoslovak industry as a whole, and thus served the

*In 1945.—*Ed.*

Western imperialists"; Dr. Jaroslav Tichy, the Director-General of the Chemical Industry, "an old devotee of fascism, a collaborator with the Nazis, and a member of the Anti-Bolshevik League, who sabotaged the development of the chemical industry"; the Deputy Director-General of the Power Industry, the cosmopolite, Barta-Bronstein, who had particularly close relations with Slansky and "used his position to sabotage the power supply of our industry"; and Svatopluk Rada, Director-General of Mines and later Deputy Minister of Industry, who "slowed up the development of fuel and ore supplies."

In light industry Frejka named Dr. Ivan Holy, "a typical product of the Bata system, a Gestapo agent," who became successively Director-General of the Leather and Rubber Industry, Director-General of the Textile Industry, and Deputy Minister of Industry. The hostile aims of the anti-State Center had been carried out by Holy in as far as he "supported the disproportionate development of light industry."

Joseph Goldman and "the international arms merchant, factory and estate owner Eduard Outrata" had been active in the field of economic planning. In the financial sector, Slansky himself had recruited the "bourgeois lawyer and Zionist Otto Fischl, who carried out Slansky's directives in the Ministry of Finance."

Control of Central Economic Commission

The conspirators had seized control of the Central Economic Commission, which was the most important economic authority, by means of Frejka's own appointment as Chairman and by the appointment of Goldman. Slansky and Frejka had also created a large number of various economic sections and commissions where the same people had held influential positions. Thus Loebl had been Chairman of the Foreign Trade Section, Fabinger Chairman of the Metals Section, Barta Chairman of the Power Section, Tichy Chairman of the Chemical Industry Section, and Holy Chairman of the Leather and Rubber Section. "These people, thanks to their various positions and plurality, combined the functions of administrative and controlling authorities and simultaneously directed the practical affairs of Czechoslovakia economic life. . . . We supplied these hostile elements with dictatorial powers for their hostile activities. . . . We also seized control of regional economic commissions. We succeeded in this mainly because Slansky and Svermova appointed people like Sling, [Jan] Fuchs, [Stanislav] Landa, [Bohomir] Lomsky, and Polac as chief regional secretaries of the Party in the most industrialized regions. They were of bourgeois Jewish origin and during the war, in London, they had the closest contacts with imperialist circles." The Central Economic Commission had been abolished in the autumn of 1948 for "hindering the socialist development of our economy. However, we managed to conceal the real reasons for the abolition of the Commission and its subordinate bodies. It was replaced in the Central Secretariat of the Party by the new Department of Industry, Commerce, and Finance, and this was placed under the direction of Josef Frank, one of our fellow-conspirators. The treacherous activities of the Economic Commission were continued by this department and by almost the same people." The conspirators had assumed control of the Central Planning Commission by appointing Frejka himself, Reiman, and Goldman as members, and "under my leadership, these men, together with other fellow-conspirators, dominated the Central Planning Commission."

Slansky had seized control of the Central Association of Industry before Frejka's return from England by appointing Reiman as General Secretary of the Association, and hostile elements such as [Vaclav] Vlk had been placed in important positions. "This Central Association of Industry and its divisions were a huge bureaucratic organization employing more than a thousand people, all of whom were old capitalist experts. During the occupation, these people ran Czechoslovak industry for the Nazis." Slansky and Frejka had kept this organization in existence right up to 1949–50 in order to have "yet another strongpoint for our hostile activities."

Relations with Zilliacus

Questioned about his relations with Zilliacus, Frejka said: "Zilliacus called on me in 1946 in my office in the Central Communist Party Secretariat. We were, of course, acquainted, and he immediately reminded me of my obligations by speaking about my imprisonment in England and my release from the detention camp. He also said that he was glad to be able to recall our co-operation in England, which he valued highly, and told me that he had come to re-establish contact with me and to ask me to supply him once again with information about our economic life, in accordance with our agreement made in England. He went on to the question of the external economic relations of Czechoslovakia and said he wanted to know about the Czechoslovak attitude toward economic relations with the capitalist West, particularly England. I informed him of the preparations for the Two-Year Plan, which was being prepared in 1946. I also informed him of the nationalization of industry and banking in Czechoslovakia, about the condition of industry and banking after nationalization, and about the difficulties which we had to face. This conversation lasted for about three hours. Zilliacus gained a detailed survey of the state of the Czechoslovak economy from me; I told him especially about its vulnerable points, by means of which the Western imperialists could exert pressure on Czechoslovakia.

"In 1947, Zilliacus again visited Czechoslovakia, and on

this occasion I met him several times, when I betrayed various valuable information about the state of the Czechoslovak economy to him. In particular I told Zilliacus about Czechoslovak foreign trade, not only with the West, but also with the USSR and the people's democracies. Zilliacus was not satisfied with my information about the types of goods in question and therefore I put him in touch with another member of the espionage Center, Loebl, and asked him to work out a detailed report about Czechoslovak foreign trade for Zilliacus. Loebl promised to do so. I informed Zilliacus about the progress of the Two-Year Plan. Zilliacus showed great interest and asked for more detailed information, not only about Plan fulfillment but also about Czechoslovak industrial potential. I therefore instructed Goldman, another of the conspirators, to prepare a report, which I personally handed to Zilliacus in the Hotel Alcron. I saw Zilliacus again in the autumn of 1948, when he told me that his stay in Czechoslovakia was ending and that he was about to leave for Yugoslavia. He supported the treacherous views of Tito on that occasion and spoke against the Cominform resolution. . . ."

PRESIDING JUDGE: "What were your views on this resolution?"

FREJKA: "I did not support this resolution because the aims of Tito in Yugoslavia were basically identical with ours. . . . In the autumn of 1948 Zilliacus showed particular interest in questions concerning Czechoslovak foreign trade, and I enlightened him, making use of the Plan fulfillment report for the first nine months of 1948."

PRESIDING JUDGE: "Were you entitled to give Zilliacus this sort of report?"

FREJKA: "No."

PRESIDING JUDGE: "That means that you violated what?"

FREJKA: "That means that I violated official secrets."

PRESIDING JUDGE: "You were in fact a link between the anti-State Center and an imperialist spy."

FREJKA: "Yes, I was such a link, but I want to state that relations with imperialist spies, particularly with Zilliacus, were also maintained by other members of the anti-State Center, above all by Slansky himself. In the autumn of 1947, Slansky, about two days after my meeting with Zilliacus, called me to his office and asked me to act as interpreter at his own meeting with Zilliacus. On that occasion we agreed that Slansky would inform Zilliacus about principles of economic policy and that I would fill in the details. Slansky also agreed with my intention to instruct Goldmann and Loebl to prepare detailed reports for Zilliacus. To enable Zilliacus to gain even more detailed information about Czechoslovak foreign policy, Slansky, in my presence, telephoned to arrange a meeting between Zilliacus and our fellow-conspirator Clementis."

Specific Acts of Economic Sabotage

Asked to specify some of the sabotage activities, Frejka said that they had slowed down the development of the heavy industry; they had failed to take into account some important iron ore and nonferrous metal deposits; they had sabotaged the power industry; they had misallocated capital investments; they had deliberately planned to utilize industrial potential below its capacity, and they had generally caused a great deal of waste. "A particularly effective means of sabotage" was the prevention of the application of Soviet planning experience. The Presiding Judge asked for details on each of these points, first of all on the hampering of the development of heavy industry.

Frejka said that the implementation of the plan for the development of heavy industry was postponed until the years 1950–52, whereby investment operations in the industry accumulated so much that it became impossible to tackle the problem. Such was the case with the construction of the Gottwald foundries in Kuncice and of a large number of other engineering plants. Investments and resources which were to have been used for these purposes were instead diverted to "various superfluous" projects in other sectors, such as the construction of a series of textile mills in Slovakia. In the Five-Year Plan itself this hostile policy was continued by the deliberate setting of low targets for the production of indigenous raw materials. Furthermore, industrial production was purposely lowered by planning for far too low utilization of available productive capacity. In the heavy engineering industry, for instance, only one shift was worked although more could have been operated, or heavy lignite cutting machinery was used for only four to five hours a day. Plans for far too low use of available capacity were also made for the cement industry; for the production of natural and artificial fibres; for foundries and the power industry.

Another act of sabotage was the misappropriation of investment capital for purposes other than the development of heavy industry. Efforts were made to prevent the application of Soviet planning experience. Both during the Two-Year and Five-Year Plan periods the task of concentrating on the fulfillment of specific production objectives was neglected, in the metal industry and the foundries in particular. As a result, in many cases items of light instead of heavy industry were produced, i.e. light electromotors instead of heavy ones, or small machine-tools instead of large ones, etc. Soviet experience was not applied in the field of planning for the use of raw materials in accordance with norms. As a result, for instance in 1950, the metal industry's percentage of copper used for the production of some materials was 2 percent in Czechoslovakia as against 1 percent in the USSR. Consequently a copper shortage arose. Industrial and foreign trade sabotage further led to the total or partial failure of heavy industry to fulfill its commitments, or to great delay.

Another act of sabotage was the introduction into the Two-Year Plan of a provision to the effect that the textile, rubber, and leather industries could use, for the purchase of raw materials and investment equipment abroad, only such foreign exchange as they could procure through their own production. Thereby these industries were directly compelled to expand their exports to the West. A variety of difficulties for Czechoslovak industries arose from that at a later date, such as raw material shortages in the textile and leather industry or thousands of millions of crowns' worth of export losses.

The building of a raw-materials basis for the foundry industry had been neglected. A large number of important deposits of iron ore and nonferrous metals were not taken into consideration when planning. In 1947 mining was stopped at the iron ore mine in Sternberk in Moravia. A lower output of iron ore was planned for 1953 than for 1948. While cutting down iron ore production, the Five-Year Plan envisaged a 70 percent increase in the production of crude iron. Thus a serious discrepancy was created and the foundry industry became even more dependent on imports of raw materials from the West. Similarly, in the production of nonferrous ores several years were wasted as a result of sabotage; during that time large quantities could have been produced. Frejka and his accomplices had further opposed the utilization of low-yield ores, and consequently geological research was sabotaged. Yet another means of keeping the Czechoslovak foundry industry dependent on the West had been the failure to create the necessary refining facilities for nonferrous metals. As a result, some of the nonferrous metals imported from the peoples' democracies had to be sent for refining to Belgium. Also neglected in the Five-Year Plan were the important deposits of pyrites in Czechoslovakia, despite the fact that the country was at that time entirely dependent on imports of these raw materials.

Frejka then explained his sabotage activities in the power industry, on which the conspirators had particularly concentrated. His own crime was, first of all, his agreement to a plan envisaging too low a utilization of available power plants. With a view to sabotaging the industry Slansky put Barta-Bronstein, a member of the conspiracy, in a high position. The latter concentrated his sabotage on arranging for excessive and widely dispersed construction of new power plants while, at the same time, neglecting and dismantling factory power plants. Slansky and Frank retarded the establishment of a separate Ministry of Fuel and Power and held up the application of a national fuel consumption policy. Another saboteur of the power industry was Fabinger, Director-General of the Metal Industry, who directed the sabotage of deliveries and repairs of electrical equipment. Power utilization figures in the Soviet Union were much higher than in Czechoslovakia, where some 25 percent of available plant as against 15 percent in the Soviet Union, were being held in reserve all the time. With the increasing demand for power during the winter months 1950–51 and 1951–52 substantial breakdowns in supply were the result of this sabotage. "These effects of sabotage in the power industry will be felt for some time yet, and it will take quite a while to remedy them."

The Presiding Judge then asked Frejka about sabotage in the field of investment planning. Frejka admitted to having carried out his sabotage activities "within the framework of the agreement on hostile investment policy entered into with Slansky," as already stated. It affected both the planning of new factories, and the reconstruction of old plants; in numerous instances establishments capable of production were destroyed and replaced by new plants, ostensibly to increase productive capacity. Asked about how this activity was carried out in the steel industry, Frejka stated that in the Konev Works in Kladno four still serviceable blast furnaces had been broken up and three new ones constructed. Similarly, in the Trinec Iron Works, still larger, still serviceable equipment had been dismantled and replaced by new machinery of approximately the same productive capacity. By this method huge losses had been caused to the Czechoslovak economy.

An expert's statement was then referred to, according to which, in the Trinec Iron Works, the value of the annual output still suitable for production, yet broken up, represented Kcs.530,000,000 [$10,600,000]; the loss suffered from 1948 to 1952 thus amounted to over Kcs.2,500-000,000 [$50,000,000], to which the value of the dismantled equipment — approximately Kcs.360,000,000 [$72,000,000]—must be added. "This approach," the statement declared, "has led to . . . the disruption of one of the main sources of the production of pig iron, steel, and rolled products, thus causing the Czechoslovak economy colossal losses." The accused then admitted "that under my control, a sum of some Kcs.9,000,000,000 [$180,000,000] was frittered away in what is called the reconstruction of Trinec. We further carried out sabotage in the planning of new factories, mainly by including in the plan the construction of unnecessarily large plants for light engineering. One of the branches thus affected was the production of automobiles, and another was the Czechoslovak leather and rubber industry."

Asked about the plan for a large automobile factory, Frejka stated that the construction of such a plant with an annual production capacity of some 50,000 vehicles had been under review. The plant had, however, not been built. He added that this harmful increase in the productive capacity of vehicles had been directly controlled by "an agent of U.S. monopolies, Alexander Taub," and by another member of the plot, Dr. Fabinger. "In 1946, with my approval, Dr. Fabinger invited the U.S. citizen Alexander Taub as a so-called consultant for the Czechoslovak motor vehicles industry. Taub then controlled the Czechoslovak motor industry until about the end of 1948. . . . We thus entrusted the control and the building of the Czechoslovak motor vehicles industry directly to an agent of U.S. monopolists, Taub, who then, through Fabinger and with our help, was responsible" for sabotaging the Plan of the Czechoslovak motor vehicle industry and for a further dovetailing of Czechoslovak economy with the capitalist West.

An expert's statement was then read according to which the harmful nature of the policy of the "imperialist agent Taub" lay in its intention to link Czechoslovak economy to the capitalist countries both as regards dependence on the import of raw materials and the export of its products. Frejka confirmed that this statement was correct. "Through their agent Taub, the U.S. monopolists had a direct influence on the development of Czechoslovak industry," he added. It was put to Frejka that he—Taub—was paid $2,000 and later $2,500 dollars a month, and in addition was given every facility to become acquainted with all large Czechoslovak metal producing plants. "Did Taub make full use of the possibilities which you granted him?"

FREJKA: "Yes. We also made it possible for the U.S. agent Taub to acquire on the spot the most confidential information and data on the largest Czechoslovak plants. When, about the end of 1948, Taub left for the U.S., he carried with him a number of secret and confidential plans and detailed data of both an economic and a technical nature about the most important Czechoslovak metal producing plants. He was therefore detained by security officials at Ruzyne Airport. On Fabinger's request, I intervened and arranged that Taub could take these papers away with him to the U.S. Thus I made it possible for our anti-State plotters' Center to gain a further contact with the Western imperialists.

"A further sector of heavy industry in which we carried out a faulty and harmful investment policy was the leather and rubber industry. There we had as co-operator

Dr. Ivan Holy, who took a substantial part in the sabotage activities affecting investment policy. Thus we included first in the Two-Year and then in the Five-Year Plan unnecessary provisions for the establishment of a tire plant in Puchov, Slovakia, for the production of light tires. A market for these products was not safeguarded either. Thus we frittered away a further several hundred millions in capital investment. Another sabotage act in this sector was to have ordered machinery for this tire factory from the U.S., which had to be paid for in advance, although it was known to me that such machinery was being manufactured in Czechoslovak engineering factories. Later an embargo was put on the export of parts of this plant by the U.S. Government, and it had to be manufactured in Czechoslovak engineering works. We were thus responsible for an unnecessary reduction of Czechoslovak foreign currency reserves amounting to some Kcs.200,000,000 in dollars [$4,000,000]."

PROSECUTOR: "But these were not your greatest sabotage acts. Tell us about your major activities."

FREJKA: "Especially extensive acts of sabotage regarding the development of Czechoslovak economy were carried out by us by including in the Plans the construction of a sheet rolling mill in the Ostrava area and of a large oil refinery in the Kadan area. About the autumn of 1947 we agreed with Slansky that the sheet mill would be bought in the U.S., although it was known to us, from the purchasing contract, that it was necessary to pay for the plant before its delivery and that the seller was not under any obligation to deliver the mill should there be a ban on the export of such goods by the U.S. Government. Such a ban was in fact later issued." The experts' statement on this matter said: "Before the contract was signed it was clear that an export licence would not be granted." Frejka, when confronted with this, stated that despite this the order had been placed, that Kcs.1,000,000,000 [$20,000,000] had been paid in dollars, but the goods had not been received. On the contrary, up to his arrest Czechoslovakia had been compelled to pay for the storage of the plant. It had been alleged that the mill was required to carry out the Plan; but "in 1951 it became evident that this was a fraud on our part, as in that year, although the mill had not been delivered, no shortage of sheet metal was felt, as it was possible to obtain what was required in the Liskovec plant."

Asked about sabotage activities affecting the oil refinery project, Frejka stated that the construction of this refinery had been provided for in the Plan, although it had been known that the necessary raw materials were not available at home and that it would have been more economical to restore the war-damaged Bratislava oil refinery, as well as to manufacture a greater quantity of petrol from coal in the Stalin Works. A further sum of several hundred million crowns had thus been unnecessarily spent. Further large sums had been frittered away in heavy engineering because existing productive capacity had not been made sufficient use of. The construction of plants had been started at unsuitable places, and work had had to be stopped and transferred elsewhere. Thus the construction of a large nitrate plant in the Ostrava Region had later to be discontinued and continued elsewhere, although even that site proved unsuitable.

There had been a whole series of similar cases, and this type of sabotage had slowed down and damaged Czechoslovak investment reconstruction, especially in heavy industry. On the one hand, tens of billions had been spent unnecessarily, and on the other, things required for the building up of socialism had been left undone.

Asked about matters which had been neglected in the Plans, Frejka referred to the steel industry, where projects providing for raw materials of home origin had been omitted. Thus there was no provision for the building of a rubber-making plant. "We made provision for the processing of natural rubber, which we intended to import from the West."

Asked for greater details of his sabotage activities, Frejka added that they had included lack of preparation and excessive dispersal. The first had resulted in the costs of the Czechoslovak building industries being 15 percent in excess of what they should have been, which had caused to Czechoslovak economy in recent years an annual loss of some Kcs.5,000,000,000 [$100,000,000]. Dispersal had resulted in the freezing of further huge amounts by delay. Losses under this heading were put by the experts' statement at Kcs.12,000,000,000 [$240,000,000] yearly. Frejka admitted his responsibility for this loss.

"Basic Conception" of Five-Year Plan Sound

PROSECUTOR: "How did you apply your sabotage intentions in the Five-Year Plan draft and in the further stages of the Plan negotiations at the expense of their positive points?"

FREJKA: "The basic conception of the Five-Year Plan is completely correct. We—the members of the anti-State plot—were unable to destroy this conception. We succeeded, however, as already stated, in smuggling into the Plan a series of sabotage acts, those acts about which I have given evidence. I have explained how we tried to justify these acts of sabotage by alleging the needs of the Czechoslovak economy and how we dovetailed them into the Plan. It was by this method that we succeeded in misleading responsible persons, in particular the President of the Republic. Later, it was [to] the President's merit that our acts of sabotage were successively exposed; they were then put right in the Five-Year Plan, in particular after the report made by the President to the February conference of the Czechoslovak Communist Party Central Committee in 1950 and 1951."

PROSECUTOR: "The sound nature of the Five-Year Plan was cleansed of your sabotaging superstructure. Was this so?"

FREJKA: "Yes, that is so."

Economic Dependence on Western Countries

Frejka was then questioned about his sabotage activities in the field of foreign trade. He stated: "In the field of foreign trade we put into effect the plotters' concept of maintaining the economic dependence of Czechoslovakia on the West, chiefly by orientating Czechoslovak foreign trade toward the West, and we acted against the development of trade relations with the USSR and the peoples' democracies. We made provision in the Five-Year Plan for excessive quantities of consumer goods to be exported to Western countries, and for excessive imports of raw materials from Western countries. We acted in this way in planning exports of footwear, textiles, and light tires, and in the import of textile raw materials, natural rubber, and leather." Frejka admitted that the losses of the Centrotex Company had amounted in 1950 and 1951 to over Kcs.3,000,000,000 [$60,000,000] as a result of the group's activities.

Asked by the Prosecutor whether the group had intentionally led Czechoslovak economy into dependence on capitalist countries, and on the other hand had sabotaged the development of trade relations with the USSR and the people's democracies, Frejka stated: "In various trade negotiations with the peoples' democracies I pressed those countries not only to buy from us investment goods which they required to set up socialism, but also quantities of consumer goods and investment goods which they did not need or which they could produce at home. In addition, I pressed for such countries, such as Bulgaria, to supply, in exchange for our deliveries, industrial raw materials which were in short supply there. Thus it occurred at times that we even turned down tobacco from Bulgaria in exchange for machinery, while we were later compelled to buy tobacco from Turkey for Western currency."

Other Evidence from Frejka

Sabotage activities against trade relations with the USSR were carried out by the accused in the autumn of 1950 during negotiations for a commercial treaty with the USSR. "In the course of these I pressed, together with my fellow conspirators, for the USSR to buy from us light industry products which the USSR did not need; on the other hand I also pressed for the Soviet offer of a greater delivery of grain to be turned down, although the economic needs of Czechoslovakia required this. By various sabotage acts of this nature we succeeded as already stated in smuggling into Czechoslovak plans extensive acts of sabotage." When these had been exposed, the Plans had had to be revised. The loss caused had amounted to several tens of billions.

Frejka was then asked about sabotage activities in the field of price and supply policy. In that sector, the accused admitted to having carried out sabotage mainly by decontrolling the price of bread and at too low a level in 1949. At that time, a fellow-conspirator, Outrata, had made a "conspiratorial" proposal to decontrol the price of flour and bread. This proposal had been supported by Frejka, although he knew that the bulk purchasing prices of animal husbandry produce were such that if the proposal was put into effect, large-scale feeding of bread and flour to animals would follow; and this had actually resulted. Frejka further stated that the result of their activities had been a serious disproportion in the relation of available supplies and rising purchasing power. The policy of reducing prices had therefore run aground about half-way through 1950. A leading role in the conspiratorial activities in the food sector had been played by Josef Frank, who had been appointed by Slansky head of the Price and Supply Commission, and it had been Slansky and later Frank who had co-ordinated subversive activities in supply matters. By various sabotage acts in this field, distrust had been caused among workers toward the Government and the Party. A further crime committed by Frejka was the introduction of the so-called SPH system, which Frejka had approved although he knew that it was a system practised by the Bata concern, and was both harmful and capitalistic. This system was responsible for slowing down the advance of socialism and for huge losses.

Relations with Titoites

Questioned about what he knew of the Titoites' plans for the establishment of an anti-Soviet federation, Frejka described a meeting in October, 1947, in Milan Reiman's apartment in Prague, at which, in addition to himself and Reiman, Loebl, Fabinger, and Goldman had been present as Czechoslovak representatives, and which the Yugoslav commercial attaché Ivo Barbalic—who was later expelled from Czechoslovakia—the Yugoslav Foreign Trade Minister Petrovic, and some other leading Yugoslav officials had attended. Various obstacles to close trade relations between the two countries were discussed. However, agreement was not reached on a number of fundamental problems and it was decided to send a Czechoslovak delegation to Yugoslavia to discuss things with [Boris] Kidric * in person. At that meeting in Prague the Titoite representatives had sketched prospects of Czechoslovak-Yugoslav economic co-operation with a clear anti-Soviet bias.

*One of Tito's closest associates and chief economic planner in Yugoslavia.—*Ed.*

Frejka, Reiman, and Fabinger had gone to Belgrade at the end of October, 1947. The Titoites had on this occasion voiced their "hostile attitude to Czechoslovakia in an even more provocative manner." Asked whether he had informed Slansky of the Titoites' hostility to Czechoslovakia and the USSR, Frejka replied that he had done so but that it had been clear to him that Slansky was fully informed of the hostile plans of the Titoites.

Slansky had nevertheless instructed him to continue the "excessive economic relations" with Tito's Yugoslavia. In reply to a further question Frejka confirmed that Slansky had repeated his instructions for "excessive economic relations" with Yugoslavia even after the Cominform resolution. That was why a trade agreement had been concluded with Yugoslavia for 1949 at roughly the same volume as that for 1948.

Frejka concluded his evidence by explaining that the conspirators had acted in this manner because their aims had been the same as those of the Titoites. "As I have here explained, we conspirators, led by Slansky, were trying, by means of sabotage, economic disruption, and espionage, to create in the economic field the prerequisites for a definite reversal of conditions in Czechoslovakia, for Czechoslovakia's severance from the camp of peace and her transfer to the camp of imperialism and war."

Evidence of Witnesses

Evidence of Ivan Holy

The first witness to be called at the session on the morning of November 23 was Ivan Holy, formerly Deputy Minister of Industry. To explain why Slansky had enrolled him in the conspiracy, Holy said: "I was a suitable person for Slansky. Slansky knew my bourgeois origin and knew about my collaboration with the German fascists during the occupation, when I acted as a Gestapo and Security Service informer and supplied them with information from the beginning of the occupation until January, 1945."

PROSECUTOR: "How did you know that Slansky knew of your activity during the occupation?"

HOLY: "This is proved by a conversation I had with Slansky at his office at Communist Party Headquarters in the autumn of 1947. He received me at a table on which there was a bundle of papers, and he said right at the beginning that he had documentary evidence of my past during the occupation, in fact about my connections with the Nazis. He hinted, however, that he would not use this material against me. Thereby he put me under an even greater obligation to carry out my hostile work according to his instructions and under Frejka's guidance."

At the request of the court Slansky here confirmed the witness's statement.

With Slansky's approval Holy had become Works Manager of the Bata Works in 1945. In 1946 Slansky had pushed through his appointment as a Communist Deputy. In 1948 Slansky had arranged for Holy's appointment as General Secretary of the Leather and Rubber Industries and later of Textiles, and later still as Deputy Minister of Industry. As a result of these favors he had been under an obligation to Slansky and had carried out all his instructions.

Holy then described the "hostile tasks" he had performed. Immediately after the liberation, in the summer of 1945, Slansky had instructed him to pursue a pro-capitalist cadre policy. On the occasion of his visits to the Bata Works in 1945 and 1946, Frejka had demanded that the Bata organization should be introduced in other nationalized enterprises. Frejka had then expressed the view that the time was not ripe for the introduction of the

Soviet Cost Accounting method in Czechoslovak economy. This view had been repeatedly uttered by Frejka, in particular in 1948 when the so-called De-Bureaucratization Commission was to recommend the adoption of the Bata organization in the economic Ministries.

Asked by the Prosecution whether Frejka had been "the principal and guiding force" in this matter, Holy replied: "No. The principal and guiding figure in the introduction of the Bata system was Rudolf Slansky." Holy then told the court how this policy had "supported Czechoslovak émigré traitors at the expense of the Czechoslovak people." In 1947 Dr. Jiri Kubelik, a former Social Democrat and a personal friend of the traitor Lausman, who was arrested for subversive activities in 1949 but was at that time still head of the Czechoslovak Leather and Rubber Industry, had signed an agreement in London with the capitalist Thomas Bata concerning deliveries of footwear, footwear machinery, and the repair of the latter. This agreement had been detrimental to the Czechoslovak economy because it had burdened it with the duty of repairing and modernizing the machinery pool of Bata's concern in the West, and had also enabled him to dominate the market with the help of regular deliveries of footwear from Czechoslovakia. In spite of the harmful character of this agreement Eugen Loebl, then Departmental Head in the Foreign Trade Ministry, had insisted on its observation.

Evidence of Vojtech Jancik

The next witness to be questioned was "Vojtech Jancik, alias Jung, in charge of the Cadre Department of the Secretariat of the Central Committee of the Party." He said that, after his return from England, Frejka had appointed him in August, 1945, to the Economic Department of the Central Committee, where he was first put in charge of Slovak affairs. In 1947, when he supported the hostile plans of Slansky and Frejka, he was put in charge of cadre policy in the Economic Department. Both had known him for a long time and knew that he had sympathized as a student with the Zionist movement, that he was of petty bourgeois descent, and that as a refugee in England he had "contact with Jewish bourgeois nationalists." Cadre policy had been laid down by Slansky and Frejka. The various sections and subsections were filled by Slansky with "Jewish bourgeois nationalists, cosmopolitans, and bourgeois so-called experts—for instance Eugen Loebl, Dr. Josef Goldman, Zdenek Rudinger, Fabinger, Dr. Ivan Holy, Svatapluk Rada, Dr. Oldrich Cerny, and other people of this type." All these people "were definite enemies of building socialism."

Asked about co-operation between Frejka's Economic Department and Tito's Yugoslavia, Jancik replied: "There was very close co-operation. In November, 1945, for instance, Frejka agreed with Slansky to send an economic delegation to Yugoslavia for the purpose of studying the situation there and gathering so-called experience. I myself was a member of this delegation."

PROSECUTER: "And what experience did you gather there?"

JANCIK: "During our one-week stay, and particularly in discussions between the leader of the delegation, Frejka, and the then Minister of Industry in Yugoslavia, Kidric, we learned that the Yugoslav Communists in no way utilized the experience of building socialism in the USSR but went the so-called special Yugoslav way, which was basically different from the methods of building socialism in the USSR." Slansky's conspiratorial Center had neglected Soviet experience in the same way; on the contrary, under the pretext of the so-called special situation of Czechoslovakia, they had worked for the restoration of capitalism and imperialism.

Examination of Josef Frank

After these witnesses, the accused Josef Frank was questioned. He pleaded "guilty of being a member of the anti-State Center which was led by Rudolf Slansky in the interests of the U.S. imperialists. I also plead guilty that I worked, together with Slansky and the other accomplices, for the usurping of power by the anti-State Center, following the example of the Tito fascist clique. I also plead guilty of sabotaging, on Slansky's instructions and on my own initiative, the building of socialism in Czechoslovakia, her economic basis, and defense capacity, and in this way of causing great material and political damage to the State. I am further guilty of having misused my office in the Communist Party to cover the criminal activities of my accomplices in the conspiratorial Center. And, finally, I plead guilty of being a war criminal and of having committed a whole number of grave crimes for the benefit of U.S. imperialists and to the detriment of the working people of Czechoslovakia, the Communist Party, and the whole peace camp."

Activities as a War Criminal

In reply to the question as to who had actually led him into this position, Frank replied: "The root of my struggle against the people and against socialism is my opportunism and my opportunistic development." He described his early development, and admitted that in 1930 he had first betrayed the revolutionary movement when he was arrested for Communist activities. At that time he had betrayed certain facts which had helped the bourgeoisie in the fight against the working class. Frank then explained at length how he had become a war criminal. In 1942 he had been appointed clerk and interpreter in Buchenwald concentration camp, which function he had "fulfilled with the utmost gusto for the benefit of the Nazis." Asked about concrete war crimes he had committed, he said that he had helped the Nazis in drawing up lists of prisoners to be sent to places of work where the conditions were even worse than in the camp, with the result that many had perished. He had beaten up prisoners "and committed war crimes." He had received the lists of prisoners to be sent on these transports from the Nazi camp authorities through the chief camp policeman [Kapo] Willi Seifert. He had given the lists their final form. "I added to the lists names of prisoners whose numbers I was given by the prisoner Jung. These added prisoners were of Russian nationality."

PRESIDING JUDGE: "We know who Seifert was; he was, like you, a war criminal. But who was this Jung?"

FRANK: "I did not know."

PRESIDING JUDGE: "You then helped the Nazis to murder people, not only in accordance with their instructions, but you actually added people on instructions from someone whom you did not even know."

Frank agreed to that. Frank then explained that he had succeeded in keeping these crimes secret from the Party and the authorities and had posed as a fighter against fascism. He had known that the War Crimes Commission was looking for him. In 1945 Slansky had appointed him to the Secretariat of the Cultural Committee. Later he had informed Slansky "of the fact that I was on the list of war criminals; I showed him the actual place in the list and asked him whether it would not be better if I took up another job in view of these facts. Slansky replied that this was unnecessary and that I could continue to work in the Secretariat." Following this hint he had continued to keep his past a secret. In this way he had become dependent on Slansky.

QUESTION: "Did Slansky make use of this dependence of yours?"

FRANK: "He harnessed me to his anti-State activities. Thus I began to take an active part in the machinations of the anti-State Center which Slansky organized in the interests of the U.S. imperialists." In this he had only gradually been involved, as a result of his dependence on Slansky, of his opportunism, of his secret war crimes, and of his moral depravity. His dependence on Slansky had grown even greater, and in June, 1949, he had been elected Secretary of the Central Committee. Hence he had fully supported Slansky and carried out his instructions, although he had been aware of their hostile aims.

Placing of Enemies in Important Posts

Asked by the Prosecutor about his part in placing and maintaining enemies of the State in important economic positions, Frank said that he had taken over the work Frejka had done on the Economic Commission after Frejka's recall. The Economic Commission was later abolished. He, Frank, had continued Frejka's policy in accordance with Slansky's instructions. The Prosecutor then wanted to know the names of the industrial directors placed by Frank. The first to be mentioned was the Director-General of the Heavy Engineering Industry, Fabinger, "an enemy of the Soviet Union." Frank said that in 1949 he told Slansky of the harmful activities of Fabinger, but Slansky had dismissed him with the remark that Fabinger was an outstanding expert who should stay in his job. Later, when, as a result of a decision of the Presidium of the Central Committee of the Party, Fabinger's activities were to be investigated, Taussigova, obviously upon instructions from Slansky, had protracted the investigation for nearly one year, whereby Fabinger was maintained in his position as Director-General until 1951.

Foreign Trade Sabotage

Asked about Czechoslovakia's foreign trade with the USSR and the people's democracies, Frank said that they undermined it and that the country was made dependent on the West, which was evident from the fact that more than 50 percent of Czechoslovakia's foreign trade was scheduled to be transacted with the West. The Presiding Judge wanted to know details about sabotage in that sector. Frank said that "sabotage on the widest scale" in foreign trade manifested itself in vast deficit transactions, to the detriment of the Republic. Loebl covered up these transactions by running a separate "M" account, which in effect served to hamstring the initiative of foreign trade officials who were trying to obtain preferential prices in negotiations with the West, and to hush up deficit business from which Western capitalists and traitorous émigrés benefited.

In 1950 the Soviet Union had increased its orders for consumer goods which could not be sold easily on the Western markets, in order to help Czechoslovakia straighten out her balance of payments, but some members of the conspiracy had refused such orders. The conspirators also used a further form of sabotage—the overpricing of goods which should have been exported to the Soviet Union so that the trade agreement could not be concluded. An injunction by Gottwald had been necessary to bring about order in the export-import companies. In 1949, Frank stated, Petr Planer had attempted to discredit Czechoslovakia's help to the People's Republic of China by suggesting that old and useless machine tools should be sold to China. Other conspirators sabotaged economic co-operation with people's democratic countries by delaying delivery of certain equipment. Thus, for example, by not delivering equipment for a cement works to Poland in time, a loss of about half a million tons of cement was caused to that country. Thus not only was foreign trade with the Soviet Union and the people's democracies sabotaged, but this also created a situation in which Czechoslovakia was economically dependent on Western markets.

Asked by the Prosecutor whether the conspirators gained through their sabotage in foreign trade funds for their conspiratorial activity and for their own enrichment, Frank stated that this was the case and that this enabled the conspirators to have accounts in Western countries. He added that he himself had such an account in Switzerland. Frank then described in detail how the conspirators sabotaged the building up of heavy industry, including the steel industry, and the conspirators' wrecking activity at various important constructions.

The Workers Cheated by Compensation

Another way of cheating the workers had been the granting of compensation for the nationalization of industries previously owned by Western capitalists. In 1948, for instance, Dr. [Ivan] Skala, from the Ministry of Finance, and Loebl, from the Foreign Trade Ministry, were sent to the U.S. to discuss compensation payments for U.S. property nationalized in Czechoslovakia. Dr. Skala betrayed the Republic and joined the U.S. imperialists. Frank himself had, after February, 1948, expressed himself in favor of granting compensation to Rothschild. He could not recall any details but remembered that Dr. Margolius had discussed compensation payment for a nationalized Czechoslovak iron ore mine in Sweden with British capitalists. When Frejka and Margolius reported the transaction at an Economic Council meeting, Frank agreed to export to Great Britain, free of charge, quantities of Czechoslovak industrial products under a five-year trade agreement with the U.K. That was to be compensation to British capitalists; in the course of five years several hundred million crowns were thus to have been paid out.

Frank was then asked about the so-called "Taub" plan concerning the purchase of a sheet mill. That was an American plan, Frank said, worked out in 1946 at the behest of Fabinger and Rudinger with the American engineer Taub and aimed at the subjugation of Czechoslovak economy to the U.S. The plan envisaged that the automobile industry was to be developed in the people's democracies. In Czechoslovakia, Fabinger and Rudinger in their posts in heavy engineering carried it into effect by hampering the development of heavy engineering and the general metal industry. They wanted to ensure that the Czechoslovak heavy engineering industry remained dependent on the West in every respect.

Sabotage in Agriculture

Asked if he had striven to preserve capitalists in other spheres of the country's economy as well, Frank stated that he and the other members of the conspiracy had done so in the countryside. They had "obstructed the socialization of the village."

In 1948, Frank explained, when a speed up in the socialization of the village had been decided on, Slansky had urged that, in view of the fundamental questions involved, the Agricultural Department of the Secretariat of the Communist Party Central Committee should be put under his personal control. He had then placed members of the conspiracy in key positions. This policy of obstructing the socialization of the countryside had been put into effect by calling off the struggle against the village rich and by allowing them to join the Party and enter agricultural co-operatives. Not only rich peasants but big landowners had been placed in important posts.

Extensive sabotage had also been carried out in the field of livestock production. The Prosecutor submitted a document in Slansky's files concerning the organization of harvest work, in which paragraphs relating to the need to fight against the kulaks were marked: "To be crossed out in the draft."

Frank recalled a conversation with Slansky in 1949 when the latter had declared, in the presence of Svermova, Geminder, and others, that the Party line about a gradual and prudent procedure in the socialization of the countryside meant in fact that the class struggle against the village rich should not be developed at all and that problems should be solved peacefully. As early as 1947 Slansky had sent directives to Regional Secretaries, recommending the enrollment into the Party of village rich, whom he had called "peasants of authority." At a conference of Agricultural Officers of Party Regional Committees in 1949 Slansky had ruled that village rich should be accepted in agricultural co-operatives. Frank added: "I was present at the time and I did not oppose his suggestion; I voted for it." Asked whether capitalist elements among the rural community had also been supported financially, Frank replied that, on Smrkovsky's instructions, the State Farms had paid out large sums to former owners of their land, as compensation under the Land Reform. Smrkovsky had earmarked Kcs.600,000,000 [$12,000,000] for this purpose in 1950, and about Kcs.150,000,000 [$3,000,000] had actually been paid out during the first half of 1950. Some landowners had reecived as much as Kcs.5,500,000 [$110,000] and others had received monthly payments of Kcs.3,000 [$60] to Kcs.4,000 [$80] on instructions from Gondar, a colleague of Smrkovsky.

Other capitalist elements, not only in the countryside but also in the towns, had been supported "through the benign handling of the release of frozen accounts, belonging chiefly to business people, manufacturers, landed gentry, etc." Thus some Kcs.5,000,000,000 [$110,000,000] had been paid "into the pockets of these capitalist parasites" in 1950. Slansky had further ordered that favorable consideration should be given to big peasants in the matter of credits. The village rich had thus been supported at the country's expense.

Frank continued: "In 1949, when the Party Chairman directed the setting up of large fattening centers for pigs on the Soviet pattern, Smrkovsky and Slansky sabotaged the construction of these centers. Smrkovsky ordered the drawing up of plans for centers for 5,000 pigs, while the economic number would have been 2,000 to 3,000. The buildings were constructed in an unsuitable manner and entailed excessive appropriations of money and materials. At the end of 1949 I drew Slansky's attention to this, but he agreed with Smrkovsky's sabotage."

End of Frank's Evidence

In reply to the Presiding Judge, Frank admitted that the conspirators had tried to undermine the Party by following "the methods of the traitor Tito." "We tried to dilute the Party by introducing non-Marxist and non-Leninist elements, by depriving it of its revolutionary character, by weakening its fighting capacity, and by robbing it of the character of the vanguard of the working-class movement. On the economic side we refused to apply Soviet experience in the development of socialism. Similarly, in the building up of the Party we rejected the experience of the All-Union Bolshevik Party; we based this theory on our notorious interpretation of the particular character of Czechoslovak conditions.

"We distorted Party directives with regard to the recruitment of new members, and thus enabled hostile and alien elements to enter the party. We accepted various non-working-class elements, time-servers, former entrepreneurs, estate-owners, kulaks, bourgeois nationalists, Trotskyites, etc. We suppressed and limited criticism and self-criticism, evaded Party democracy, introduced dictatorial methods, made decisions without referring to elected authorities, distorted the Party line, postponed the solution of urgent problems, and smothered the activity of basic Party units. Honest citizens who pointed to the harmful activities of the Zionists we labeled as anti-Semites, and terrorized them."

Frank also stated that Slansky intentionally isolated the Party Chairman, Gottwald, and tried to prevent anyone, except Slansky himself and other members of the conspiracy, from informing Gottwald about the state of affairs. In this manner Slansky wanted to become the decisive factor in the Party. "Slansky continually spoke about the President's illness and so wanted to prepare the ground for the moment when he would be able to cause the unnatural death of the Party Chairman."

Turning to the security sector, Frank stated that "Slansky concentrated all questions of security in his hands and no one was permitted to interfere in security matters. In this sector we placed Karel Svab, who cooperated closely with Slansky from 1945 onward. Slansky succeeded in getting the International Brigade member turned general, the Londoner Pavel, appointed as Deputy Minister of National Security, and [Osvald] Zavodsky as head of National Security. Of course, these associates of ours were exposed and arrested. In spite of the efforts made by Slansky and the rest of us we did not succeed in attaining our shameful aims, although we used a great variety of means in our struggle against the Republic and Party, such as sabotage, espionage, subversive activity, etc. The Communist Party and the Czechoslovak people led by Klement Gottwald went on to further great successes in the building up of socialism, and in the end we were exposed and rendered harmless."

Examination of Eugen Loebl

At its evening hearing on Sunday, the Prague State Court heard evidence from Eugen Loebl, formerly Deputy Minister of Foreign Trade. Loebl declared his guilt. Asked in what his guilt consisted, he said: "I am guilty principally in that, as a member of the subversive espionage conspiracy built up and headed by Slansky, I carried out extensive hostile, subversive, and harmful work in Czechoslovak economy." He had first become a member of the conspiracy on returning to Czechoslovakia from his exile in Britain in 1945, "as an ally of the treasonable Benes clique with which I was connected through the imperialist agent Hubert Ripka." Right up to his imprisonment, continued Loebl, he had maintained espionage connections with representatives of the Western intelligence services and passed to them information covering the whole field of Czechoslovakia's economic life and foreign trade.

Binding Czechoslovak Economy to the West

Questioned by the Prosecutor as to the agents and intelligence services with which he had been in touch, Loebl named "the U.S. spy Herman Field with whom I first got in touch in 1949 in Kracow," the old officer of the British intelligence service, "Konni Zilliacus," with whom he had been in contact in 1946 and 1947, and "the spy Godfrey Lias," with whom he had maintained connections from 1945 to 1949. Elaborating his offenses, Loebl explained that, in collaboration with Slansky and in particular with Frejka and Margolius, he had pursued the object of "tying Czechoslovak economy to the capitalist West and making it dependent on the West." This was to have been done mainly by exporting light industry manufactures to the capitalist countries and importing from them the raw materials necessary for the manufacture of these articles. In this way Czechoslovak industry was to have been made dependent on Western materials and the excessive development of the light industries, entailed by this plan, was to obstruct the promotion of the country's heavy industry.

The Ueberall Scheme: Profits for Israel

One aspect of this had been the Ueberall Scheme, the idea being to increase the production and export of light industry manufactures to the West "in such a way that the profits of the work of Czechoslovak industry should accrue to Israel." A "similar fraudulent scheme" had been the so-called dollar offensive, the purpose of which had been to retard the building of socialism in Czechoslovakia. This plan had been agreed between Loebl and "the U.S. agent and Israeli Minister Ueberall." It was to have been put into effect with the help of U.S. capitalist Zionists. Loebl continued: "Just as, in the course of negotiations with the capitalist countries, I tried to tie Czechoslovakia's economy to the capitalist West and to damage Czechoslovak economy, I also acted, at negotiations with the popular democratic countries, in such a way as to damage them so that they lost interest in concluding trade agreements with Czechoslovakia.

"Thus I tried systematically to tear the Czechoslovak Republic away from its natural economic ties with the countries of the peace camp."

Loebl's Espionage Contacts

Loebl next spoke in detail about his espionage contacts. "Before the fascist occupation I emigrated to England via Poland. Before leaving for England and while I was in Kracow, I made the acquaintance of the U.S. spy Herman

Field, who was at the time head of the Trust Fund set up by the British Committee. I had daily contacts with Field and helped him with his work in the British Committee. It was then that I began to understand that the Anglo-U.S. espionage services were using the Trust Fund as an organization for the selection and enrollment of spies from among our refugees. That the Trust Fund served the British intelligence service was proved by the fact that it was financed by the British Home Office. In return for my help with his work in the British Committee, Field enabled me to get to Britain as early as August, 1939, and to enter the services of the Trust Fund. From my collaboration with Field in the British Committee in Kracow and from my own work in the Trust Fund in England I learned what methods the Western espionage services used. Under the pretext of charitable activities they had founded an organization for the winning over and enlistment of agents and spies who were subsequently employed in the peoples' democracies to disrupt them from within and to bring them back under the thumb of the Western imperialists."

Activities in Britain

Asked to describe his treasonable activities in Britain, Loebl continued: "I adopted Benes's argument about the resurrection of the pre-Munich capitalist Czechoslovakia, a country which would have the closest ties with the capitalist West. This pro-Western bourgeois-nationalist concept I propagated in lectures at different Trust Fund hostels. I was employed by the Trust Fund until 1941 when I became Secretary of the Friendship Club. Naturally, my work as Secretary of the Friendship Club was also marked by this hostile concept. Although the London Executive of the Party drew my attention to the fact that I should make the Club into a center of mutual understanding, a place where all political parties could work together in the struggle against fascism, I betrayed the Communist Party and the idea of making the Club into a center of mutual co-operation. Instead, I drove the Club into the services of Benes, Ripka, and their reactionary clique. Through this treason I gained the confidence of the reactionary Benes clique and in the autumn of 1943 I was appointed a member of the Government delegation to the UNRRA Conference in the U.S. At this Conference I committed a further act of treason. In many talks with representatives of reactionary governments, I emphasized that neither I myself, nor any other representative of the Communist emigration in Britain, intended to build up a socialist order of society in Czechoslovakia, but that we were prepared to continue the Republic's pre-Munich foreign policy. When it became clear that the U.S.-British circles intended to misuse UNRRA for the political penetration of the liberated countries in Europe, I agreed with Benes that I should conceal this intention from the representatives of the Party and that I should describe UNRRA as an unselfish aid scheme of the Americans and as a model of postwar international co-operation. In recognition for my keeping this promise Benes later appointed me top official of the Ministry of Economic Reconstruction set up in London."

Questioned about details, Loebl said that, while still in London, he had promised several UNRRA representatives, such as Sir Frederick Leith-Ross, Corvin and others, that he would set up a special office in Prague for UNRRA, with contacts in all economic ministries, to enable UNRRA "to penetrate them and influence them." Asked since when he had pursued his avowed aim of tying Czechoslovakia to the capitalist countries, Loebl said: "I began to work along these lines during my London exile, with direct support of the Economic Commission, whose members were also Jewish bourgeois nationalists under Frejka's leadership. At our last meeting before returning to the liberated homeland, I agreed with Frejka that, under the pretext of needing persons with a knowledge of the West, we would continue to keep the circle around the Economic Commission, and in fact, enlarge it with further 'Londoners' whom we would place in economic key positions with a view to realizing our concept of shackling Czechoslovak economy to the capitalist West. Furthermore, I agreed with Ripka, whom I met by chance in London in March, 1945, and whom I congratulated on that occasion on his appointment as Foreign Trade Minister in the Kosice Government, that I would co-operate with him. Ripka made some very flattering references to my co-operation with him and told me that he wanted to make me a departmental head in his Foreign Trade Ministry. I gladly responded to Ripka's hint and assured him that he could count on me as a follower."

Loebl's Activities after his Return to Czechoslovakia

Turning to his activity after his return to Czechoslovakia, Loebl said: "The realization of my plans was made easier by a meeting I had with Frejka in Prague at the end of June, 1945. Frejka told me he had just seen Slansky, who had entrusted him with the control of the Economic Commission of the Party and with the office of Chairman of the Economic Department. He was very pleased since this new post would make it easier for him to implement our London agreement about placing members of the Economic Commission in key positions with a view to realizing our concept of tying Czechoslovakia's economy to the capitalist West. We set ourselves two tasks from the outset. On the one hand, we would place enemy cadres into key positions and on the other, we would cover up their hostile activities. Frejka and I decided that we would staff the Economic Department with 'Londoners,' people trained in the British economic school such as Goldman and Zionists such as Levcik, Jancik, [Frantisek] Kollar, and others. We did not confine ourselves to people who came back from the West, but also used people whose anti-Communist political past was a guarantee to us that they would work along our lines. Frejka took this proposal to Slansky. When I met Frejka after his conversation with Slansky, he told me that Slansky had approved this proposal. This fact made me suspect that Slansky entertained a hostile attitude to the Party. To confirm this suspicion, I agreed with Frejka that we would set up a special consultative body in this Economic Department, to be named, according to the London model, the Economic Commission. We also agreed that into this Economic Commission we would take only enemies of the Party, cosmopolitans, Zionists, bourgeois nationalists and people nurtured on capitalism. When Frejka told me that Slansky had approved even this patently hostile proposal it was quite clear to me that Slansky was an enemy of the Party just as I. It was clear to me that Slansky was surrendering all economic positions in the Party to capitalist elements, and that he was doing so deliberately and systematically. When I knew that Slansky himself was an enemy of the Party, just as I, and when he had entrusted me with a highly important post in Czechoslovak economy, I decided that I would act in accordance with Slansky's orders. Thus, I became to all intents and purposes, a member of his anti-State conspiracy."

PROSECUTOR: "But you also had obligations toward Ripka. What did this mean?"

LOEBL: "This was very favorable because I could now, in my new post as a member of the Economic Commission and with the direct support of Slansky, carry out even more easily the promise I had made Ripka in London, that I would fight against the popular democratic order."

Asked about details of his work along Ripka's directives, Loebl said: "I upheld Ripka's thesis in the Economic Commission, the thesis of the vital necessity for Czechoslovakia's foreign trade to proceed along the classical lines of exporting our light industry manufactures, which meant increasing light industry output at the expense of heavy industry. This line of Ripka's, which I carried into the Economic Commission, was identical with Slansky's line and his instructions which were carried into the Economic Commission by Frejka."

The Prosecutor then asked about Loebl's espionage work. Loebl stated: "In the UNRRA Mission in Prague there worked, among other people, the Anglo-Americans Corvin and Bergiton. I maintained very close relations with them. We met not only in my office but also in cafés and private homes."

PROSECUTOR: "What concrete espionage information did you give those spies?"

LOEBL: "I explained to Corvin and Bergiton the bottlenecks of Czechoslovak economy; I informed them of the transfer of some industrial establishments from Bohemia to Slovakia and I betrayed to them Czechoslovakia's foreign exchange situation, especially with regard to dollars, Swiss francs, and sterling. Moreover, I arranged for Corvin, Bergiton, and other Anglo-U.S. UNRRA officials that they would be permitted to visit establishments of Czechoslovakia's heavy industry so that they could carry out economic espionage on the spot."

PROSECUTOR: "Were these spies, Bergiton and Corvin, the only ones with whom you were in touch?"

LOEBL: "No. I had espionage connections with a number of others."

PROSECUTOR: "Such as?"

LOEBL: "Such as the U.S. spy Field."

PROSECUTOR: "Who else?"

LOEBL: "The officer of the British intelligence service Konni Zilliacus."

PROSECUTOR: "Who else?"

LOEBL: "*The Times* correspondent, the Englishman Godfrey Lias."

PROSECUTOR: "Who else?"

LOEBL: "*The Times* correspondent in Vienna, [Peter] Smollett."

PROSECUTOR: "Who else?"

LOEBL: "The U.S. professor [Fred Warner] Neal * and others."

Loebl's Contacts with Godfrey Lias

Asked when and how his contacts with Lias started. Loebl replied: "My espionage connection with Godfrey Lias, with whom I collaborated closely, began in the autumn of 1945. It happened at Hubert Ripka's request. Ripka told me in his office that, in view of our London agreement about subversive collaboration, it was necessary for me to maintain contacts with a number of Western correspondents and to give them information on Czechoslovak economic and foreign trade matters, so that the Anglo-U.S. businessmen would get an accurate picture of Czechoslovakia's economic position. Ripka actually named *The Times* correspondent Godfrey Lias whom he said he had known in London; he said he attached much importance to my maintaining contact with him. A few days later I made Lias's acquaintance and through him I was linked to the espionage Centers. During our very first talk, Lias told me that he was most interested in Czechoslovakia's economic problems and particularly in her foreign

*An American specialist in Eastern European affairs and Professor of International Relations at the Claremont Graduate School in California.—*Ed.*

trade. He also told me quite openly that not all the information he received was meant for publication. From this it was quite clear to me that Lias passed these reports on to the British espionage service. We then agreed that I would regularly supply him with espionage reports, which he could either come and collect from my office or send someone to collect. We agreed that he would come to see me at my office a few days later. I reported to Ripka about my arrangment with Lias and he was most satisfied and approved of what I had done. He also told me that he had already heard about it from Lias direct."

PROSECUTOR: "What kind of espionage reports did you give Lias?"

LOEBL: "I informed him on all confidential and secret matters concerning Czechoslovak economy and foreign trade."

PROSECUTOR: "How many reports roughly did you give him?"

LOEBL: "In writing I gave him about eight or twelve espionage reports, but considering that I have given him a very great deal of information I cannot remember what I gave him orally and what in writing."

PROSECUTOR (*with a sneer*): "Was there any secret at all that was known to you and that you did not betray to Lias?"

LOEBL: "I betrayed to Lias all secret information that interested him or that had great significance for the British Government's discriminatory campaign against the Czechoslovak Republic."

PROSECUTOR: "What further services did you render Lias?"

LOEBL: "At Lias's request I saw to it that the Aloron firm, in which Lias was financially interested, was exempted from nationalization, which was against the law and damaged Czechoslovakia. I also arranged a number of import permits for him for jewelry, furs, and other things from Switzerland and Britain."

PROSECUTOR: "When did you break off espionage contacts with Lias?"

LOEBL: "I did not break off espionage connections with Lias voluntarily. Our relations came to an end when his espionage activities were unmasked in 1949 and he had to leave Czechoslovakia."

Loebl's Espionage Connections with Herman Field

The Prosecutor then asked Loebl to speak about his connections with Herman Field.

LOEBL: "My espionage connections with Herman Field began in 1939 in Krakow, where he was engaged in selecting and recruiting agents and spies from among our émigrés. In the summer of 1947 he sent me a card from the U.S. to tell me that he intended visiting Czechoslovakia as the leader of a delegation of architects and asked me to help him. I replied telling him I was willing to help him. Thus the U.S. spy Field came to Czechoslovakia with my help and resumed his old espionage contacts. I informed him about all our postwar reconstruction problems so that he learned from me everything he needed to form a full picture of conditions in Czechoslovakia. I told him everything I knew from my position as Departmental Head in the Foreign Trade Ministry."

Contacts with Smollett

Loebl then spoke of his contacts with Smollett: "In 1946, André Simone, editor of *Rude Pravo* and a member of our conspiracy, introduced me to *The Times* correspondent Smollett. I maintained very close connections with him and gave him information about Czechoslovak foreign trade and economic matters—information which was very valuable to the British espionage service."

PROSECUTOR: "Did you perform any other services for Smollett?"

LOEBL: "At Smollett's request I arranged for him to be appointed Austrian representative of the nationalized Koh-i-noor firm. I arranged this business deal to enable Smollett to pursue his espionage and subversive activity in Czechoslovakia more effectively under the cloak of lawful business. I also gave him detailed information about the Koh-i-noor firm without the Government's approval."

Asked about further espionage contacts, Loebl continued: "In the course of my work at the Foreign Trade Ministry, I was visited by very many representatives of Anglo-U.S. circles. I informed them about all questions concerning Czechoslovak economy and foreign trade."

PROSECUTOR: "Did Clementis recommend a spy to you?"

LOEBL: "In the summer of 1949 Prof. [Fred Warner] Neal was recommended to me by Clementis's office. Neal was interested in economic problems, especially in the planning of foreign trade, and I gave him information at three meetings."

At this stage the prosecution submitted a letter from Neal appreciating Loebl's assistance, as well as a photograph of Prof. Fred Neal. Loebl identified Neal.

Sabotage of Foreign Trade

Loebl was then questioned about his sabotage in the field of foreign trade. In this sphere, too, he admitted, he had "carried out a whole string of sabotage acts." One of them had been the Ueberall Scheme. Ueberall had come to Prague even before he was appointed Israeli Minister, as "an American agent and representative of Zionist organizations." With him and with other members of the conspiracy Loebl had "worked in favor of that U.S. outpost in the Middle East—the State of Israel."

Asked about the details of his work with Ueberall, Loebl said: "On one occasion Ueberall came to me with a concrete proposal. He said it was possible to get dollar credits from U.S. Zionists on the condition that Zionist émigrés would be allowed to transfer their property."

PROSECUTOR: "How did you react to this?"

LOEBL: "I reacted favorably because this proposal was in line with Slansky's instructions to use Zionist organizations for tying the country to the U.S. That is why I agreed on the scheme Ueberall proposed."

Asked to explain the "sabotage character" of the proposal, Loebl said the dollar credits were to have made Czechoslovakia economically dependent on the U.S. Since the credits were meant for the purchase of investments, the scheme would have also made Czechoslovak industry technologically dependent on America. Lastly, as the credit would have been repaid by exports of light industry manufactures, it would have obstructed the development of Czechoslovakia's heavy industry.

PROSECUTOR: "What further considerations were you guided by?"

LOEBL: "Considerations for the Zionist émigrés and the transfer of their property, as this affected many of my friends and relations."

Another campaign of the same character was the so-called "dollar offensive," which in fact was a continuation of the Ueberall plan. It had been decided to use the dollars for the purchase of investment goods, thus increasing Czechoslovakia's dependence on U.S. monopolies. Loebl admitted that he had given instructions for such imports without regard to the damage they might cause to Czechoslovakia's economy. He had also instructed Czechoslovak exporters to sell to the West even at a loss. In consequence Czechoslovak manufactured goods were frequently exported at below cost prices. In these activities Loebl had co-operated with the "U.S. spy, the Zionist Alexander Taub." He had agreed with Taub on a propaganda campaign of lectures to be given in U.S. synagogues and Zionist societies.

The Prosecutor at this point submitted to the court a letter from Taub to Loebl in which Taub had informed Loebl that he intended to discuss the Ueberall plan with the Israeli Minister in Washington, Epstein, to make sure that it was accepted. At the beginning of 1949, Loebl said, Ueberall had visited him together with members of the Israeli trade delegation. At this meeting they had discussed how to "misuse the prepared trade agreement with Israel for the support of Zionist emigration and property transfers on the part of the Jewish bourgeoisie and the Zionist emigrants."

Export to Israel of Machinery for Production of Pencils

Loebl then described another of his "sabotage acts," his support of the plan for the export to Israel of machinery for the production of pencils. A joint stock company was to be formed, and payment for the machinery was not to be made in foreign exchange but in shares in the company. This plan was intended to damage Czechoslovakia in two ways: first by tying her to a company in the capitalist world, and secondly by depriving her of urgently needed machinery. At this point the Prosecutor submitted an expert's report on the plan to set up a pencil factory in Israel. The report stated that eight Czechoslovak subjects who intended to emigrate to Israel and one Israeli had been trained in the Koh-i-noor Works in Budejovice in the manufacture of pencils. The vigilance of the workers, however, prevented the execution of this plan. Despite Loebl's endeavors the machinery was not sent to Israel. Loebl then admitted that after the nationalization of smaller industrial enterprises, following the February events of 1948, he had permitted the export of factory equipment to Israel, although it would have been his duty to examine every case of the export of machinery as to whether this machinery was needed in Czechoslovakia. In order to support Czechoslovak dependence on the capitalist West, he had been instrumental in the purchase of machinery for the production of artificial fibers from a U.S. company. He had forced the National Bank to make payments in dollars before the machinery was delivered. Later the U.S. Governement had prohibited the export of this machinery, and the dollar payments became a frozen asset.

The Prosecutor remarked at this point that Loebl had also negotiated loans with Western countries at exorbitant rates of interest.

The Accounting System Used in Trade with the West

Loebl then described a special system of accountancy call the "M accounts" which was designed to conceal the disadvantages of Czechoslovak trade with the West. He had instructed exporters to fix prices for the West below production cost, while the USSR and the people's democracies were charged much higher prices. The losses in this trade with the capitalist countries were then offset by the exorbitant prices charged to the USSR and other friendly States. During trade negotiations with the Soviet Union in Moscow in 1947 Loebl had forced the USSR to accept from Czechoslovakia second-rate goods, while high-quality products were reserved for capitalist countries. Prices charged to the USSR, particularly in respect to electric motors, generators, oil pipes, and similar goods, were much above the world market level and in some cases as much as 30 percent higher than prices charged to the capitalist countries. To prove Loebl's guilt on this point, the Prosecutor submitted an expert's report according to which certain machinery was offered to the USSR for Kcs.560,750 [$11,015], a price that was later reduced to Kcs.400,000 [$8,000]. On Loebl's instruction the same machinery had been sold to Sweden for Kcs.362,635 [$7,253]. Loebl then proceeded to describe sabotage which he committed in connection with oil purchased in Hungary in 1946. Part of the purchase price, amounting to Kcs.5,000,000 [$100,000], was not paid to Hungary but remitted to Switzerland, where it fell into the hands of the "treacherous Hungarian émigrés."

Asked by the Prosecutor in what other ways he had assisted enemies of the Republic in their fight against the Czechoslovak people, the defendant admitted that he had built up a net of Czechoslovak trade representatives abroad consisting of enemies of the popular democratic regime who had fled abroad after February, 1948. Those people had used the high commissions earned from Czechoslovak trade for the fight against Czechoslovakia. They were "inveterate capitalists, Zionists, and bourgeois nationalists, who were not interested in Czechoslovakia's progress." His intention had been to assist these enemies of the Republic and to have, should the popular democratic regime be overthrown, a net of capitalist representatives abroad. Loebl then named representatives appointed abroad.

Compensation for Unilever

The Prosecutor again submitted an expert's report on the arrangements made by Loebl with the "émigré, Guttmann, the former owner of the Ostrava coal mines." Guttmann had been paid a commission of 3 to 4 percent, although international usage was only 1 to 1½ percent.

Moreover, Guttmann was paid a yearly salary of Kcs. 250,000 [$5,000]. Loebl affirmed that those arrangements had been made by him. The Prosecutor then quoted the case of one Nacht, who had later Americanized his name to Nash, who with the help of Loebl, had earned commissions of Kcs.49,000,000 [$980,000] on the export of rolling stock. Loebl admitted that he had authorized this commission and went on to describe an agreement which he had concluded with one Hansard, who represented Czechoslovak export trade to the Gold Coast, where "the Unilever concern owns big enterprises." He had arranged with Hansard that Unilever would only pay 80 percent for Czechoslovak goods, and the remaining 20 percent was to be used as compensation for nationalized Unilever property in Czechoslovakia. This concerned the Schict Works in Usti. Loebl admitted that Unilever was not entitled to compensation for those factories, since they had been confiscated because the Schichts had been Nazis. Loebl also stated that he had given to Hansard "espionage reports on the strategy of Czechoslovakia foreign trade." He had also assisted Hansard by agreeing to a certain surcharge on the import to Czechoslovakia of raw material for the margarine industry. This surcharge was also paid on account of compensation.

In reply to a question by the Prosecutor, Loebl admitted that he had made possible the continued existence of capitalist firms in Czechoslovakia even after the nationalization of foreign trade. He had given instructions in the Foreign Trade Ministry to the effect that agents of capitalist firms were not to be nationalized, and he had advised many importers and exporters to register as representatives or agents to evade nationalization. This had made possible the continued existence of several hundreds of capitalist firms in Czechoslovakia, "which caused great damage to Czechoslovak economy."

Loebl's Relations with Yugoslavia

Asked by the Prosecutor to describe his relations with Tito's Yugoslavia, Loebl said that long before the publication of the Cominform resolution, the conspiratorial Center had been aware of the fact that the Titoites were leading Yugoslavia into the camp of the U.S. imperialists. He personally had convinced himself of this during his negotiations with Kidric in 1946 and in autumn 1947, when he spoke with the Yugoslav Commercial Attaché [Ivo] Barbalic in Reiman's flat in Milan. In his presence and that of Frejka, Fabinger, and Reiman, Barbalic had said that Czechoslovakia must help Yugoslavia even if it harmed Czechoslovakia. The conspiratorial Center was supporting Yugoslavia's anti-Soviet policy by increasing export of capital goods. When Slansky and Clementis had learned about these arrangements with Yugoslavia, they had expressed their complete satisfaction. Even after the Cominform resolution, on Slansky's instruction transmitted by Frejka, he had assisted Titoite Yugoslavia by continuing the export of capital goods, although Yugoslavia was not fulfilling her obligations under the trade agreement. Slansky's group of conspirators had evolved a theory of "Czechoslovakia's special road toward socialism" similar to that of Yugoslavia, which was in reality the road leading toward the re-establishment of capitalism. The role of Tito in Czechoslovakia was to be played by Rudolf Slansky.

At this point the Presiding Judge asked whether any of the other defendants had any questions to ask. Thereupon a voice was heard to say: "A statement."

PRESIDING JUDGE: "A statement! Please come forward. Defendant Loebl, make room at the microphone."

The following statement was then made by an unnamed defendant (whose voice was clearly Slansky's):

"I fully agree with the evidence given by my associate, Loebl, and I declare that I am fully responsible for all his crimes."

Evidence of Two Witnesses

Evidence was then taken from Dagmar Kacerovska, a former clerk of the U.S. Embassy in Prague, sentenced some time ago by the Prague State Court for the crime of espionage. Kacerovska confirmed Loebl's co-operation with Godfrey Lias to whom he had regularly given espionage reports. These reports Lias had sent to the intelligence service in London through the British Embassy's diplomatic pouch.

The next witness was Josef Hoffman, an official of the Foreign Trade Ministry, who described "the methods used by Loebl against those who drew attention to his rackets. Honest people were being intimidated, sacked, or transferred to posts where they could not observe Loebl's dirty activities."

Examination of Rudolf Margolius

The morning's proceedings on November 24 opened with the examination of Rudolf Margolius. He said: "I was recruited for subversive work by Eugen Loebl in October, 1948, when I became a member of the anti-State group." On the instructions of this group he had conducted in the Foreign Trade Ministry "extensive espionage and sabotage activities aiming at the disintegration of Czechoslovak economy." He had deliberately negotiated unfavorable trade agreements and had enforced payments to foreign capitalists as compensation for nationalized property. He had also arranged for the payment of debts contracted by the pre-Munich Republic. His own and the conspiratorial Center's final aim was the restoration of capitalism in Czechoslovakia. He also pleaded guilty to having maintained espionage contacts right up to his arrest with representatives of imperialist States. These were Vera Micheles-Dean, representative of the U.S. Foreign Policy Association, the agent of the British imperialists, Konni Zilliacus; the Jewish international businessman and Czechoslovak émigré, the Zionist, Brenner, and the representative of Swedish capitalists and former Minister to Czechoslovakia, Otto Wilhelm Winther. With the help of these agents he had supplied important and detailed information on Czechoslovak economy to the U.S. and British espionage services, particularly as regards Czechoslovak foreign trade. He had done this knowingly and deliberately, thus enabling the Western imperialists to cause damage to Czechoslovak economy. In the interests of Western imperialism he had also deliberately held up the development of economic relations between Czechoslovakia and the Soviet Union and the people's democracies in order to separate Czechoslovakia from the socialist camp and to subordinate her to the influences of the Western imperialists. "Finally I plead guilty that I placed hostile Zionist elements as Czechoslovak trade representatives abroad."

By means of exorbitant commissions and other tricks, he had enabled the "treacherous émigrés in the capitalist West" to acquire funds for their hostile activities against Czechoslovakia. He had granted various advantages to these émigrés and he had also helped many enemies of the Czechoslovak popular democratic regime to emigrate to capitalist countries.

Margolius described a meeting in Frejka's office in 1948, at which Goldman had also been present, when Frejka had told him that, according to Slansky's instructions, no changes were to take place in Czechoslovak foreign trade and that it was to be administered in the same way as was done before by Ripka. From this he had realized that it was Frejka's policy to increase Czechoslovakia's dependence on the capitalist West. Shortly after this meeting he had been told by Loebl that he would be appointed Chief of the Bureau of the Foreign Trade Ministry. This appointment had been made because Loebl knew that he, Margolius, fully supported the Western trade policy. From then on Frejka and Loebl had openly given him directives on how to conduct the anti-Czechoslovak policy. They had told him that it was necessary "to sabotage the decisions of the Council of Mutual Economic Aid," * that the peoples' democracies must be treated harshly. Both Loebl and Frejka said that these decisions had been made directly by Slansky. He had been made aware of Slansky's sabotage intentions by the fact that leading positions in the country's economic machinery had been given to hostile elements, particularly Jewish bourgeois nationalists and Zionists.

More Questions about the Ueberall Scheme

The Prosecutor asked Margolius for details about the so-called "Ueberall Scheme." Margolius said that the campaign was initiated by the former Israeli Minister to Czechoslovakia Avriel (Ueberall) at the beginning of 1948. Avriel had appeared in Czechoslovakia in 1947 under the name of Ueberall and then "he organized and directed Zionist organizations in Czechoslovakia." Margolius admitted to having been in constant touch with Ueberall, and they had both openly confided to each other their hostility to popular democracy. The purpose

*Established in 1949 by the Soviet Union and the other Communist countries in Eastern Europe in part as a countermeasure to the Marshall Plan.—*Ed.*

of the Ueberall campaign had been the "complete tying of Czechoslovak economy to the imperialist camp, especially the U.S." One of its specific aims had been to hamper the switch-over to mainly heavy industrial production in Czechoslovakia. It was for this purpose that Loebl tried to secure credits from Jewish capitalists in the U.S. so as to create financial and economic dependence on the U.S. Industry was to become dependent on imports of raw material and important equipment. It was planned to repay by light industry exports to the U.S. If that was to be achieved the switch-over to heavy industry would have to be sabotaged. The profit was to go to the Jewish capitalists in the U.S. and especially to Czechoslovak émigrés who were to become the key export-import agents and mediators in trade with Czechoslovakia. Thereby it was intended to help them to amass wealth while at the same time Czechoslovak economy would be damaged.

The Prosecutor then submitted a photograph which the defendant recognized as a picture of Alex Taub, "a representative of the U.S. Zionists and a U.S. agent," who had been in Czechoslovakia since 1946. He had been conducting espionage and sabotage in his capacity as adviser to Fabinger in the automobile industry. Taub was a Zionist, the representative of General Motors in the U.S., and before he became Fabinger's adviser he was an adviser on Chiang Kai-shek's General Staff. Margolius also recalled Taub's hostility toward Czechoslovakia's new regime. He had met Taub in the summer of 1948 at a Prague conference with Loebl at which it had been agreed that Taub should work out a concrete plan of campaign to undermine Czechoslovak economy.

The Prosecutor then had a document entitled: "Program of the Ueberall Campaign" dated June 18, 1948, identified by Margolius. The defendant was asked to give details about the so-called "dollar offensive." He said that the purpose of that offensive was to create Czechoslovak dependence on the U.S.A. Exports to the U.S.A. were effected at "tremendous loss" to Czechoslovakia because of the very low prices, frequently below production cost. The dollar offensive project had been drafted by Margolius himself in co-operation with Loebl on instruction from Slansky. The defendant gave some details: In 1948 Margolius and Loebl supported a "harmful proposal" of Dr. Hoesslein, an Israeli Zionist and Czechoslovak émigré, providing for Czechoslovakia to help with the construction of a pencil factory in Palestine. Under the pretext that the machinery to be exported was old equipment Margolius and Loebl arranged for the transfer to Palestine of machinery from the nationalized Koh-i-noor Hardtmuth factory in Cskebudejovice; the machinery was worth over Kcs.10,000,000 [200,000]. "The transfer was not carried out because the plan was unmasked," Margolius said; the Prosecutor added: "by the workers who prevented your sabotage."

Margolius went on to specify machinery exports to Palestine in 1948–49 when "Jewish bourgeois elements" had emigrated to Palestine. In those years exports were made with the agreement and knowledge of the Commission of Foreign Trade attached to the Secretariat of the Central Committee of the Party and including Loebl, Fischl, and Margolius; ostensibly old but in fact very well preserved and usable machinery was exported, mostly taken from factories formerly owned by Czechoslovak capitalists who had already emigrated or who intended to emigrate to Palestine. Those people were thus enabled to reacquire production equipment the export of which was not permitted. Those transactions caused Czechoslovakia damage running into many millions, and not only because important equipment was lost to the country but also because the machinery was taken out of the country at very low prices.

The Presiding Judge then questioned Margolius on the 1950 trade agreement between Czechoslovakia and Israel. The defendant, who was instrumental in the conclusion of that agreement, described it as yet another act of sabotage of Czechoslovak economy; its harmfulness lay in the fact that 17 percent of the exports to Israel remained in effect unpaid for, while at the same time the transfer of property which the Government did not allow to be exported was made possible.

The Prosecutor then made the following observation: "How was it possible for you to conclude such harmful agreements? You knew that Czechoslovakia does not shut herself off from trade agreements with the capitalist countries, provided certain conditions are observed, i.e., the agreements must be based on the principles of equality, mutual advantage, and either party's sovereignty. We are not closing the door to such agreements with the capitalist countries."

Margolius submitted that his sabotage had consisted in subordinating the interests of Czechoslovakia to those of the capitalist countries. He gave examples: In talks with Denmark in 1950 he had agreed to exports of heavy machinery, especially power plants, steel, etc. to Denmark in exchange for less important and essential commodities such as various foodstuffs and spices. Similarly damaging agreements were concluded with Sweden, Norway, Belgium, Holland, Iceland, etc. Each of these treaties envisaged the imports of large quantities of fish and fish products. All this was in accord with the policy of maintaining Czechoslovakia's dependence on the capitalist West. Margolius was particularly against imports from Poland, although the country could easily have met Czechoslovakia's fish demands. He had sabotaged by his policy the aforestated postulates of trade between Czechoslovakia and other countries.

Export of Television Tubes to Britain

The same line was taken in arranging a trade agreement with Britain, under which Czechoslovakia was to export television tubes to the U.K. This "directly endangered Czechoslovakia's defense potential." Margolius not only agreed to the export of the tubes but in later years even actively supported it, notwithstanding the fact that he had been warned by the Ministry of Defense that these tubes could be used for military purposes. He thereby deliberately weakened Czechoslovakia's and strengthened Britain's defense capacities. He agreed to the Prosecutor's submission that he had thereby endeavored to add to the war strength of the capitalists.

Sabotage of Trade with the USSR

Prosecutor Ales then asked defendant to explain how his foreign trade sabotage had supported Tito. Margolius agreed that deliveries to Yugoslavia of aircraft engines and coke at very unfavorable terms to Czechoslovakia were continued after the Cominform resolution.

PROSECUTOR: "You knew then, and even before the Cominform resolution, that Tito openly adhered to the imperialist camp?"

MARGOLIUS: "Yes, I did."

PROSECUTOR: "In short, step by step, every one of your actions in the field of foreign trade dragged Czechoslovakia further into the war camp?"

MARGOLIUS: "That is so."

PROSECUTOR: "You also knew that you enabled the Western imperialists to pursue a policy of discriminating interference in our economy by your systematic exhaustion of our credits with the capitalist countries. Tell us more about that."

Margolius admitted his guilt in this respect and added that "this hostile trade policy was the very opposite to that practiced by the Soviet Union." He also admitted that, in order to enrich capitalists, he had deliberately used capitalist firms as commercial intermediaries.

Margolius was then asked for details about sabotage of foreign trade with the USSR and the people's democracies. He repeated that he had endeavored to hamper the development of such trade relations, and the main form of sabotage had been to force capitalist trading methods on the people's democracies and the USSR. "We did not adhere to contractual conditions; in particular we did not abide by delivery time limits, and finally we conducted a hostile price policy." Exports to the capitalist countries were consequently priced very low, at times even lower than production costs. The prices demanded from the democratic camp were substantially higher. The discrepancy between those two price levels amounted to anything from 40 to 90 and even more percent. The Prosecutor wanted to know how Czechoslovak nationalized industries were in a position to know the price at which their products were exported.

MARGOLIUS: "They could not find out, and we made it impossible for anyone to check up on our sabotage export trade."

Defendant was then asked to illustrate the case of the exports by the Kovo national enterprise. He said: "Kovo, for instance, demanded for electric motors supplied to the USSR 400 percent more than from capitalist States." Margolius then told the court how he sabotaged the supply of paper for Hungary. In 1951 Hungary had requested an additional 1,000 tons of newsprint. He had refused this request, untruthfully asserting that the paper was not available. At the same time he had exported newsprint to Brazil at lower prices. In negotiations with Poland on scientific-economic aid in 1948 he had supported the wrecking attitude of Frejka and Loebl, who had demanded cash payment for such aid. The Polish representatives had indignantly objected, as such an attitude was in contradiction to the spirit of co-operation between States building socialism, "and they rightly invoked the example of the USSR, which grants scientific-technical aid free of charge."

Examination of Otto Fischl

The next to be questioned was Otto Fischl, former Deputy Minister of Finance, described by the announcer as "a bourgeois nationalist, son of a rich merchant, and collaborator of the Nazis." Fischl pleaded guilty "to having been a member of the anti-State hostile Center, led by Rudolf Slansky. As an accomplice of Rudolf Slansky and a Jewish bourgeois nationalist, I took part in the Center's hostile actions, which were organized by the Anglo-U.S. imperialists and their agents in Israel, headed by Ben Gurion, actions aimed at enriching the Jewish bourgeoisie." His tasks had been set by Slansky. He had also collaborated with Geminder and had been in direct contact "with the U.S.-British agents sent to Czechoslovakia by Ben Gurion."

PRESIDING JUDGE: "Who were these agents?"

FISCHL: "They were the Israeli Minister Ehud Avriel, Dr. Felix, and Ben Schalom."

PRESIDING JUDGE: "Explain why you had such a hostile attitude toward people's democratic Czechoslovakia."

FISCHL: "Your Honor, I could not possibly have another attitude but a hostile one."

PRESIDING JUDGE: "Why?"

FISCHL: "I am a Jewish bourgeois nationalist."

He had been a partner in the Mautner law firm, which catered mainly to the Jewish upper class. He had received large sums for his work and in this way his interests had become identical with this class. He had been a member of "the Jewish bourgeois-nationalist organizations KAPR and the League of Czech Jews." During the occupation he had maintained his link with the bourgeoisie and collaborated with the Nazis "and all this led me after the liberation on the path of hostility to the people's democratic regime."

Fischl continued: "When I saw, after the liberation in 1945, that the Communist Party would be the decisive force in Czechoslovakia, I joined it and, in order to be entrusted with high offices, I forged the date of my joining; I pretended to have been a member of the Party since 1928." As a result of this successful forgery, he had first been given employment in the Svoboda printing works, and in 1946 he had been appointed Head of the Economic Department of the [Party] Secretariat. He had known Slansky for a long time and Slansky had known that he, Fischl, had not been a prewar member of the Communist Party. In spite of this, he had appointed him to the Economic Department and had also entrusted him with administering his private property.

Fischl was then asked about the sabotage he had carried out in the economic and financial sphere. He had begun this sabotage while working at the Central Committee of the Party by "supporting the endeavors of the Zionists and of the Jewish-bourgeois-nationalistic elements to get hold of the National Administration of Property." The National Administration of Property had fallen into the hands of Jewish reactionaries who had used it for "strengthening the bourgeois-nationalist and Zionist position in the State by allocating the property mainly to Jewish bourgeois nationalists and Zionist elements."

The Prosecutor submitted depositions by experts from which it appeared that Fischl had caused damage amounting to Kcs.10,000,000,000 [$200,000,000] in the Administration of Property, of which sum the working people had been deprived. He then asked Fischl how he had managed the national economy when working in the Ministry of Finance. Fischl said that he had been appointed to the Ministry by Slansky. "At that time there was emigration on a large scale to Israel and to the big capitalist countries by the Jewish bourgeoisie, and it was my task to help this bourgeoisie to transfer its property and by doing so to steal more of the property of our workers."

The Prosecutor then asked Fischl why the Jewish religious communities were interested in this transfer of property. He replied that this was so "because they were dominated by Jewish reactionaries, Zionists, cosmopolitans, and other hostile elements. These elements in the end went so far as to misuse the cloak of the Jewish religion for carrying on Zionist, hostile activities."

Continuing his evidence, Fischl said that through illegal exportation of property the Czechoslovak people had suffered losses amounting to billions. Asked by the Prosecutor to explain why he had allowed Jewish capitalists to export huge fortunes while he had been very strict with applications submitted by poor people, the accused said that by his strict attitude toward the poor he had covered his permits to the rich. The accused had put aside a report submitted by the controlling organs of his Ministry, which had drawn his attention to the heavy losses resulting from the exportation of vast fortunes. He went on to describe "action Baycha" under which the illegal transfer of Jewish reactionary elements as well as their property, not only from Czechoslovakia but also from Poland, Hungary, and Romania had taken place. Transport from Slovakia had been directed to Vienna, where it had left for Israel and other capitalist States. People who had been sent in this way had also included individuals wanted by State security organs. They had been sent under false names and their documents had been falsified by the Central Zionist Organization, which had stamped them with false stamps of the district court in Bratislava. While this action was in progress, the accused told Slansky that it had caused great losses to Czechoslovakia, without giving him any figures. Slansky, in the presence of Frank and Geminder, had told the accused that this did not matter and that Zionist actions in Czechoslovakia should be given a free hand.

In the next part of his evidence Fischl described the case of the Ander family, which had owned multiple stores in Czechoslovakia's leading cities, as well as abroad. This family had caused the country damage amounting to Kcs.70,000,000 [$1,400,000] through tax and currency frauds. Further intrigues by this family had cost the State another Kcs.16,000,000 [$320,000]. The accused had intervened in the trial which had then ensued, which he had stopped on condition that the Anders would give up their business interests. This had happened at a time when the Anders' stores had already been nationalized and, therefore, were not owned by them. In this way the accused had saved the Anders their vast private fortunes. A similar course had been adopted by the accused in the case of the firm Arnstein and Pick, whose partners had been the Vogl brothers, international capitalists. Richard Vogl had escaped abroad after the February events. The other brother was already in the U.S. at the time. Through the firm in America they had been engaged in various currency frauds which had caused Czechoslovakia considerable losses. When these frauds had been unearthed and two leading employees, Koblich and Waldstein, arrested, the accused had arranged their release. Later they had escaped abroad. In this way, Fischl said, he had helped criminals who had robbed the Czechoslovak people of Kcs.80,000,000 [$1,600,000]. Asked by the Prosecutor whether he had discussed this case with Slansky, the accused said that he had not, but later on he had told Svab, because he had known that he had intervened on behalf of the conspiratorial Center and that nothing would happen to him. It was possible that Slansky and Svab had discussed the matter. The Prosecutor then read a statement by Svab taken during a preparatory hearing from which it transpired that this was so.

Asked by the Prosecutor what he had wished to achieve through his activities, Fischl said: "In this manner we undermined economic and political conditions in Czechoslovakia and prepared the ground for our criminal intentions, which were to change from the people's democratic regime to capitalism; to lead Czechoslovakia into the capitalist camp; and in this way we in fact worked for war."

Examination of Otto Sling

The examination of Otto Sling opened at 16.00 hours [4 P.M.] on November 24. Sling's attitude was "insolent and cynical." He admitted without any regret his espionage activities and his destructive work, and in front of the microphone he adopted an orator's pose and frequently cut short the questioners.

PRESIDING JUDGE: "We are now continuing the trial with the examination of the defendant Otto Sling. Do you know the indictment?"

SLING: "Yes."

PRESIDING JUDGE: "You know with what crimes you are being charged?"

SLING: "Yes."

PRESIDING JUDGE: "Do you plead guilty?"

SLING: "Yes, I plead guilty to all counts of the indictment. I admit to having been a member of the anti-State conspiratorial group headed by Rudolf Slansky. This group consisted of elements hostile to popular democratic Czechoslovakia, coming from the ranks of bourgeois nationalists, Trotskyites, collaborators, and similar enemies.

We conducted our disruptive activities in all sectors of political, economic, and public life, in the National Security Corps, and in the Army. I have particularly in mind the hostile cadres policy, the sabotage of national economy. I admit that during my stay in England from 1939 to 1945 I was engaged in hostile, opportunist activities. During the same period I established espionage contacts with officials of the British Committee, later the Trust Fund. These organizations were in fact parts of the British and U.S. espionage services."

At the request of the Presiding Judge, Sling described his "adventurous past and his dirty work during his residence in England." The Prosecutor then asked Sling to describe the activities of the British Committee and Trust Fund and Sling's own work inside these organizations.

SLING: "Officially the British Committee was explained as a charitable organization which was meant to give material assistance to refugees from Czechoslovakia. In reality the British Committee induced émigrés to work for the U.S. and British espionage services. This was done for the purpose of implementing future hostile imperialist plans in Central Europe, in particular during the postwar era."

Trust Fund's Co-operation with British Labor MP's

Sling went on to describe how the Trust Fund co-operated closely with the Labor Party in order to recruit agents among the Right-wing trade unionists. He also outlined how the American espionage service trained these agents on behalf of the international reactionary trade union center in America and how these activities were facilitated by the leading officials of the Labor Party's Central Secretariat, the then international secretary of the Party, Willis, and the MP's [Philip] Noel Baker, Davis, and others.

Sling's Return to Czechoslovakia

Sling then described his return to Czechoslovakia from England via Moscow. He had stayed on this journey in Moscow for two weeks, where he had realized that the Communist Party was going to play a leading part in Czechoslovakia. He therefore endeavored to make contacts with leading Czechoslovak Communists in Moscow. These contacts were more important both for the purpose of his career and his subversive work than his old contacts with the Benes people. "I became a member of Slansky's conspiratorial group in 1945, when I was appointed leading secretary of the Communist Party's Regional Committee in Brno."

Sling had arrived in Brno in May, 1945, where he was appointed by Svermova as representative of the Communist Party Central Committee. In June, 1945, he had visited Slansky in Prague to obtain directives with respect to the treatment of Communist officials who had betrayed the Party during the Nazi occupation. On that occasion Slansky had told him that use should be made of all these people, "including such semi-Trotskyites as Milan Reiman." This instruction of Slansky's he had interpreted as a directive to continue his hostile activities inside the Communist Party. Another interview with Slansky, in August, 1945, confirmed this impression. During this interview Slansky had told him that he, Sling, was to act in his position as regional secretary strictly in accordance with Slansky's directives. "I realized that Slansky was trying to isolate Klement Gottwald, the Chairman of the Communist Party. I accepted these directives and I became associated with Slansky's hostile activities." Thus this period represented the real beginning of the era when Slansky collected enemy elements around himself with a view to implementing his conspiratorial plans.

The filling of important positions with Trotskyites, as practiced by Slansky, Geminder, Taussigova, and other members of the conspiracy, including the defendant himself, had provided them with a secure foundation for their disruptive work. They had used the same tactics as the Titoite clique in Yugoslavia and their aims had been essentially the same. Under cover of the slogan of "Czechoslovakia's road to socialism" they had in fact tried to drag Czechoslovakia into the imperialist war camp and to obstruct the establishment of socialism.

Sling's Intentions vis-à-vis the Armed Forces

The Prosecutor then turned his questions to the conspirators' intentions with regard to the armed forces. Sling stated that late in 1945 "the Jewish bourgeois nationalist Bedrich Kopold," then an Educational Officer, had called on him at the Regional Secretariat and told him that it might be possible to win over a number of influential senior officers. Kopold had named Generals [Jaroslav] Novak, Kouril, and others. In reply to Slansky's questions Kopold had told him that they were "reactionary bourgeois officers, and participants of the counter-revolutionary putsch in Russia, and had fought actively against the Red Army in the ranks of the Czechoslovak Legion." Sling said he had informed Slansky of his talk with Kopold and that Slansky had stressed the need for him to gain more such bourgeois officers with a view to strengthening the positions of the conspiracy within the Army. Slansky's instructions had been clear and the accused had therefore enabled Generals Novak, Kouril, Trnka, [Rudolf] Bulandr, Budin, Pasek, and others to join the Communist Party. Early in 1946 Slansky had instructed him to form these senior bourgeois officers and generals into an organized group and to remain in close touch with them. He had done so. Through Kopold he had maintained contact with "the circle of generals" and had called regular meetings of them in private apartments. At these meetings he had emphasized the need for gaining more bourgeois officers for the Party. He had stressed the need to fill responsible Army posts with bourgeois experts, justifying his argument by referring to the many bourgeois experts used in all sectors of the country's economy.

"The aim was to render impossible the creation of a new popular democratic Army, to lower the fighting value of the Army, and to ensure the absolute influence of the conspiratorial Center within the Army. This was to have been done by me, and was in fact done by me, with the help of these bourgeois officers and generals." In his work Sling had had the assistance of "the Jewish bourgeois nationalist Reicin," whom Slansky had appointed Deputy Defense Minister for that very purpose.

"These are the crimes I have committed, jointly with the chief of the conspiracy, Rudolf Slansky, and the other conspirators—crimes against the Czechoslovak State, the Communist Party of Czechoslovakia, and the Czechoslovak people. The anti-State conspiracy represented the main force within popular democratic Czechoslovakia in favor of U.S. warmongering imperialism. We conspirators were in fact tools of U.S. war policy. Our anti-State group meant for the U.S. imperialist warmongers the concentration of all bourgeois-nationalist, Trotskyite, and similar forces on which they could count in the event of an attack on us."

Examination of Karel Svab

Svab, former Deputy Minister of National Security, was questioned.

PRESIDING JUDGE: "Are you guilty in the sense of the indictment?"

SVAB: "I am guilty of having shielded the hostile group concentrated around Slansky from being unmasked."

PRESIDING JUDGE: "This is one part of your guilt. What else?"

SVAB: "I am further guilty of having made possible the activities of Anglo-U.S., Yugoslav, and other hostile espionage agencies in Czechoslovakia. I have covered the wrecking activities of the Troskyites, Zionists, bourgeois nationalists, and other hostile groups. I have undermined the security apparatus by placing—either directly or with the help of others—unreliable and hostile persons into leading positions of our security and also persons who were incapable of dealing with the enemies of the Republic. I have further undermined the security apparatus by hampering Party political work in our security system."

The Presiding Judge asked him whether it was true that he had on various occasions shielded the Slansky group against unmasking and also carried out hostile activities against the people's democratic regime and the Communist Party.

SVAB: "That is correct. I was one of this group and together with them I carried out anti-State activities. I did so because I myself was a member of the anti-State Center."

PRESIDING JUDGE: "This means that you carried out those activities as a conspirator. What led you to do this?"

Svab's Activities in Sachsenhausen

Svab explained that his hostility went back to the time when he was imprisoned in the concentration camp at Sachsenhausen. There he had co-operated with the Nazis and had been promoted to foreman. As a Nazi henchman, he had "helped the Nazis to maintain their Nazi order by torturing my fellow prisoners and by stealing their food. For this purpose, I used all the methods I had learnt from the Nazis." On one occasion he had been instrumental in the beating up of a prisoner who had taken a piece of bread. He had himself beaten two fellow prisoners. "They were of Russian and Ukrainian nationality." His fellow prisoners had openly condemned his behavior.

When he returned—as a war criminal—after the war, he had expected to be punished. "This did not happen, thanks to Slansky, who used my treachery in recruiting me for his anti-State Center." His former fellow prisoner, Jaroslav Herman, had written to Slansky about Svab's crimes. Slansky had not reacted in such a way as might have been expected from the Secretary-General of the Communist Party. "On the contrary, in order to bind myself to him for ever, he ordered me to give a written report of all my crimes." The Prosecution at this point submitted a photostat of Herman's letter to Slansky, which Svab identified. Svab's report to Slansky on his crimes in the concentration camp, dated September 20, 1945, was similarly submitted and identified. He added: "This report is in reality my written and signed pledge of my co-operation with Slansky." On the basis of this Slansky appointed him to the leading security position in the Secretariat of the Central Committee and ordered him to take instructions from himself only. Slansky thus had a person in this position who was dependent on him and at the same time he had a guarantee that the security apparatus would work for his hostile ends.

"Our conspiratorial Center, led by Slansky, worked for the liquidation of the people's democratic regime in Czechoslovakia, for the implementation of the Anglo-U.S. strategic plans, for the preparation of a new war."

The Frejka Clique's Sabotage

From the very beginning of his job, Svab had received reports gravely incriminating individual members of the conspiratorial Center. "All this material I handed to Slansky, and together with him I liquidated it. Furthermore, on Slansky's instructions, I warned each of the incriminated individuals. I thus enabled them to continue their hostile activities." He had, for instance, found out that ever since 1945 Frejka had concentrated round himself "members of his London group of so-called economists from the ranks of former leading personalities of capitalist cartels and other large enterprises or direct employees of the British ruling circles. I knew that this Frejka clique not only sabotaged our economy but also spied. This latter activity I shielded by handing all reports on it to Slansky. We liquidated them. Slansky knew, for instance, that Goldman and Frejka were sabotaging the preparations and the implementation of the Two- and Five-Year Plans; we also knew that not only Frejka and Goldman but also Loebl were collaborators of the U.S. spy, Noel Field, who was unmasked during the trial of Rajk in Hungary. Frejka and Goldman gave this U.S. spy important reports on Czechoslovak economy and its planning, and Loebl reported on foreign trade.

"As early as 1947, I received important evidence condemning Loebl of hostile co-operation with the imperialist agent, Ripka. In co-operation with Slansky, I destroyed this evidence and warned Loebl. We also knew that Clementis was an agent of the French Secret Service, the leader of a group of bourgeois nationalists in Slovakia, and an agent of Benes. We had a letter from Ripka to Benes from which it was clear to us that Clementis had a treasonable attitude." These and similar documents they "liquidated" in this way: Slansky kept the most incriminating himself and the others Svab filed in secret archives.

Asked how he and Slansky had shielded the U.S. spy Noel Field, Svab said: "Field, the U.S. spy who was unmasked at the Rajk trial, said that he had maintained a wide espionage net in Czechoslovakia. As his collaborators he named the Jewish bourgeois nationalists Frejka, Goldman, Loebl, Hajek-Karpeles; in Slovakia, [Laco] Holdos, Pavlik-Pollitzer, and others who, on his instructions, supplied him with important espionage information from all spheres of their activities."

PRESIDING JUDGE: "How did you keep this evidence of Field from the courts?"

SVAB: "As Slansky and I could not destroy this testimony of Field's, Slansky ordered that the investigations be carried out in such a way that they were only a formality and that during the investigations all members of the Center be informed of the extent of Field's evidence so that they could prepare their defense."

PRESIDING JUDGE: "When did you learn that Noel Field was a spy?"

SVAB: "I learned that in 1947 from a document submitted to me by the Zionist Stepan Placek. This letter, written by the imperialist agent Allen Dulles himself to Field, requested espionage co-operation. This important document we kept secret, even when in 1949 Field was unmasked as a spy."

Prosecutor Kolaja asked Svab what other hostile groups Svab had shielded. He said that he and the Center had supported "Zionist organizations and their terrorist gangs." These Zionist organizations had maintained continuous contact "with the imperialist agents who worked at the Israeli Legation in Prague and also with the 'Joint' espionage organization. I knew from numerous reports which I received that this whole conspiratorial movement was financed by U.S. agencies which used the Zionist organizations as one of their channels for spreading imperialist influence in the peoples' democracies."

Kolaja then asked why they had supported these Zionist organizations. Svab said that one of the reasons for this was that "Slansky, who led the conspiratorial Center, is himself a Jewish bourgeois nationalist and a large number of other members of our Center are also Jewish bourgeois nationalists or even directly Zionists. The main reason for our support, however, was that the Zionists were the most reliable imperialist agency, which gave Slansky the best opportunity for maintaining his link with the imperialist West.

"The anti-State Center's preparations for the restoration of capitalism in Czechoslovakia made use of Tito's experiences and relied on a group of Trotskyites and other renegades who had been exposed before the war. Slansky knew the hostile character of these elements very well, and from May, 1945, onward he made their re-entry into the Party possible under the slogan 'Come back; all is forgiven.' I helped him in this."

Slansky had transferred Svab from the Party Secretariat to the national security sector after the conspirators had consolidated their positions in the Secretariat. Slansky had full confidence in Svab and, therefore, had entrusted him with this new task. "Particularly full support in undermining the National Security Corps was given by a group of Trotskyite former volunteers of the International Brigade in Spain."

PRESIDING JUDGE: "Tell us what particular danger was caused by the activities of the anti-State Center in case of an attack against the Czechoslovak Republic."

SVAB: "In case of an attack against our Republic by the imperialist West the anti-State Center represented a danger in as far as it would have acted as a fifth column to the detriment of the Republic's defense potential, thus facilitating the realization of the imperialists' aggressive plans. Rudolf Slansky realized very well the importance and significance of the security sector and, therefore, devoted great care to making it subject to the interests of the anti-State Center. At the right moment this would have enabled him to become a dictator like the U.S.-

British agent, Tito, to undo the development of socialism in Czechoslovakia, to dissociate the Republic from the USSR and the camp of peace. Despite our concentrated efforts we failed to get the security sector completely into our hands and to remove its honest members, who were devoted to the interests of the Czechoslovak people, the Communist Party, and Gottwald and who step by step exposed our hostile activity and upset our plans."

Examination of Bedrich Reicin

Reicin's examination began shortly before midday. The session on November 25 was attended mainly by members of the National Security Corps and the Army, who had thus been able to follow the examinations of Svab, former Deputy-Minister of National Security, and Reicin, former Deputy-Minister of National Defense.

PRESIDING JUDGE: "Do you plead guilty in accordance with the indictment and are you guilty of the crimes detailed therein?"

REICIN: "Yes."

(Note: At first Reicin appeared to be suffering from emotional stress and spoke slowly; later his voice sounded more controlled.)

According to Reicin his betrayal of the working-class movement and of the Czechoslovak people had started in the autumn of 1938, after the dissolution of the Czechoslovak Communist Party by the Agrarian * and reactionary Benes clique. "In these decisive and difficult times my political and moral decomposition became evident." After his arrest by the Prague Gestapo in April,

*The Agrarian Party was the strongest in Czechoslovakia before the war. Many of its leaders participated in the rump governments set up by the Nazis and it was not re-established after the war.—*Ed.*

1939, the Germans "made use of my cowardliness and gradually I became a collaborator of the fascist Gestapo, betraying my knowledge of the Party and its officials."

The Gestapo had examined Reicin with respect to the affairs and leadership of the Federation of Proletarian Physical Training, as he had been the Sports Editor of *Rude Pravo*. The Presiding Judge mentioned a deposition by an unnamed witness who had been Reicin's cellmate in 1939 and who had stated that Reicin had written a report for the Gestapo in his cell. Reicin confirmed this, saying that the Gestapo Commissioner Elbers had asked him to give details about the working-class PT [Physical Training] movement.

"My examination by the Gestapo led to the exposure of the underground Party Central Committee and its leading officials." Reicin had given information about Party officials of the Central Secretariat, the Komsomol Central Committee, and the Party First Region, together with reports on the editorial staff of the Party press, particularly of *Rude Pravo* and *Halo Noviny*, and on officials linking the Party with the Comintern. Reicin had also told the Gestapo about printing presses used by the Party for the production of illegal pamphlets.

"My treason, my shameful treason, helped the Gestapo in its extermination campaign against the Czechoslovak Communist Party, for my statements enabled it to effect the physical liquidation of those whom I betrayed." Many had paid with their lives. In reply to the Prosecutor's remark that he had betrayed the national hero [Julius] Fucik, Reicin admitted that he had furnished the Gestapo with reports about Fucik after his own release from prison. He had also betrayed his contacts with the Party leadership through a bookshop in Prague where the Gestapo had then placed its own agent Freisleben. This Gestapo agent had confirmed Reicin's guilt, according to a statement in the hands of the Prosecution. "In view of my betrayal and my cowardice the Gestapo regarded me as a willing instrument and released me on condition of further collaboration. Elbers also knew that I had the opportunity of emigrating to the USSR, as I had informed him of this. The Gestapo wanted to make use of this opportunity and to send me as its agent to the USSR. I accepted this proposal of the Gestapo. In my selfish desire to get out of prison at any cost I stooped even to this shameful betrayal and signed an undertaking for Elbers pledging my future co-operation with the Gestapo."

After his release on October 14, 1939, acting in accordance with Gestapo instructions, Reicin had tried to gain the confidence of the Party in order to ensure his own dispatch to the USSR. He had furnished reports on his contacts with Fucik and others. In December, 1939, Vaclav Kren, a member of the underground Central Committee, had instructed him to abstain from further Party activities as he had become known to the Gestapo. All this Reicin had betrayed to Elbers, who had told him to obey these instructions in order to retain the Party's confidence, which would enable Reicin to go to the USSR and to work against the émigré leadership of the Party.

The Prosecution then produced four letters written by Fucik mentioning his contacts with Reicin and Reicin's own postwar declaration affirming his wartime contacts with Fucik.

PROSECUTOR: "Tell us how the German fascists enabled you to go to the USSR."

REICIN: "In view of my tasks in the USSR, the Gestapo passed me on to a higher authority in the Sicherheitsdienst at the beginning of 1940. I was given an emigration passport to China via the USSR. After discussing my tasks in the USSR I openly left Prague for Moscow on October 13, 1940, via Berlin, Koenigsberg, and Vilna."

PROSECUTOR: "How did you fulfill the instructions given

to you by the German fascists after you arrived in the USSR?"

REICIN: "On my arrival in Moscow I reported to the émigré leadership of the Czechoslovak Communist Party, but I kept silent about my betrayal and my Gestapo tasks." He had been placed in a home for political émigrés near Moscow and at the beginning of 1941 Slansky had asked him to co-operate temporarily in the Czechoslovak transmissions of Radio Moscow. In February, 1942, Reicin had joined the Czechoslovak Army in the USSR and at the beginning of 1945 he had become head of military intelligence in the First Czechoslovak Corps. After the liberation he had become Chief of Czechoslovak Military Intelligence and later Deputy Minister of National Defense. "I recruited cadres from the ranks of old bourgeois officers of the pre-Munich army and its intelligence service—bourgeois nationalists and other unreliable elements on whom I relied in my later hostile activities. The U.S. spies Col. Woldike, Col. Koenig, and their British colleague Col. Mullens received important information as a result of my activities. This information contained reports on the state of the Czechoslovak Army at that time."

The Prosecutor then presented photostat copies of documents from the secret archives of the General Staff which "prove that information about the Army was given to the Anglo-U.S. spies." Reicin recognized these documents as valid. Reicin's espionage activities, he went on, had been aided by Gen. [Antonin] Bocek, former Chief of the General Staff, and Gen. Rasla.

Western Military Representatives' Visits

Reicin continued: "I also agreed to visits by representatives of Western capitalist armies to Czechoslovak military training establishments and special units. On these occasions these Western spies, covered by their diplomatic office, learned of facts which should have been kept secret. Acting on instructions issued by Gen. Bocek, Gen. Marko, the Officer Commanding Signals, accompanied an English officer on a tour of signals units and acquainted him with the progress of training, organization, fighting preparedness, and other circumstances affecting these units. During these visits Gen. Marko told the Englishman about top secret matters affecting the Czechoslovak Army, its internal organization, conditions, etc. In Benesov he even acquainted him with all the officers of the unit and particularly pointed out to him the intelligence officer, whom he described on the sly as: 'this is our intelligence spy.' Gen. Bocek and I talked this over, but we took no action against Gen. Marko for in effect he only did the same thing as we were doing."

Reicin had covered up the activities of officers "who had been caught in the act of espionage . . . and recruited them for further services for U.S. and British espionage." He had supported officers who had opposed the application of Soviet methods in the Army and "the whole reactionary gang was under the protection of Benes, the agent of the U.S. imperialists. He issued orders prohibiting action against officers who had espionage connections with representatives of the U.S. or other Western armies."

REICIN: "Dr. Benes gave open instructions prohibiting action against reactionary pro-Western officers, who, together with representatives of the U.S. Army and other Western capitalist armies, carried on hostile activities in the Czechoslovak Army and undermined the defense of the people's democratic order. Benes himself approved and aided the hostile activities of Western espionage agencies in Czechoslovakia. In 1947 I myself took part in a military conference with Benes in the [Hrdcany] Castle * when I presented a report on the state of the Czechoslovak Army from the point of view of military intelligence.

*Official residence of the President of Czechoslovakia.—*Ed.*

This report contained definite information about the subversive doings of high Czechoslovak officers connected with Anglo-U.S. spies, about their relations with Western spies, etc. On that occasion Dr. Benes gave us his hostile instructions. He opposed action against reactionary pro-Western officers who carried out espionage in the Czechoslovak Army in the interests of the Americans and their allies."

Benes "Worked Systematically" against the Kosice Program

PROSECUTOR: "This means that Benes, in agreement with the interests of the Anglo-U.S. imperialists and you and your clique of bourgeois officers, prepared conditions in the Army for the creation of a fifth column?"

REICIN: "Yes. Benes worked systematically from 1945 against the implementation of the Kosice program on the cleaning up of the Army leadership. He tried to preserve the pre-Munich personnel. Through us, his collaborators in the Army, he packed the command with reactionary, Western-minded officers."

The Prosecutor then submitted that the fact that Benes had openly spoken in front of Reicin proved that he had enjoyed Benes's confidence.

REICIN: "That is so. At this secret conference Benes really openly expressed his anti-Soviet and pro-Western tendencies. He did so because he trusted me and relied on me, as on Gen. Bocek. In this way my whole shameful past brought me not only into close relations with Dr. Benes and his lackeys but also into the anti-State plot led by Slansky."

Reicin was then asked when he had become a member of Slansky's conspiratorial Center. He replied: "It began at the end of 1945 or at the beginning of 1946 when on the occasion of my visiting the Secretariat of the Central

Committee of the Communist Party Slansky told me that he knew of my treasonable activities in the Gestapo in 1939. This was a shock to me and I expected an investigation into the matter, but this did not happen. On the contrary, Slansky began to be considerate to me, he furthered my career even more than hitherto, and in this and other ways he tried to make our relations closer. I recognized in Slansky my savior and protector and I began to accept his line fully. In this way Slansky bound me to him."

PROSECUTOR: "Your treacherous character led you to be simultaneously in hostile contact with the Benes clique and with the Slansky gang. Is this so?"

REICIN: "That is so. . . . Slansky tied me more and more to his own person by supporting my criminal and sabotage activities in connection with the hostile Army command. Slansky did so particularly by agreeing that we should grant espionage facilities to Anglo-U.S. agents among the ranks of Czechoslovak officers and foreign diplomatists and connive at their machinations."

Sabotaging the Czechoslovak Army

Reicin also confirmed that Slansky "knew of the espionage activities which were carried out by his clique in the Army command against the Soviet Union and the people's democracies. I had no secrets from Slansky as regards questions of hostile activities within the Army. My conversation with Slansky when he invited me to his office in the building of the Central Committee of the Communist Party in August, 1948, was particularly characteristic. On this occasion Slansky expressly said to me that it was his wish that I should become deputy of the Minister of National Defense, with responsibility for cadre matters. Slansky told me that he supported my candidacy so that I should direct the cadre activities in the Czechoslovak

Army in conformity with the previous line of procedure. He asked me to ask for his advice in all questions and directed me to continue my disruptive activities in the Army. I agreed with this."

Asked about the important positions held by his group in the Army, Reicin declared: "Slansky, in co-operation with me and the bourgeois clique in the Army command to which belonged the Chief of Staff Gen. Bocek, Gen. Zdenek Novak, and a number of others, controlled the key positions in the Army. This fifth column, linked with a number of other bourgeois-nationalist, Zionist, and other hostile elements, hampered the building up of the Army in every way. This continued up to February, 1948."

After February, 1948, "Slansky installed further criminal cadres in important Army posts in order to attain a further safeguarding of leading posts in the Army and to establish a 100 percent rule over them. In conformity with directives issued by Slansky, Sling, another member of the Center of plotters, acted in Brno on the same lines. Hostile bourgeois cadres which had not been entirely compromised up to February, 1948 by obvious reactionary activities were left in the Army even after the February purge. They were promoted and thus enabled to continue the hampering and sabotaging of the building up of the Czechoslovak Army from the posts in which we had placed them." Reicin admitted that "only a formal purge took place in the Army in 1948 and it was advantageous to Slansky and the bourgeois leadership that many enemies remained in their Army posts."

As an associate of Slansky, Reicin settled cadre questions concerning the Czechoslovak Officers' Corps in conformity with the requirements of the gang. That was why Slansky had decided to push Reicin into the post of Deputy Minister of National Defense responsible for cadre matters. Thus decisions on cadres were concentrated in Reicin's hands. In addition Reicin had deliberately and systematically sabotaged the implementation of the Kosice Government Program concerning the Army. Reicin had also sabotaged the training of the Czechoslovak Army and had weakened its defense capability.

Espionage Contacts with Yugoslav Agents

Speaking about the co-operation and the espionage contacts of the Slansky Center with the Titoites, Reicin admitted that, for the sake of the implementation of the conspirators' plans for the restoration of capitalism in Czechoslovakia, the members of the Center had employed the same methods as the criminal, traitorous Tito gang in Yugoslavia. "Slansky and I were in contact with Titoite agents in Czechoslovakia, who were in the service of U.S. espionage agencies, and in conformity with the directives received from these agencies we built up a hostile network in Czechoslovakia. I established direct contacts with Yugoslav agents at the end of 1945 in my office on the occasion of the official visit of the Yugoslav Military Attaché in Prague, Col. Ivanovic. Col. Ivanovic expressly told me on this occasion that the Yugoslav intelligence service was well acquainted with my co-operation with the Gestapo during the occupation period. He said that I would certainly understand what the betrayal of this fact would mean to my person. Then Ivanovic declared that I must co-operate with the Yugoslav espionage service in Czechoslovakia on this line. I entered into this co-operation in view of the fact that the Yugoslavs knew of my traitorous co-operation with the Gestapo. I was thus forced to co-operate with them. In the course of the negotiations with Col. Ivanovic I fully realized that he was sent to Czechoslovakia not as an ally but as an enemy. In a further conversation Col. Ivanovic told me that Czechoslovakia was not the only country in which the Americans were interested through the medium of their Yugoslav helpers.

He declared that the same methods were also applied in Hungary, Bulgaria, Romania, and Poland."

Documents shown to Reicin during his interrogation before the trial were here stated to have proved that Titoite spies were given important secret military information even after the publication of the Cominform resolution. "I confirm that the Titoites were not only given very important secret military information, even after the publication of the Cominform resolution, by leading personages in the Ministry of National Defense, but were also allowed to import military materiel."

The Chief Prosecutor's Speech

Dr. Urvalek, the Chief Prosecutor, said, "Our people's democratic court has never before dealt with a case concerning such criminals as those who are in the dock today." Day by day the Czechoslovak people had witnessed "a chain of treason" without parallel in the country's history. The hearts of the working people were filled with the deepest indignation and just anger. The accused had tried to abuse the Party and had sold the country's interests to the Western imperialists. They had undermined Czechoslovakia's friendly relations with the USSR, the shield of the country's freedom. They had deliberately caused damage to the country's economy amounting to many thousands of millions. The Czechoslovak Army "was made incapable of dealing with aggression." Espionage agencies were set up in the Ministries and an attempt was made to make the security apparatus an instrument of their sinister plans. "All this was done with the sole aim of introducing a Tito fascist regime in our country with all its consequences, i.e. to restore capitalism, to hand our homeland once more to the imperialists as a colony, and to transform her into a base for the war against the

Soviet Union and the people's democratic countries which is now being prepared."

The trial had enabled the Czechoslovak people not only to see the moral baseness of the accused in its full nakedness, but also to realize the full extent of the danger which had threatened the country as a result of their criminal activities. It had also become clear that many obstacles and difficulties which had been thought to be merely accompanying development toward socialism were in fact the outcome of the deliberate disrupting activities of the accused. The great anger of the people, which had become obvious in the course of this trial, was proof of the fact that the people were firmly resolved to smash everybody who dared to cause harm to the freedom and independence of the homeland. The people would deal mercilessly with anybody who might make an attempt to disrupt Czechoslovakia's firm alliance with the Soviet Union.

The accused were not only dangerous individually, but above all as a group backed by the U.S. imperialists. "They are, above all, so dangerous because the whole of the Center of plotters, with its sabotage, espionage, and treasonable activities, is closely linked with the intensified war preparations of the U.S. imperialists, and it has thus become a fifth column in the crusade of the imperialists against world peace. In the pay of the U.S. imperialists the plotters were ready to carry out any order given to them. The trial has shown what sort of methods are being employed by the imperialists for the recruitment of their agents and what sort of people are being enlisted. It is in this respect that the trial is of great international significance."

The plotters' Center was born in the West in the course of the Second World War and "in close connection with the aims of enslavement pursued by the Western imperialists during the war. It is notorious that the Western imperialists planned and prepared an entirely different development and result of the war than that which materialized in the end." They had failed to destroy the Soviet Union with Hitler's help. They had, in vain, delayed the opening of the second front in the hope that the Soviet Union would bleed to death. Stalin's predictions of 1934 on the final outcome of a Second World War had proved right in every respect. The Soviet Union had defeated both Germany and Japan and her economic, military, and political power, as well as moral authority, had grown. As a result of the Soviet victory, governments representing the bourgeoisie and the owners of big estates were liquidated in many parts of the world, including Czechoslovakia. The imperialists, however, did not give up their criminal intentions to restore their rule over the countries in which the people had taken power into their hands. The imperialists had, above all, not scrapped their old criminal plan to destroy the Soviet Union, whose very existence and successful reconstruction filled them with horror. The U.S. imperialists, those successors of Hitler, were making the greatest possible efforts to prevent their own extermination. They were employing the most barbarous means to enslave the free nations and were preparing a new war.

During the Second World War the Anglo-American imperialists had financed a number of reactionary émigré governments and employed them as their agencies. It was their intention to use these governments for the restoration of their power after Germany's defeat. The liberated countries were to be ruled by the bourgeoisie and used as assembly grounds for an aggressive war against the Soviet Union. In Czechoslovakia this task was allocated to a clique led by Benes, an old agent of the West, and his associates, Ripka, Lausman, and others. This explained why these persons were given money in London that was promised to the Republic at the time as a miserable compensation for the Munich betrayal. Out of this so-called Munich fund benefits were paid to émigrés in the West. After liberation the Benes agency occupied prominent positions in the Republic. This agency acted under the direction of Western diplomats, above all the U.S. Ambassador Steinhardt, as was proved in the trial of Horakova. In the course of 1947 and 1948 these open agencies of the imperialists were unmasked. This happened in Czechoslovakia in February, 1948, when an attempt at a counter-revolutionary putsch was liquidated and the representatives of the Western imperialists were driven from their positions. "Thus the first agency, consisting of the most reactionary bourgeois-nationalist and fascist elements, was smashed. Experience has shown, however, that the imperialists were playing another false card in their base juggling with the fate of the people of the countries liberated by the Soviet Army." The Cominform resolutions of 1948 and 1949 had fully revealed the treachery of the Tito clique in Yugoslavia. The case of Yugoslavia had shown in every respect how dangerous was this juggling of the imperialists. The Cominform resolution had shown that the bourgeoisie had continued its old-established practice of recruiting spies and provocateurs within the Party.

"Strategic Reserves" of the Imperialists

By these methods the imperialists had endeavored to disintegrate the Party from within. They were attempting to use the same methods as in the case of Tito's Yugoslavia. The Titoite clique which, according to the imperialist plans, was to cover the left flank in the case of an attack against the USSR, was unmasked in time, thanks to the historical experiences of the Soviet Communist Party. "However, the cunning imperialist plans were not confined to Yugoslavia. In other countries too, which had been liberated by the victorious Soviet forces, the imperialists instructed their agents to recruit spies, informers, and traitors inside the Communist Parties." Thanks to the vigilance of the working population and the Communist Parties, the treacherous gangs of Rajk, Kostov, and others had been unmasked in time. All these traitors were to turn their countries into imperialist military bases in the case of war against the USSR. The trials of these Western agents had proved that the imperialists had begun laying their plans against the Soviet Union at the very beginning of the Second World War. In addition to their usual spies and agents, the imperialists had created "a second reserve, planted inside the Communist and Workers' Parties." These second reserves had become particularly active at the time when the Western imperialists started their frontal attack against the camp of peace with the help of diversionists and murderers, paid out of the $100 million voted by the U.S. Congress at Truman's request.

"It would have been surprising if the Western imperialists had left out our own country from their plans, for Czechoslovakia, by virtue of her wealth and economic potentialities and owing to her strategic position, forms a serious obstacle to aggressive plans. However, we cannot complain about insufficient interest in our country on the part of the imperialists. The imperialist protectors of the pre-Munich bourgeois Republic left nothing undone to win power in our country. Indeed the present trial shows that the imperialists did not fail to create in Czechoslovakia their strategic reserve inside the Communist Party." The trial had proved that the imperialists had started implementing these plans with respect to Czechoslovakia right at the beginning of the Second World War. "Can it be a mere coincidence that, in addition to the agents recruited at a later date, there returned after the war six of the present defendants with long-term tasks given them by their imperialist masters? These are: Clementis, Loebl, Sling, Frejka, Hajdu, and André Simone. Is it a mere coincidence that in 1939 agents of the British bourgeoisie, which so hates communism, hurried at the behest of the agent Ripka to the assistance of two Communist Deputies, Slansky and Clementis? Is it a coincidence that Clementis was aided by British peers in 1939, when he found himself in a French internment camp? No, all this is no coincidence, just as it is no coincidence that the so-called charitable Trust Fund was recruiting spies in Poland at the beginning of the war through its agent Herman Field. A similar organization was set up in Switzerland by Noel Field, the closest collaborator of the agent Allen Dulles, who was in charge of American espionage in Central and Eastern Europe."

Sling's and Frejka's evidence about the true character of the Trust Fund had fully confirmed these facts. The imperialists had already planted their agents inside the Czechoslovak Communist Party before the war. These imperialist agents had maintained close connections with Benes in London. "After the liberation all these spies indicted in the present trial and other Trotskyite and Zionist agents and traitors flooded Czechoslovakia. Sling has confirmed that they all returned with well-defined treasonable plans. At the head of all these hostile elements the imperialists placed Rudolf Slansky, who has been unmasked in this trial as an inveterate agent of the bourgeoisie and a vile enemy of the people. By order of the American imperialists, Slansky gathered around him this whole gang and became its chief. Rudolf Slansky is the creator and head of this conspiratorial Center."

Slansky's Background and Activities

The Prosecutor then proceeded to describe Slansky's background. He was the son of a wealthy businessman and he had wormed his way into the Communist Party despite his bourgeois origin. He had never severed his links with the bourgeoisie. In bourgeois courts of law before the war he had acted in a cowardly and opportunist way, disclaiming his membership in the Communist Party. In 1927 he had defended Trotskyism, and in 1935 he had advocated co-operation with the Right-wing leaders of reformist parties and with Benes in connection with the National Front problem. In the files of the bourgeois police he had been described as a follower of Trotsky, for the police knew that, even when Trotsky had been unmasked in the Soviet Union, Slansky had still hailed him at public meetings in Czechoslovakia. Slansky had rightly said during his examination in the present trial: "I never was a real Communist." "It has been proved in this courtroom that Slansky has been an agent of the American espionage service since 1930 and has betrayed the interests of the Communist Party and the revolutionary workers' movement.

"Mordecai Oren has corroborated Slansky's close connections with Zionist organizations and with the Israeli Legation. Oren also confirmed that all Zionist campaigns were conducted under Slansky's protection. The witness Oskar Langer, an international Zionist agent, also confirmed that Slansky was the patron of all Jewish bourgeois nationalists and that he had expressly said that it was necessary to fill important positions in economic, political, and public life with Zionists and Jewish bourgeois nationalists. According to Slansky their bourgeois background could be disregarded. His closest associates from the days of his youth were Geminder, Frejka, Reicin, and Sling—all Zionist agents. Slansky cannot deny his Jewish bourgeois-nationalist character. If we realize the true meaning of Jewish bourgeois nationalism, from which descend the international Zionist organizations, the most important agencies of American imperialism, we understand why

Rudolf Slansky finds himself today before a people's court, charged with the heaviest crimes in our penal code."

The Prosecutor then turned to Slansky's activities during the war in the USSR and his betrayal of the partisan movement in Slovakia. He repeated the charge in the indictment that Slansky, co-operating with Benes and Benes's Military Attaché in Moscow, Gen. Pika, had given away important secrets concerning the organization of the partisans and had tried to subordinate partisan units to Golian's reactionary command. The Prosecutor then dwelt at great length on Slansky's vile action with respect to the removal of the national hero, the darling of the Party and the people, Jan Sverma, Gottwald's closest collaborator. Describing Sverma's death, Dr. Urvalek repeated the charge that Slansky was responsible for it. "Slansky's guilt for Sverma's death reveals him as a monster and as a hardened enemy who knows no mercy." Sverma's death had enabled Slansky later on to describe himself as the main protagonist of the partisan struggle and finally to obtain the position of Secretary-General of the Party. "Slansky is a man who is prepared to walk over corpses to achieve his ends.

"For years Slansky denied that he had concluded a pact with the traitor Lausman, who deserted to the imperialists in order to be Slansky's quartermaster. He built up a false legend about his work as a partisan, following in this respect the example of Tito." Cunningly deceiving the Party and its leading personalities, Slansky had built up his conspiratorial group. The leaders of this anti-State plot were now in the dock. "Who are these men? Josef Frank, a war criminal who should have been tried by a War Tribunal for torturing Soviet and French prisoners in German concentration camps, an adventurer, thief, and embezzler who for years, under Slansky's protection, disguised his criminal past. Bedrich Geminder, one of Slansky's closest friends, devoted to him and prepared to betray our country and our people at any moment in the interests of his master—this man without a country was entrusted by Slansky with the International Secretariat of the Party's Central Committee. Ludwig Frejka, an agent of the American spy Herman Field, an inveterate cosmopolitan, who with Slansky's help became Chairman of the Party's Economic Commission and created the legend that he was an indispensable economist with Marxist training. This swindler and traitor surrounded himself in the Economic Commission with similar enemies of the people, Goldman, Jancik, and others. Karel Svab, another war criminal who tortured prisoners in German concentration camps, was Slansky's reliable instrument for the domination of the National Security Corps. Vladimir Clementis, one of Benes's closest friends and agents, an old agent of the British, American, and French espionage service, a Slovak bourgeois nationalist, an enemy of the people and of the Soviet Union, who quickly accepted Slansky's anti-popular treacherous platform. This renegade was appointed Foreign Minister.

"With Slansky's assistance Vavro Hajdu, a Zionist and agent of the intelligence service, became Deputy Foreign Minister; and the Trotskyite Artur London, an agent of the American espionage service, became Deputy Foreign Minister in charge of cadres. In the Ministry of Foreign Trade Slansky planted as Deputy Minister the Zionist Loebl, Field's prewar agent and later an agent of the intelligence service, and the cosmopolitan Zionist and agent of the British intelligence service, Rudolf Margolius. These saboteurs turned the Ministry of Foreign Trade into a trade agency of the Western capitalists. The post of Deputy Minister of Finance was filled by Slansky by the collaborator and protector of Nazi war criminals, the adventurer and organizer of Zionist disruptive campaigns, the leading agent of the Israeli espionage service, Otto Fischl. As Deputy Minister of National Defense Slansky appointed Bedrich Reicin. This Gestapo agent and contemptible traitor, whose black conscience is burdened with guilt for the death of members of the illegal Committee of the Communist Party and editors of *Rude Pravo*, among them the national hero Julius Fucik, beloved by our people and by all progressive people throughout the world, became after the defeat of the Nazis Slansky's valuable assistant and an agent of the American, British, and Yugoslav espionage services. Otto Sling, son of an industrialist millionaire, remained throughout his life a capitalist, alien to the working class, closely connected with British and American imperialists and with Benes's clique, an agent of American and British espionage; this traitor was made by Slansky and Svermova Regional Secretary of the Party in Brno, one of the most important regions of the Republic. To this assembly of criminals belongs also André Simone, an old Trotskyite and spy. His criminal past fitted him well for the part of Slansky's 'Court writer' and servant on the staff of *Rude Pravo*."

All these contemptible enemies of the people had penetrated with Slansky's help into the most important positions in State and Party, and in their turn planted hostile elements in their own Departments. Frejka, Frank, and Jancik planted as so-called experts sworn enemies of the working class and the USSR, capitalist agents, as directors-general in various branches of production. Among them were Fabinger, Rada, Holy, Smrkovsky, Vlk, and an endless stream of others. Similar appointments were made in foreign trade by Loebl and Margolius. Capitalist, anti-popular, Zionist elements were planted in State trade monopolies.

"Exactly the same were the activities of Reicin in the Army and Svab in the security sphere." The same treacherous work was done in the regions by the Regional Secretaries, in particular by Sling in Brno. This grand scheme to get hold of the Party was, however, unmasked in time, but the extent of the plot showed how dangerous it had been. "This conspiracy grew and affected all important positions like a cancer.

"Through the whole life of Slansky his Trotskyite line runs like a red thread. His best friends from childhood were Trotskyites. His closest collaborators after the liberation were Trotskyites. . . . But Slansky is not a greenhorn as a bourgeois agent in the working-class movement. He knows well how the Trotskyite plot worked in the USSR. But he does not draw on the experiences of the Soviet people and their Party but on the experience of the Trotskyites. From this experience he learns the lesson that he must camouflage himself better than the Soviet Trotskyites. He and his gang do not come into the open with their own platform—be it ever so false and hypocritical. From the experience of Soviet history it was clear that they could never come before the masses with any mendacious platform. For this reason they seemingly accept the correct decisions of the Party and Government. Ostensibly they bow to them. But they carry them out in their own wrecking fashion. In their heart of hearts they remained all the time sworn enemies of the people, and of the Communist Party, and allies of the most aggressive of imperialist powers. As Trotsky had sold the Soviet country to Nazi Germany and the Mikado's Japan, in the same way the Trotskyite Slansky and his accomplices tried to sell their country to the successors of Hitler, the U.S. imperialists."

Activities of Clementis: Slovak Separatism

Clementis, a Western spy and lackey of Benes, was at the same time the representative of bourgeois nationalism. "Clementis, this henchman and favorite of Benes, this traitor in the grand style who had made such a good impression on the English lords, wore in vain the mask of a loyal Slovak. How is it possible that Clementis, this 'loyal Slovak,' was Benes's henchman? After all, it was well known that Benes despised the Slovak nation and its language, that Benes was an advocate of the false theory of Czechoslovakism, that he denied altogether the existence of a Slovak nation, that he proclaimed Slovak to be a mere dialect. How can it be explained, then, that Clementis formed such a close alliance with this Benes? The explanation is simple. Benes and Clementis both fought, not for the rights of the people, but for the exploiting interest of the bourgeoisie. They both believed that the U.S. Army would occupy Czechoslovakia and, in that case, they hoped Czechoslovakia would become a U.S. protectorate." Czechoslovakia would have become an object of exploitation by the U.S. monopolists. This development had been prevented by the liberation of the country by the USSR.

The Party had fought even during the First Republic against Benes's nationalistic and chauvinistic policy toward the Slovaks. The Kosice program had fully safeguarded the rights of the Slovak people, as also did the Czechoslovak Constitution. Clementis and the other bourgeois nationalists wanted to serve their U.S. masters and in their interest strengthen the position of the Slovak bourgeoisie. "Slovak separatism in Clementis's version means the handing over of Slovakia to the U.S. imperialists. They are all on the same anti-people's platform, together with such Slovak reactionaries as the traitors [Josef] Lettrich, [Jan] Ursiny, Turcansky, and even [Karol] Sidor *; and together they aimed at the overthrow of the people's democratic regime, the splitting of our Republic, the restoration

*Leaders of the Slovak Democratic Party, except for the latter who had been a prominent leader of the Nazi-supported clerical fascist state established in 1939 and continued until the defeat of Germany.

of capitalism, and the return of want and hunger to the Slovak people. They wanted to hand over to the Americans the essential rights of the Slovak people."

The Slovakia of want and emigration had gone forever; the country was developing and becoming industrialized at an unprecedented pace, and the living standard of its people was approaching that of the people of Bohemia. To create the conditions for this upsurge was the expression of real and genuine love for the Slocak people. These conditions were a firm link with the Czech working class and a common unbreakable link with the USSR. Clementis and his bourgeois-nationalist allies had worked against these very conditions. They, together with the other members of the conspiratorial Center, had aimed at severing the Slovak from the Czech working people, at restoring capitalism, at handing the country over to the U.S. imperialists and transforming it into a U.S. war base. These were the common aims of Clementis and Slansky and the basis of their co-operation. And finally, how could this self-styled Slovak patriot be a spy at the same time? His being a spy showed up his patriotism for what it was worth.

The Zionist Movement

"It will be necessary for me to go into details of this so-called Zionist movement. One of the reasons for this is that eleven of the defendants have been trained by Zionist organizations. A further reason is that the trial shows to all Communist and Workers' Parties the menace of Zionism as an agency of U.S. imperialism. The Zionist organizations have always had close links with world capitalism, and therefore have been dangerous enemies of the liberation struggle of the working class. The menace of the international Zionist organizations increased after the setting up of a U.S. satellite, the so-called State of Israel. Even after the setting up of this State the main seat of Zionist organizations remained in the U.S., where the Zionists are strongly represented among the U.S. monopolists who are laying down the whole aggressive policy of the U.S. The Ben Gurion Government . . . is transforming Israel into a military base for U.S. aggression. The Zionist agents in Slansky's conspiratorial Center served by their criminal activities mainly the U.S. aims of world domination and aggression, and not the working people of Israel. Cosmopolitanism and Jewish bourgeois nationalism are in fact only two sides of the same coin, and a debased coin it is at that."

The building of socialism was contrary to their class interests. "The Zionist movement is not some kind of an idea, some sort of an ideology—even if a wrong one. It is—and this trial has shown it clearly—identical with the Zionist organizations in the U.S.A., plus the ruling clique of the State of Israel, plus the Zionist capitalists throughout the world, bound by close links to the capitalist imperialists. The evidence of the U.S. spy, the Zionist Orenstein, has shown that this link is directly based on a secret agreement between Truman, Acheson, and Ben Gurion; that the consequence of this agreement was the Morgenthau-Acheson plan, which laid down the conditions for U.S. support in setting up the State of Israel. The representatives of Israel agreed that Israel would fully support the plans of the U.S. imperialists to attain world domination and to use the Zionist organizations not only in the U.S. but throughout the world [as arms of espionage activity]. In our country the implementation of this agreement lay in the hands of the Israeli Minister, Ehud Avriel Ueberall." The trial had shown the smooth cooperation among the representatives of Israel, the Zionist organization, and the Slansky gang in stealing the people's property and handing it over to Israel by various means.

Prosecutor's Speech Continued

The Prosecutor then dealt with Fischl who, he said, had collaborated with the Nazi during the war, and after the war had saved Nazis and murderers, even people guilty of the massacres of Lidice and Lezaky. He was a Zionist. And he had protected the murderers of Jews and was an ally of the neo-Nazis. "This is their real face. In the same way, Ben Gurion's Government in Israel, which sold out to the U.S. imperialists, is becoming an ally of Western Germany. Many of the defendants unscrupulously misused the fact that the Czech and Slovak peoples despised anti-Semitism, all the more as Hitler had massacred the Jews in his concentration camps. And this very fact was misused by various Jewish racketeers, industrialists, and bourgeois elements for working themselves into the Party, preventing any criticism, and hiding their real face behind the sufferings of the Jewish people at the hands of the Nazis. Our people know that our Party will never give up its proletarian internationalism, that in this trial the defendants are anti-State criminals, international Zionist racketeers in a grand style, agents of Western imperialism."

It was only logical that Slansky had planted Zionists in the most important positions of economy and Party and supported the Zionist organizations and their criminal activities in connection with emigration, which had caused such tremendous damage to the Republic. "This trial has shown up the dangerous character of Zionism in its full depth. And the international significance of this trial is based, among other things, on the fact that it warns not only our Communist Party but also the other Communist and Workers' Parties against this dangerous agency of the U.S. imperialists, Slansky, himself a Zionist, a Trotskyite, and a lackey of the bourgeoisie in the First

Republic and of the imperialists, in his further development gathers round himself a group of people of his own type; people of whom he knows that they have nothing to do with the interests of the working people, enemies of the people like himself, who he knew would willingly fulfill his orders and implement his counter-revolutionary plans."

These people he had found among those who had returned after the war from the West, where they had become spies; among the Zionists, Trotskyites, bourgeois nationalists, collaborators, and other enemies of Czechoslovakia. He had packed the State and Party organizations with such elements with the utmost craftiness. "Slansky knew very well that in the struggle for socialism in our country, that greatest struggle in history, and in the victory of the new social order the decisive role would be played by the revolutionary Party of the working class, the Communist Party, which follows the teaching of Marx, Engels, and Stalin. Hence he and his fellow-conspirators concentrated their endeavors on gaining control of the Party and on transforming this instrument of the working class for building socialism into an instrument for restoring capitalism." For this purpose he had sabotaged all those basic principles which made the Party an effective weapon of the working class. "They replaced by dictatorial methods the systematic and patient persuasion and mass political activities; they suppressed the principles of democratic centralism and democracy within the Party, the principles of criticism and self-criticism."

They had planned at the right moment to hand over the Republic to the U.S. imperialists, following Tito's example. For this purpose it was necessary to pack the Party with bourgeois elements, thereby destroying its proletarian class character. The recruiting campaigns for the Party organized by Slansky were best characterized by his instructions to the Communist officials of the National

Committees of August 15, 1947, which spoke of the recruitment of people of standing, the lower middle class and the bourgeoisie. Workers and small peasants were not even mentioned. They had covered up their sabotage within the Party for a long time by pretending that these were all minor affairs and that it was not necessary to bother the Party leadership with them. The Party Control Commission, which was to investigate, was in the hands of Jarmila Taussigova, another member of Slansky's conspiratorial Center. The evidence had shown how she had succeeded in sabotaging the investigations against Sling in Brno.

The case of this bourgeois Sling showed best how this sabotage of the work of the Party had been done. What Slansky did on a national scale, Sling and the other regional secretaries appointed by Slansky did in their regions. Thanks to Slansky and Svermova the secretaries in the most important industrial regions were all Zionist adventurers and hostile elements alien to the Party.

People like Sling were to be in control of the Party in the regions and guarantee the implementation of the plotters' schemes. But the wreckers, despite their efforts to alter the Party's revolutionary character, to gain control over it, and to render it incapable of fulfilling its historic mission, failed to realize their plans. "If we remember that shortly after the February events the plotters' network began to crack, we notice that no position occupied was of any avail and that they were exposed and rendered harmless after a short period, including their leader, Rudolf Slansky. The Party, all its honest members, stood firmly behind their beloved leader, Klement Gottwald, and behind Gottwald's Party leadership." The Party directives had been clear. They had mobilized the people and pointed out the correct road. They had been the most serious obstacle to the wreckers' success. Honest Party members had protected its purity. Only for a short time had the plotters been able to silence the warnings from below. They had not succeeded in silencing criticism. The Party, led by Gottwald, "was locked in continuous struggle with them from the very beginning." The various criminal elements had been exposed one after another. Today they were standing trial. "The Party has been victorious, as could not have been otherwise. The Party and its Bolshevik leadership are continuing to lead our people along the victorious path toward socialism."

The criminals had not ignored the fact that the Party, enriched by Soviet experience, was devoting all its efforts to the advance of the country's economy, and to a higher standard of living. Therefore, in their criminal attempt to discredit this endeavor in the eyes of the people, to thwart the advance of the country, to make it dependent on Western imperialists, and finally to hand it over to the U.S. aspirants to world hegemony and their aggressive plans, they carried out extensive sabotage activities in the fields of planning, industrial, and agricultural production, supply, and foreign trade—in short everywhere.

Damage to the Czechoslovak Economy

In the course of the trial it was proved that the plotters had caused Czechoslovak economy the loss of many billions. They had thus carried on in a different guise where the U.S. imperialists, with their air raids at the end of the war, had stopped. On April 17 and 18, 1945, the U.S. imperialists had destroyed 70 percent of the Skoda works; in 1949 the accused Margolius had signed an undertaking to pay the so-called Skoda Loan negotiated by the Czechoslovak capitalists under the First Republic. After the liberation of Czechoslovakia by the Soviet Army the imperialist agency of Slansky and Frejka had established itself in Czechoslovak economy. Its elements provided for the imperialists by their bourgeois-Zionist attitude a guarantee to the effect that they would carry out instructions issued by U.S. monopolists. A cleverly concealed network of plotters, directed by Slansky and Frejka, had been set up in the Czechoslovak economy. Their criminal aim had been described by one of the most influential U.S. warmongers, George Kennan, head of foreign policy planning in the U.S. State Department: "The basic aim of U.S. foreign policy is to win over the peoples' democratic countries to its side by both political and economic pressure."

The aims of the so-called UNRRA mission, controlled by Loebl, as well as the plan of a "bridge" as conceived by Ripka, the work of Slansky and Frejka, the endeavor to Marshallize Czechoslovakia, and, after this had failed, the policy of discrimination and blockade, had all rested on that idea. The same aim had been followed in various other schemes, such as "Ueberall," "the dollar offensive," and others. The plotters had entered the struggle against the people armed with such fraudulent arguments as that Czechoslovakia abounded with poor ores, that her industry was advanced and of a peculiar structure, and so on. Behind all those fraudulent arguments there lay their endeavor to subordinate the country to the capitalist world, and to intensify her dependence on capitalist countries. With that in view, they had purposely neglected the utilization of the country's natural resources, ignored the unlimited Soviet and peoples' democratic industrial potential and aid; they had not been guided by considerations for the interests and needs of the Czechoslovak peoples but by the endeavor to subordinate Czechoslovak economy to the predatory interests of U.S. imperialists, the endeavor to harm and weaken the country.

It had been revealed that the roots of the criminals were anchored in the breeding ground of foreign intelligence services. All those Frejkas, Loebls, and others, by giving away secret data on the economy, had helped U.S.

imperialists to effect economic and political pressure and to intensify economic discrimination. The plotters, aware of the decisive significance of economic planning in a country advancing to socialism, attempted in the first place to sabotage that particular field. Millions of workers had been fighting for the Plan, yet behind the backs of Party and Government another treacherous scheme was being put into operation, aimed at making the building of socialism impossible. The plotters had endeavored to subordinate Czechoslovak economy to capitalist countries, to thwart co-operation with the USSR and the peoples' democracies. With this in view, planning methods had been introduced aiming at rendering effective control impossible and at eliminating both Party and Government from decisions on the most important questions.

The Prosecutor then went on to list the various crimes committed by the accused in the economic sphere. Despite the country's wealth in both ferrous and nonferrous ores the plotters had failed to make provisions in the Plan for adequate development in these fields. They had not only confined themselves to local plans of ore extraction, but had even gone so far as to liquidate mines near Sternberk. No mention had been made either in the Two-Year or the Five-Year Plan of exploitation of nonferrous metals. For the development of Czechoslovak metal production the plotters adopted the conception of Taub, a U.S. spy and adviser to Chiang Kai-shek, under which the basis of engineering was to be motor vehicle production. Through this production, not safeguarded by raw materials available at home, Czechoslovakia was to have become an appendix of capitalist countries. As regards the chemical industry, there had been no attempt to produce materials which would have replaced imported raw materials, in particular fuel, synthetic rubber, and other synthetic materials. The Plan had made provision for an increase in production of such sectors as required imports of raw materials from capitalist countries. To do away with dependence on capitalist countries it would have been necessary to promote co-operation with the USSR and the peoples' democracies. This would have required a change of structure, particularly increased productive capacities of plants, chiefly in steel production. The plotters, however, had sabotaged these basic requirements of industry. They had made excessive provision in the Plan for the textile, light engineering, and rubber industries. That approach had threatened the advance toward an improved standard of living, as it would have necessitated more imports from capitalist countries and at the same time increased exports of those goods. As a result of that policy a large percentage of raw materials imported from capitalist countries had been re-exported to those countries at highly unfavorable prices.

Most serious had been the effects of the plotters' sabotage in capital investment. Investment goods had not been allocated to sectors capable of relying on raw materials available at home, but to fields where Czechoslovakia possessed no raw materials, and where the utilization of investments would have been tied to increased imports, chiefly from capitalist countries, as well as to markets in those countries. Thus the appropriation for the textile, leather, and rubber industries under the Two-Year Plan had amounted to thirty-nine times as much as was provided for the utilization of ore deposits at home. The advance toward socialism had been slowed down by incorrect allocation of capital investment and by its dispersal. Home production of iron ores had been allocated a mere 0.08 percent of the investment total planned for industry. No provision had been made for a synthetic rubber plant, nor for an aluminum plant; and insufficient provision had been made for the development of the Stalin works.

The plotters had treacherously planned excessive investments in sectors in which existing productive capacity remained unused, with the result that huge plants were built prematurely for which engineering and steel requirements were not available. Instead of concentrating investment capital, it had been dispersed. This had manifested itself chiefly in power production and had caused shortages of power. Appropriation of investment had been effected without previous project planning and frequently without a clear-cut production program in the plant which was to be built. Thus Kcs.48,000,000 [$960,000] had been frittered away in Martinov; in Zablati, near Trencin, Kcs.37,000,000 [$740,000] had been lost. At the same time, under the pretext of reconstruction, plants still capable of production had been destroyed. In Trinec the damage caused by the plotters' reconstruction scheme had amounted to Kcs.9,000,000,000 [$180,000,000], in addition to which the productive capacity of the plant had been reduced during this period. In Kladno, the dismantling of four blast-furnaces had caused the loss of Kcs.1,500,000,000 [$30,000,000]. The enormous damage caused by the plotters' activities had been of a material, moral, and political nature; they had also slowed down the development of socialism in those peoples' democratic countries with which Czechoslovakia had entered into contracts for the delivery of plant and machinery, which were not carried out.

The execution of the plotters' sabotage scheme had also affected the defensive ability of Czechoslovakia. It had as its aim the weakening of the country, the destruction of her effective defensive ability in the event of an attack by the imperialist aggressors. "The plotters aimed at weakening the strength of the entire camp of peace, thereby putting themselves fully at the disposal of those who planned a new world war."

However, "despite all intrigues, the malignant growth planted by the saboteurs in the healthy body of the Five-Year Plan was destroyed in the course of the execution of the Plan by our working people. The treacherous plans to paralyze our development have suffered inglorious failure thanks to the Party and to the workers' constructive enthusiasm. After the February session of the Central Committee of the Communist Party in 1951, industrial production was raised not by 57 percent, but by 98 percent. Production of iron ore will be 2.7 times higher than orginally planned; the investment development of heavy industry will exceed the original plan figure by almost 75 percent."

The trial had exposed the roots of a series of deficiencies. It had been proved that the plotters had caused difficulties in power supply, an unsatisfactory state of affairs in meat supplies, and had necessitated a rise in meat prices on the free market. It was by these methods that the plotters had endeavored to cause dissatisfaction and to carry out the task entrusted to them by their imperialist masters.

Trade Relations with Capitalist Countries

They had also been responsible for vast losses in the field of foreign trade, where they had for an extensive period carried out their subversive activities. It was particularly in this orbit that they had taken a series of harmful steps, such as the "dollar aid scheme." "They conspired with Zionists from capitalist countries and agreed upon subtle schemes to defraud this country. Thus unfavorable and harmful agreements were entered into. . . . Czechoslovakia never has refused—neither does she now—trade relations with capitalist countries. There is, however, one condition: that the principle of equality among contractual partners is safeguarded. Under this condition differences in economic systems can form no obstacle in the development of international co-operation. In the field of foreign trade, however, the plotters violated this principle intentionally and entered into agreements in which Czechoslovakia was neither an equal partner nor benefited from the agreements." One of those agreements had been the so-called "dollar offensive," which had revealed the hostile conception aimed at subordinating Czechoslovak economy to U.S. monopolists. Under that scheme goods had been exported from Czechoslovakia at prices so low as even to astound U.S. customs officials. A further harmful act had been the agreement and payment of compensation for nationalized property in Czechoslovakia to foreign capitalists.

One of the most characteristic instances of that kind was the agreement with Unilever in 1948, when the plotters fraudulently enforced an agreement under which Czechoslovakia was to pay compensation for the former property of George Schicht's capitalist German company, a bastion of Nazism in the pre-Munich period. According to law the Schicht works should have been liable to confiscation; despite this an agreement was entered into under which an unlawful payment of over Kcs.63,500,000 [$1,270,000] was made. Another violation of the principle of equality and mutual advantage had been the agreement with Britain in 1949, involving a long-term obligation to compensate Britain for nationalized property in Czechoslovakia and recognizing all old debts, including wartime credits. A whole series of agreements had thus been concluded which constituted a fraud on Party and Government. The plotters had welded Czechoslovak economy to that of capitalist countries by negotiating loans from private capitalist firms, such as Hambro in London. They had used every opportunity to rob the working people. Thus, under an agreement with Zionist-Israeli circles, 17 percent of the total Czechoslovak exports to Israel had in effect not been paid for. In the course of the trial a number of treacherous acts had been exposed, including intentional support of Tito's economy even after the

Cominform resolution. Negotiations in Czechoslovak imports and exports had been entrusted to treacherous émigrés, Zionists, international sharks, and other leeches who drew colossal profits from Czechoslovak economy.

It had further been proved that in agricultural production also the plotters had endeavored to put obstacles on the path to socialism and to thwart socialist reconstruction in the countryside, by supporting kulaks and landowners and carrying out sabotage on Czechoslovak State farms and on schemes aimed at increasing agricultural productivity. To conceal their activities they had invented a series of theories, such as that State farms could not be run at a profit—put forward by Smrkovsky—or that of the permanent indebtedness of Czechoslovakia to capitalist countries.

The exposure of huge losses in foreign trade and the robbing of the people's democracies had been rendered possible by the introduction of the fraudulent "M Account" by Loebl. The plotters had collaborated with people like Taub and Ueberall; they had relied on Zionist circles in the capitalist world; and endeavored to interfere with the fraternal relations with the USSR and the people's democracies, thereby plotting against the country's independence and sovereignty. They had intentionally neglected the priority needs for the development of heavy industry and engineering. They had been responsible for the artificial creation of unequal progress in the national economy, thereby aiming to bring about in Czechoslovakia that state of affairs which Tito had created in Yugoslavia. "In the course of the trial, Tito's and Slansky's common aims were exposed. The trial has shown that all the wreckers' acts of robbery against this country were aimed at putting into effect the plan in which UNRRA failed, and to bring about the state of affairs which the Marshall Plan has effected in the satellite countries: to create in an impoverished country the conditions for a restoration of capitalism and to hand her over defenseless to the yoke of U.S. monopolists."

Concluding his speech Urvalek stated that the innumerable messages received by the court during the past few days displayed the firm resolution of the people to undo the damage caused by the agents of the imperialists in the shortest possible time. The road to the continuation of peaceful reconstruction was cleared. The ranks of the Party were closer than before.

"In the name of our nations against whose freedom and happiness the criminals took their stand, in the name of peace, against which they shamelessly plotted, I demand the death sentence for all the accused. Let your verdict become an iron fist without the slightest pity. Let it be a fire which burns out the roots of this shameful abscess of treason. Let it be a bell ringing throughout the whole of our beautiful country for new victories on the march to the sunshine of socialism."

Speeches for the Defense

Following the speech of the Chief Prosecutor, the court rose, and after resumption of proceedings Counsel for the Defense pleaded on behalf of the accused. The first to address the Court was Dr. Bartos defending Slansky and Margolius, who was followed by Dr. Posmura, defending Geminder, Svab, and Loebl. The next was Dr. Ruzicka, defending Simone, Frejka, and London, who was followed by Dr. Stastny, defending Frank, Clementis, and Reicin, and finally, by Dr. Synek, defending Hajdu, Sling, and Fischl. All Counsel emphasized that the court proceedings had proved the evidence against the accused to be irrefutable and that the crimes were proved and confirmed by the fact that all the accused had admitted their guilt in every respect. Individual Counsel for the Defense referred to the fact that the accused Slansky was the leader of the Center of plotters, who had issued orders to individual members of the conspiracy, and that the latter had then worked in conformity with these orders. This, they said, was an extenuating circumstance. The day's sitting of the Court was concluded with final statements of the accused. They all had no other choice but to admit and to confirm their crimes once again.

Verdict and Sentences

At about 10 A.M. on November 27 the Presiding Judge rose to pronounce the Court's verdict:

"In the name of the Republic, the State Court in Prague tried from November 20 to 27, 1952, the criminal suit against the leaders of an anti-State conspiratorial Center, Rudolf Slansky and accomplices, on charges of the criminal offenses of high treason, espionage, sabotage, and military treason." The Presiding Judge then went in detail into the reasons which had guided the Court in arriving at its decisions. Bearing in mind these facts and guided by Article 161 of the Criminal Procedure Code, the Court had decided: "The accused are all guilty of the following offenses carried out over a prolonged period up to the date of their arrest, both in Prague and elsewhere:

"(1) That in collaboration with one another and with further persons they tried to destroy the independence of the Republic and the people's democratic order guaranteed by the Constitution; that in doing so they jeopardized this order to a considerable extent; and that Slansky, Reicin, and Sling misused the Armed Forces for these offenses;

"(2) That Slansky, Geminder, Frejka, Clementis, Reicin, London, Hajdu, Loebl, Margolius, Sling, and Simone (Katz) collaborated with one another and with other persons in getting in touch with a foreign power or with foreign agents with intent to betray State secrets, that they did in fact surrender State secrets to a foreign power, and that they committed this offense although the duty of keeping State secrets had either been expressly imposed on them or else derived from their very position; that they committed these offenses in a particularly dangerous manner, on a considerable scale and over a prolonged period; and that Frejka, Clementis, Reicin, Hajdu, Sling, and Simone (Katz) committed this offense as members of an organization whose aim it is to spy out State secrets;

"(3) That Slansky, Frejka, Frank, Loebl, Margolius, and Fischl did not fulfill but violated the duties arising from their positions, with intent to thwart or impede the implementation of a concerted economic plan and to cause grave damage to the work of the authorities, public organizations, and enterprises, and that as members of a group they committed acts which did in fact render more difficult the implementation of a concerted economic plan in sectors of special importance, and that their work did in fact greatly disrupt the work of the authorities and extensively damaged the interests of national defense.

"(4) That Slansky, Frank, and Reicin secured advantages to the enemy during the Second World War, and that they did so under especially aggravating circumstances.

"They have thus committed the following offenses:

"(1) All the accused have committed the criminal offense of high treason; Loebl under Article 12 of the Penal Code, and under Article 1, Paragraph 1, Sections A and C; Paragraph 2; and Paragraph 3, Section 1 of the Defense of the People's Democracy Act (Law No. 231 of 1948); all the other accused under Article 78, Paragraph 1, Sections A and C; Paragraph 2, Sections A and B; and Paragraph 3, Section B, of the Penal Code; the accused Slansky, Reicin, and Sling also under Paragraph 3, Section D, of the named Law.

"(2) Slansky, Geminder, Loebl, Clementis, Reicin, Frejka, Margolius, London, Hajdu, Sling, and Simone (Katz) have committed the criminal offense of espionage; Loebl under Article 12 of the Penal Code and under Article 5, Paragraph 1, and Paragraph 2, Sections B, C, D, and E of the Defense of the People's Democracy Act (Law No. 231 of 1948); the other accused under Article 86, Paragraph 1; Paragraph 2, Sections A and B; and Paragraph 3, Sections B, D, and E of the Penal Code; Clementis, Reicin, Frejka, Hajdu, Sling, and Simone (Katz) also under Paragraph 3, Section C of the named Law.

"(3) Slansky, Frank, Frejka, Loebl, Margolius, and Fischl have committed the criminal offense of sabotage; Loebl under Article 12 of the Penal Code and under Article 36, Paragraph 1; and Paragraph 2, Sections B and C of the Defense of the People's Democracy Act (Law No. 231 of 1948); the other accused under Article 85, Paragraph 1, Sections A and B; Paragraph 2, Sections A, B, and C; and Paragraph 3, Section A of the Penal Code.

"(4) Slansky, Frank, and Reicin have committed the criminal offense of military treason under Article 6, Paragraph 1, of Law No. 50 of 1923.

"For these criminal offenses sentences are passed on them as follows: Rudolf Slansky, Bedrich Geminder, Ludvik Frejka, Josef Frank, Vladimir Clementis, Bedrich Reicin, Karel Svab, Rudolf Margolius, Otto Fischl, Otto Sling, and André Simone (Otto Katz) are sentenced to death under Article 78, Paragraph 3 of the Penal Code; all of them, except Karel Svab, also with reference to Article 22, Paragraph 1 of the Penal Code.

"Artur London and Vavro Hajdu, under Article 78 of the Penal Code and with reference to Article 22, Paragraph 1 of the Penal Code, and Eugen Loebl, under Article 1, Paragraph 3 of the Defense of the People's Democracy Act, Law No. 231 of 1948, and all three also under Article 43 of the Penal Code of 1852 in so far as this applies to Article 22, Paragraph 1 of the Penal Code and all three under Article 29, Paragraph 2, and Eugen Loebl also under Article 12 of the Penal Code, are sentenced to imprisonment for life.

"All the accused are moreover declared forfeit of their citizenship. In the case of those sentenced to imprisonment their time spent under detention, from the moment of their arrest, shall be computed as part of their imprisonment.

"Concerning the gravity of the sentences:

"The death sentence in respect of Slansky, Geminder, Frejka, Frank, Clementis, Reicin, Svab, Margolius, Fischl, Sling, and Simone is due to the depth of their betrayal of the people's trust, the extent of their cunning and infamy, and the exceptional danger created by their criminal acts to our society, which is building socialism, and to all peace-loving people fighting for world peace and democracy.

"Against these facts, which the court considers aggravating circumstances, the only extenuating circumstance is the confession by the aforementioned defendants. The Court has therefore not applied, in the case of these defendants, the provisions of Article 29, Paragraph 2 of the Penal Code, believing them unjustified in this case. For the defendants are such enemies of the working people that it is necessary to render them harmless by removing them from human society.

"On the other hand, the Court did apply the provisions of Article 29, Paragraph 2 of the Penal Code in the case of Artur London, Vavro Hajdu, and Eugen Loebl. Although the danger of the criminal acts of the defendants Artur London and Vavro Hajdu to society is considerable, one cannot overlook the fact that they held no leading function in the anti-State conspiracy, although they had been placed by Slansky in the responsible posts of Deputy

Foreign Ministers. In this respect the Court took into consideration the fact that they received orders to commit their criminal offenses from Bedrich Geminder and Rudolf Slansky on the one hand, and from their immediate superior, Vladimir Clementis, on the other. Within the leadership of the anti-State conspiracy they did not fully develop their own initiative, but both of them were merely links in the long chain of conspirators.

"When deciding on the sentence in the case of Artur London, the Court took into consideration the fact that the period of his criminal activities was shorter than in the case of the other defendants.

"With respect to the sentence of imprisonment in the case of the defendant Loebl, the Court took mainly into consideration that this defendant was the first member of the plot to be arrested, namely on November 24, 1949. This defendant spontaneously confessed after his arrest and thus substantially contributed toward the unmasking of the other members of the conspiracy. Only the fact that Karel Svab and Rudolf Slansky, by misusing their office in the interest of the conspiracy, as mentioned above, prevented the investigation of the criminal offenses of the members of the conspiracy.

"In view of the above-mentioned facts and considerations the Court came to the conclusion that the penalty laid down for the criminal offenses of which Artur London, Vavro Hajdu, and Eugen Loebl were found guilty would be disproportionately severe in relation to the guilt of the other defendants. For this reason the Court applied in the case of these defendants Article 29, Paragraph 2 of the Penal Code and, instead of the death penalty laid down by the law, sentenced them only to life imprisonment, which the Court considered as fully appropriate to their guilt."

The Presiding Judge then informed the defendants in detail of their legal right to appeal and adjourned the session to give the defendants an opportunity to confer with their Counsel. After a short recess the defendants once more appeared before the Court and one after the other declared that they accepted the verdict and waived their right of appeal. The Public Prosecutor reserved his right to submit his opinion within the legal time limit.

Part III

The Supreme Court—"Rehabilitation Statement"

Judgment in the Name of the Republic

The Supreme Court comprising a president, Dr. Jaroslav Pastorka, and two judges, Dr. Otakar Balas and Dr. Jan Hlavicka, on this 24th day of May, 1963, in open session, pronounces as follows upon the case brought against Eugen Loebl by the Public Prosecutor before the Judicial Court in Prague in accordance with § 268 Abs. 2, § 269 Abs. 2, and § 271 Abs. 1.

I. Insofar as the judgment of the previous Judicial Court on November 27, 1925, G.Z.6 Ts I 91/52, found the accused Eugen Loebl guilty of

high treason under § 1 Abs. 1, lit. a/, c/, Abs. 2, Abs. 3, lit. e/;
espionage under § 5 Abs. 1, Abs. 2, lit. b/, c/, d/, e/;
sabotage under § 36 Abs. 1, Abs. 2, lit. b/, c/ of Law 231/48 Slg.

and for these crimes condemned him to life imprisonment and loss of civil rights

this was a violation of the Law according to
§ 2 Abs. 3 StPO Law No. 87/50 Slg. § 1, § 5, and § 36
Law No. 231/48 Slg.

This judgment in the case against Eugen Loebl is thus revoked in its entirety.

Furthermore, the decrees of the Prague State Court which were based on this judgment are similarly revoked, that is:

the decree of March 2, 1961, G.Z. 4 Nt 565/56 refusing the application to reopen the case against Eugen Loebl, as well as the decision of June 17, 1960, according to which Eugen Loebl was included in the amnesty of the President of the Republic dated May 9, 1961, and the remainder of his sentence remitted on condition that he commit no willful misdemeanor for a period of ten years.*

II. The accused Eugen Loebl
born on May 14, 1907, in Holic, District Senica, former Deputy Minister of Foreign Trade, last resident in Bratislava, Budovatelska ul. 4. is

acquitted

of the charges under § 226 lit. a/, b/StPO of the crimes of

1. High treason under § 1 Abs. 1, lit. a/, c/; Abs. 3 lit. e/;
2. Espionage under § 5 Abs. 1, Abs. 2, lit. b/, c/, d/, e/, and
3. Sabotage under § 36 Abs. 1, Abs. 2, lit. b/, c/ of Law No. 231/48 Slg.

according to which over a considerable period prior to his arrest both in Prague and elsewhere he

*The Court statement was made at the height of Antonin Novotny's regime as President of Czechoslovakia and First Secretary of the Communist Party.

1. gradually allied himself with other persons in order to attempt to destroy the independence of the Republic and the popular democratic system guaranteed by the constitution, whereby he to a considerable extent endangered this system;

2. conspired with other persons and made contact with a foreign power with the intention of betraying secrets, and willfully betrayed such secrets to a foreign power, committing this offense although the duty to keep secrets of state was specifically laid upon him and was also a corollary of his position; his offense involved particularly important secrets of state and was of a particularly danger ous nature, committed over a lengthy period and on a large scale;

3. together with the other accused, failed or neglected his duties with the intention of hindering the implementation of the integral economic plan and of causing difficulties for it, and of seriously disturbing the activities of officials, public organizations, and undertakings; in this as a member of an association he committed crimes that hindered the implementation of the integral plan in very important sectors and seriously interfered with the activities of the officials. In this way he to a large extent hazarded the interests of the defense of the country.

Grounds:

In his plea that the Law had been violated the Public Prosecutor complains in the first place that the judgment of the former Judicial Court of November 27, 1952, G.Z. 6 Ts I 91/52 including the proceedings against Eugen Loebl was based on such preliminaries and evidence that there was no possibility of a just assessment of offenses as is the duty of the Court under § 2 Abs. 3 StPO of 1950. As a result of this the Court was uncritical in its assessment of the results of the main proceedings and drew its conclusions regarding the charges of high treason, espionage, and sabotage on the basis of insufficient evidence—in essence on the accused's own confession.

The plea of violation of the Law further adduces facts that later became obvious and these show that if the Judicial Court had been more careful in testing the credibility of the evidence presented in the main proceedings, it would have discovered that the whole of the preliminary proceedings prior to the main trial were illegal, their results having been obtained by the use of illegal methods of interrogation by members of the Security Services.

For this reason the Procurator-General makes application for the judgment of the former Judicial Court to be held a violation of the Law and the sentences imposed by it, including that pronounced on Eugen Loebl, to be reversed in their entirety and Eugen Loebl declared not guilty of the charges of high treason, espionage, and sabotage, because on the one hand it has not been proven that he committed the culpable acts of which he was accused and on the other hand the rest of the charges are not themselves culpable acts.

In accordance with § 267 Abs. 1 StPO, the Supreme Court has examined the entire judgment and also the preliminary proceedings and finds that the judgment was a violation of the Law.

In the former Court's judgment the individual acts that led to the conviction of the accused Loebl for high treason, espionage, and sabotage were not detailed individually.

As far as the crime of high treason is concerned, in the case of Loebl this is only mentioned generally in the grounds adduced for his conviction, namely that he was a member of a treasonable center of conspiracy headed by Rudolf Slansky, in the framework of which he sought by Trotskyite methods to obtain power over the apparatus of Party, State, and the economy, to cause the overthrow of the political system of the State, and to restore capitalism in our country. The judgment further states that all the accused, thus the accused Loebl as well, had together created an apparatus with wide ramifications for putting their hostile intentions into practice, that all the conspirators were united by a common aim, and that they kept one another informed of what had been done to co-ordinate their efforts to realize their treasonable plans.

Where the conviction for espionage is concerned, here, too, the acts and deeds concerned are not detailed or gone into. According to the judgment the accused Loebl maintained intelligence (espionage) contact with three spies, Herman Field, Lias, and Cernaj in order to divulge to them secret and top secret information about our economy and foreign trade.

The same thing applies to the question of sabotage. The judgment states that in the case of the accused Loebl, he, together with others of the accused, caused billions of crowns' worth of damage to the foreign trade of the Republic by deliberately entering into unprofitable transactions with capitalist states, by paying unjustified compensation for nationalization of concerns to foreign capitalists, by supporting capitalist elements abroad, and in numerous other ways. This damage was further increased by foreign exchange transactions, also involving billions of crowns, favoring members of the Zionist bourgeoisie who had emigrated from Czechoslovakia both legally and illegally. According to the judgment the aim of these activities was to tie our economy to one side and so put obstacles in the way of cementing and developing economic relations with the USSR and the other countries of the Socialist camp. These activities were alleged to have thwarted the Two-Year Plan and to have caused considerable harm to the activities of the officials, public officers, and undertakings subordinate to the accused, including the accused Loebl. However, as the judgment fails to state the evidence on which the Court concluded that these charges had been proved, the proceedings of the trial force one to the conclusion that it was based on the confessions made during their interrogation and at the trial by Loebl and his fellow accused Rudolf Slansky, Frejka, and Margolius, as also on the testimony of the witnesses Kacerovska and Hofmann and the evidence of the commission of experts, and, finally, on the documents attached to the record of the examination of the accused, Loebl.

According to § 2 Abs. 1 and Abs. 3 StPO of 1950 it is incumbent upon the Courts to see that in criminal cases the laws of the popular democratic Republic are adhered to, that they are applied in agreement with the interests of the working people, and that offenses are justly judged. Neither the Judicial Court at the time in question nor before it the Public Prosecutor or the Security Service has complied with this stipulation.

It is unequivocally evident from the proceedings of the main trial that the Judicial Court—like the Prosecutor and the Security Service before it—both in the marshaling of the evidence during the trial and during the examination of the accused Loebl, was guilty of bias against the accused. This is confirmed above all by the fact that the Court admitted not even one piece of evidence in favor of the accused, that the Court made no effort to produce facts illuminating the positive side of the accused's activities, which certainly must have existed and which would have helped to arrive at an objective judgment of the evidence adduced against them.

Again, during the hearing of the evidence, the Court did not make sufficient efforts to go into the individual charges of which Loebl was accused, but was content with a general statement that the accused, Loebl among them, had inflicted immense damage to the country's economy in one sphere or the other, though nothing was said about the circumstances in which this was to have taken place. The alleged charges ought to have been examined more exactly if only because the majority concerned economic matters about which the accused, for all their high positions in Party and State, were not able to decide on their own. Finally, the Court accepted the evidence of the exhibits attached to the examination statements of the accused quite uncritically, although they are either inadmissible as evidence of an offense—e.g. the photographs of foreigners allegedly the agents of hostile states which have been taken from the files of the Ministry of the Interior—or speak more in favor of the accused than of the prosecution. This is the case, for example, with respect to items 7 and 8 in the case against Loebl. Document No. 7 is the original of a letter from the accused Loebl to ambassador Dr. Kratochvil in London sending him documents concerning the commercial treaty with the USSR of October 8, 1948. These documents were called "secret" by the Security Service, although they are stamped "confidential." Similarly, the letter accompanying them was alleged to be concerned with transmitting espionage information to Zilliacus. In it Dr. Kratochvil is alleged to have been reminded to pass the material on to Zilliacus. Yet nothing of the kind can be found in the letter. On the contrary, the letter mentions the progressive attitude of [Professor] Neal and his sympathy for Czechoslovakia. This is also apparent in the facts mentioned in the letter that on his visit to Czechoslovakia Neal was impressed by many things, but especially by the amount of political freedom. Apparently he was of the opinion that the American press campaign against Czechoslovakia would not last forever.

The Court also attached the wrong value to the testimony of the accused, in basing its judgment largely on this testimony. The statements of the accused to the Court and in their examination prior to the trial are couched in such a way that ridicules their value as evidence. In most cases they are statements full of phrases (the accused speak of themselves solely as hardened enemies, spies, and saboteurs of our system); any information that was to be passed to anyone termed a spy thus became an intelligence report, without any attempt being made to examine its contents; any concrete economic measure in the implementation of which the accused were concerned and which was regarded as a mistake was presented as a deliberately damaging act and thus these cases were not examined in their context. The Court should not have overlooked the fact that although the accused Loebl had been under detention for three years prior to the trial there was only one statement in the record of his examination, namely that of November 7, 1952, that is to say, two weeks before the trial; and this being of 57 pages could not possibly have been obtained in the course of one day. An appendix to the statement itself of two pages is dated November 19, 1952. The other statements obtained from the accused Loebl during the three years of his detention for examination were not presented to the Court, although they would have demonstrated the course taken by the entire examination and thrown light on the credibility of the results of the preliminary investigation.

The facts demonstrate that also in the case of the accused Loebl, the Court arrived at the sentence of guilty on the basis of errors in the trial proceedings and of faulty evaluation of the evidence.

The Court was guilty of a further error in that it called an action high treason, espionage, or sabotage under § 1, 5, or 36 of Law No. 231/48 Slg. even though this law only came into force on October 14, 1948, while the incriminating actions according to the judgment took place in 1945 or later, but before this law came into force. The Court's judgment nowhere says under which laws the accused Loebl is liable for actions performed before the law mentioned above came into force, nor does it state the reason why the actions of the accused prior to this law coming into force are to be regarded as culpable actions, the law condemning them having not yet come into force. The Court certainly quotes § 12 StPO of 1950 in its condemnation of Loebl, but this says that the culpability of an act is to be judged in accordance with the laws in force at the time of its performance, and that a criterion established subsequently can only be applied if it is to the advantage of the accused. The Court only respected this in regard to Law No. 231/48 Slg. and Law No. 86/1950 Slg., which were in force at the time of the trial. This, however, was not taken into consideration in judging the actions of the accused Loebl prior to Law No. 231/1948 Slg. coming into force.

The activities of Loebl up to the time when Law No. 231/1948 Slg. came into force should have been judged under Law No. 50/1923, according to § 2 of which high treason, if proven, ought to have been qualified as preparation for a plot and for this the maximum penalty is ten years imprisonment.

As far as the betrayal of State secrets is concerned, this should have been judged as betrayal of citizenship according to § 5 Abs. 1 of the law in question, and for this too the maximum penalty laid down is ten years imprisonment. The actions represented as sabotage when committed between July 18, 1946, until the Law 231/1948 Slg. came into force should have been regarded as a breach of § 3 Law No. 165/1946 Slg. (law concerning nationalized concerns under State control) and here too the maximum penalty allowed was ten years. Thus in no event should Law No. 231/1948 Slg., which came into force subsequently, have been applied to actions which the accused Loebl allegedly committed prior to October 14, 1948, since the application of this law was not to the advantage of the accused, but very much to his disadvantage.

All this proves that in condemning Loebl of high treason, espionage, and sabotage the Court violated § 2 Abs.

3 StPO of 1950 and §§ 1, 5, and 36 of Law No. 231/1948 Slg., for which reason the sentence pronounced on the accused Loebl must be repealed in its entirety as contrary to the Law, as must all subsequent orders based on this finding.

Apart from finding that the Judicial Court violated the rules for the conduct of trials, the Supreme Court in view of evidence later laid before it in further proceedings came to the conclusion that there was no evidence for the statement made in the indictment that the accused Loebl had been guilty of high treason, espionage, and sabotage, the trustworthiness of which was beyond doubt.

The testimony of B.D. [Doubek], who between 1949 and 1953 was one of the heads of the Security Service, given to officers of the Procurator-General during the proceedings taken against him convinced the Court that in reality no such hostile Center ever existed, that it was a fiction worked out by the Security Service for which they used testimony extorted by illegal means from persons already under arrest. According to B.D.'s testimony these illegal methods mostly took the form of exerting mental and physical pressure on those who would not admit offenses until they gave in and were prepared to admit whatever their interrogators wanted them to say; the interrogators drew up the record of the examination of an arrested person in advance, the statements the accused made in Court were prepared by their interrogators prior to the trial, and the accused, including the accused Loebl, signed these and had to learn them by heart and repeat them in Court. Measures were taken to ensure that there should be no attempt to deviate from this testimony on any essential point. The accused Loebl, who in the early stage of his examination denied having committed any offenses, had pressure put on him by means of a threat to illegally arrest his wife.

This is all confirmed by the testimony given by V.K.

[Kohoutek] in the proceedings brought against him (and later in the joint proceedings brought against him and B.D.). V.K., a former official of the Security Service, was head of the group that examined a number of persons, including the accused Loebl, in connection with the so-called treasonable Center of conspiracy. He himself repeatedly interrogated Loebl, and he confirmed that illegal means were used in the examination of Loebl in order to obtain the testimony that was needed.

The testimony of these former members of the Security Service confirms the defense of the accused Loebl and in particular the evidence produced subsequently in conjunction with his application for the 1961 trial to be reopened according to which his statement admitting high treason, espionage, and sabotage had been extorted by illegal means. In view of this important fact no credibility can be attached to the testimony of the accused Loebl given during his examination and in the proceedings during the trial, it being inadmissible as evidence in a court of law.

The same thing applies to the testimony of the other accused, Rudolf Slansky, Ludvik Frejka, and Rudolf Margolius, which was also put forward as evidence in the case against the accused Loebl. The officers of the Security Service mentioned above have stated that the same or similar illegal methods of interrogation were used in examining these persons and that their statements are also inadmissible as evidence.

The Supreme Court further decided on the basis of the testimony of B.D. that the opinion of the so-called Commission of Experts similarly adduced as grounds for sentencing the accused, including Loebl, were not objective but formulated in advance so as to support this conception of a treasonable Center of espionage and of the harm allegedly inflicted on the State by the accused. They were so phrased as to avoid any discrepancy between them and the testimony of the accused or the witnesses.

The falsity and lack of objectivity of these experts' opinions is also demonstrated by the fact that they were worked out after the examination of the accused had been concluded and immediately prior to the trial. If it had been wanted to obtain an objective picture of what had happened, as soon as it was suspected that wrong measures had been taken in our foreign trade for which the accused Loebl was allegedly partially responsible, each individual incident should have been investigated, independently of Loebl's testimony, by the qualified experts of the Court. Only after this, on the basis of the facts objectively established in this way, should conclusions have been drawn as to the responsibility of the accused Loebl. Here, of course, the accused Loebl should have been given the opportunity of seeing the statements and the inferences made and of defending himself against them.

Recent expert opinion obtained during the appeal against the sentences on Goldman and others have demonstrated how false and lacking in objectivity the opinion of the original commission of so-called experts was. The opinion of the Deputy Minister of Finance, Drahomir Dvorak of the deputy departmental head of the Ministry of Finance, Julius Hajek, and of a director of the National Bank, Josef Malat, given on March 9, 1963, concerning the foreign trade side of the individual charges brought against Loebl and others is that:

1. Erection of a Pencil Factory in Israel

The erection of a pencil factory in Israel was indeed planned. Negotiations took place between 1947 and 1949 and the [Party's] Economic Commission and the National Bank gave their provisional approval of the project. In March, 1949, however, the Ministry of Industry refused to grant an export license. Minutes of a conference held in the Ministry of Industry on May 13, 1949, show that final approval was refused on the intervention of the accused Loebl, who would not permit the export of the machinery in question from the Czechoslovak Republic. This confirms the defense of the accused Loebl of April 17, 1963, in which he stated that his provisional approval of the project was given in the belief that the machines concerned were surplus and that, when he learned that this was not the case, he refused to allow the deal to go through.

2. 1949 Trade Agreement with Great Britain

The opinion of the experts is that this agreement involved economic considerations of considerable importance, in that the British made the agreement conditional on payment of compensation for nationalized property and repayment of war credits. Negotiations were conducted at the highest government level and the bodies concerned also ratified the resulting treaty. Although the terms of the treaty, especially the financial ones, were onerous for us, it cannot be said that it was wrong to conclude the treaty. For this reason and because the accused Loebl was only one of many who took part in the preparations for this treaty, it is not proven that what he did in preparing the treaty was in any way culpable.

3. Export of TV Tubes to Great Britain

The experts have stated that the export of TV tubes was in no way harmful, but on the contrary advantageous because they were produced from domestic raw materials. There was no need to refuse it on strategic grounds as is proved by the fact that the first refusal of permission for their export made by the Ministry of Defense was gone into thoroughly and, on November 3, 1950, withdrawn. This, then, is another case where no damage was inflicted on our economy.

4. The 1948–1949 Dollar Offensive

The experts examined this case in detail and commented on its wider implications. They showed that fundamentally there were three possibilities of overcoming the difficult situation caused by a shortage of dollars which were needed for buying in foreign markets. However, they came to the conclusion that the procedure that was chosen at the time was the only one possible and economically the right one. Although in putting this action, about which the accused Loebl was not the only one to decide, into effect certain losses were incurred, the whole undertaking as such cannot be regarded as wrong in principle. The experts reached the conclusion that there was no evidence that the dollar offensive was intended to serve Loebl's alleged objective of orienting our economy toward the capitalist world. On the contrary, an analysis of the Five-Year Plan showed, according to the opinion of the experts, that the endeavor was to change the orientation of the foreign trade of the Czechoslovak Republic toward those countries with planned economies, above all the USSR.

5. The "M" Account

The experts came to the conclusion that although it would have been been possible to choose other ways of settling the difference between foreign trade and budget, setting up the M Account could be regarded as basically correct. Here then, too, the experts have confirmed the defense put forward by Loebl in his appeal for retrial, that in view of the state of the economy at the time, the so-called dollar offensive and the setting-up of the M Account were necessary and in no event harmful.

6. Procedure in Fixing Prices for Goods Exported to the Soviet Union

The experts find that at the time in question the accused Loebl was responsible for determining the prices of trade with the USSR. They point out, however, that in the case of the USSR the question of price-formation has still not been definitely answered, even though certain points of view and criteria have been accepted. Thus the experts are of the opinion that it would be wrong to draw conclusions from a few examples taken out of their context—as the previous Expert Commission did—and to say that the procedure adopted in trade relations between Czechoslovakia and the USSR was wrong and the price structure deliberately such as to upset trade relations between the two countries.

This case, too, is thus not an example of relations between our Republic and the countries of the Socialist camp being upset.

7. Foundation of Merkuria

The foundation of this trading company which was to have taken an important place in our international trade, was, according to the experts, right in principle. The deficiencies that occurred were caused in the first place by the personnel. The rightness of the idea is also confirmed by the fact that in 1958 the place of Merkuria, which ceased to exist in 1952, was taken by a new foreign trade company with similar tasks and objectives. In his examination on April 17, 1963, Loebl stated that Merkuria was set up on his initiative, but that the plan was approved by his superiors.

Thus Loebl had not made himself culpable in this case either.

8. Conclusion of Implementation of the Agreement between Czechoslovakia and the State of Israel in March, 1950

The very fact that the Treaty between the two states was concluded on March 20, 1950, and the accused Loebl arrested on November 24, 1949, shows that Loebl could not have been concerned with more than the preliminaries. The experts who have now been called in consider the Agreement an unusual one, in that here trade was linked with a transfer of capital and this in practice amounted to material support for the émigrés who were mostly of the middle class. The experts point out, however, that the people accused of concluding this agreement, among them the accused Loebl, made no secret of this disadvantage when laying the proposal before those who had to decide about it.

The facts as established show that here, too, the accused Loebl had not done anything culpable.

9. Agency Agreement between Centrotex and Tirax of New York

This agreement came into force on October 1, 1949. The agency existed for a short period; it was to promote the sale of artificial flowers, a very profitable export article.

This project was part of the so-called dollar offensive. On the evidence available the experts have concluded that the idea of selling artificial flowers to the U.S. was a good one, but that there were deficiencies in the personnel running the agency. The question of personnel, however, was the responsibility of Centrotex, which was responsible for implementing the agreement.

Thus no legal responsibiilty for losses incurred in dissolving the agency in March, 1950, that is to say, after the arrest of the accused Loebl, can attach to him.

10. Trade in Tires with Belgium, 1948–1949

The experts are of the opinion that the original judgment, according to which our State suffered losses amounting to 36 million crowns [$1,380,000] because of this trade, was wrong. The sum mentioned is the total value of the goods imported and thus cannot be held to be the damage incurred, since the imported articles in question were used until worn out. The purchase from Belgium was also conditional on that country supplying rubber to Czechoslovakia. The prices paid for these products were those prevailing in the world market. The experts have not been able to discover any inefficiency here.

11. Establishment of a Branch of Schweizer Surveillance AG, Geneva, 1949

This agency was approved on October 8, 1949, on the instructions of the Ministry of Trade. Several other ministries, including the Ministry of the Interior, agreed to the establishment. The institution in question was set up in accordance with existing Czechoslovak regulations. It has not been possible to establish any hostile activity that could have harmed the country. Although the judgment of the first Court stated that the firm in question was in contact with an American intelligence service, nowhere in the judgment is it suggested that the accused Loebl was aware of this. The experts who have now been called in are of the opinion that in such circumstances this could have been true, as it must be assumed that such firms maintain contact with some intelligence services. The criminal responsibility of the accused Loebl was in this case deduced because of his being the representative the Ministry of Foreign Trade at the conference, in which a number of central departments took part, and in that capacity—as did the other representatives—he agreed to the branch being allowed to be set up. This fact itself makes the conclusion referred to seem inadmissable, as it is at variance with the law.

12. Exceeding Credit Limits

Here, too, the experts are of the opinion that at that critical period this practice in foreign trade with the capitalist countries of the West did not harm our economy, but on the contrary in the situation then prevailing brought us considerable advantage.

This point is only in favor of the accused Loebl, and not to his discredit as stated in the indictment.

13. Scientific-Technical Aid to Poland

Here again the experts can find nothing incorrect in the behavior of the accused Loebl, since the agreement as to the ways and conditions, especially the recovery of costs, of mutual scientific-technical aid between countries of the Socialist camp was not concluded until 1949 in Sofia.

Thus it cannot be said that the accused Loebl did anything culpable in requiring compensation for concrete scientific-technical documentation as he did from Poland in 1947, though this was not in line with the agreement subsequently made in 1949.

14. The Hambro's Bank Credit

In the opinion of the experts this case cannot be judged in isolation, but only in the context of the whole economic situation at the time. In the period after 1945 our need of pounds sterling for rebuilding our economy considerably exceeded the credit of five million pounds granted us by the British Government. The credit of one million pounds given by Hambro's Brank enabled us to import pyrites and other important raw materials which our industries needed. Quite apart from this, the credit was approved by high government circles. The experts consider that the rate of interest to be paid was not higher than what is usual for bank credits. Thus, here again the accused Loebl had not done anything which could be regarded as culpable. Loebl's own defense that this credit was of great importance to our economy and that he had had no influence on the conditions on which it was granted, as these were negotiated by representatives of the Ministry of Finance, the Zivnostenska Bank, and the National Bank, is thus confirmed.

15. Payment to Lever Bros. and Unilever, London, of Compensation for the Nationalization of the Schicht Concern, 1948–1952

In their written opinion the experts have stated that negotiations for concrete compensation had gone on for a long time, in practice ever since 1945, when the firm put forward its claim for compensation for nationalization of its property. Until 1948 nothing came of the negotiations. Altogether three agreements were reached in this matter: the first in 1948, the second in 1949, and the third in 1950, each showing an improvement on the terms originally agreed. From the material available to them the experts have reached the conclusion that the main reason for making these agreements, which were not advantageous to our economy, was that we anticipated the aid of the British firm in question in importing raw materials which at the time in question were in short supply on the world market and that we should obtain these at better prices than would be the case if they had to be bought through a variety of middlemen. The experts have also stated that the initiative for concluding this agreement did not come from Loebl; thus the responsibility for harm that our economy may have suffered as a result of the agreement, cannot be laid on the accused, Loebl, all the more so as this was another case where the final decision was not his.

The experts confirm the defense subsequently put in by the accused that he was not responsible for this agreement, since he took part neither in the conferences nor in the resolutions deciding on its preparation. If he made any contribution to it, this consisted of a suggestion that was very advantageous and one that was in fact accepted, that compensation should be paid not in foreign exchange, but through the export of products of our light industries.

These facts are unequivocal proof of the rightness of the defense put forward by the accused that he never consciously failed in his duty as Deputy Minister of Foreign Trade either in the sphere of foreign trade or finance. The opinion of the present experts confirms this in all essentials. For the reasons given here, then, the accused Loebl could not be held guilty of the offenses alleged against him in the indictment.

The situation is the same as regards the allegations of espionage made against the accused, Loebl. According to the indictment Loebl's espionage activities consisted of his having gradually allied himself with the other accused and with others, and having gotten into contact with a foreign power, with the intention of betraying secrets of state, and that in fact he did betray secrets to a foreign power. He did this although it was his duty, specifically laid upon him, to safguard secrets, as was also implied by the fact of the position he occupied. The secrets involved were ones of particular importance and the betrayal was especially dangerous both in extent and duration.

There is very little put forward to substantiate this point in the indictment. Loebl is stated to be Agent IS, but there is no material to substantiate this. Later he is said to have been in contact with Herman Field from 1939 to 1949, having been recruited for espionage work by him in Kracow in 1939 and to whom he supplied extensive and important intelligence information up to 1949. Further it is stated that the correspondent of *The Times*, Lias, was active as a spy in Czechoslovakia and that Loebl was in touch with him. The indictment also states that Loebl was in touch with [Darko] Cernaj and in the autumn of 1947 gave him a specially written report on the course of the Soviet-Czechoslovak trade negotiations. This shows that the State Prosecutor's department has not adequately grounded or explained its accusations. There is nothing in the indictment to indicate what was the evidence and testimony on which the Prosecution had reached its conclusions. Among the material attached to the report of the examination of the accused Loebl, purporting to be evidence against him, were photographs of G. Lias and Noel Field, but as these came from the files of the Ministry of the Interior they could not possibly be regarded as proof that Loebl had acted as a spy for these persons. In the case of the brothers Field, the Prosecution had even got things muddled, for while the photograph is of Noel Field, the indictment asserted that it was his brother, Herman Field, for whom Loebl spied. The accompanying material includes photographs of K. Zilliacus and F. Neal, obtained from the same source, with whom, according to the documents, Loebl was in contact as their spy, though there is nothing about this in the indictment. If documents 7 and 8 purport to prove a relationship between Loebl and Zilliacus and Neal, no such conclusion can be drawn from them; indeed they are more to be regarded as favoring the accused, Loebl, than condemning him.

It has already been pointed out why the testimony of the accused Loebl given during his interrogation and in which he admits spying cannot be the basis for arriving at a judgment; that is why it is worthless as evidence. Yet even if it had not been shown that Loebl's testimony had been extorted by illegal means, one could not conclude from it, as the indictment does, that the accused had been engaged in espionage. The accused's testimony, as far as individual facts are concerned, is so general that it is quite impossible either to discover what the information allegedly transmitted was, or to judge whether it was secret or top secret. For example, in his statement Loebl says that he was in contact with Lias from 1945 to 1949, and he states that he let Lias have secret information concerning foreign trade; that in 1946 he gave him information about our trade with Sweden, in particular: how much ore we had imported and the extent of our consumption, and also that he had informed Lias about the course of our negotiations with Poland, about the division of the production program and the production of ball bearings, locomotives, commercial vehicles, etc. In 1948 and 1949 he gave Lias information about the trade agreements with Switzerland, Belgium, the Netherlands, and other countries and told him that we were making compensation deals with those countries and that it would be a good thing if Great Britain too would agree to this way of doing business. The terms in which the accused tells of giving information about the 1947 negotiations in Moscow for a trade agreement are similar.

Speaking of his espionage deals with Herman Field, the accused Loebl states that he made contact with Field in 1939 in Kracow, where Field was engaged in recruiting agents among the emigrants there. He met Herman Field in the home of V [ilem] Novy, where he gave him details of the effect of UNRRA's activities on our foreign trade and of our difficulties in rebuilding our economy. He also betrayed to Field all the secret and confidential information about our foreign trade that he knew by virtue of his position as head of a department in the Ministry of Foreign Trade. He is supposed in 1949 to have told Field about the co-called "catholic action," the action committees of the National Front, and Czechoslovakia's foreign trade.

Loebl's testimony about his espionage dealings with Zilliacus and Neal is phrased in the same way, while his testimony does not even mention his espionage dealings with Cernaj.

Similar, too, is the testimony of Kacerovska, who had been the secretary of Lias and V. Novy, in whose apartment the meeting between Herman Field and Loebl is supposed to have taken place.

Finally, among the documents there is no adequate evidence that the persons whom Loebl is supposed to have supplied with espionage material were themselves in the service of foreign powers and their espionage systems. If, in the case of Herman Field, this is assumed because of his conviction for espionage by a Hungarian court, it must be remembered that this conviction was legally reversed in 1956. In the same way, it has subsequently been shown that Zilliacus was neither a spy nor an agent of a foreign intelligence service.

These facts together show that there is nothing to substantiate the Prosecution's assertion that the accused, Loebl, engaged in espionage activities.

Since it has been demonstrated that the so-called treasonable Center of espionage headed by Rudolf Slansky, of which Loebl is supposed to have been a member and in the framework of which he committed high treason, never existed; as the concrete acts which the indictment asserts were acts of espionage and sabotage either did not take place or were not in themselves culpable, the accused Loebl is in accordance with § 226 lit. a/, b/ of StPO acquitted absolutely of the charges of high treason, espionage, and sabotage.

No appeal against this judgment will be allowed.

Prague: May 24, 1963

President of the Senate
Dr. Jaroslav Pastorek
Stamped with the stamp of
The Supreme Court

Index

L

M

T

U

V

W

Z

About the Author

About the Author

Dr. Eugen Loebl was born in Slovakia in 1907, and by the early 1930's was among his country's leading Marxist economic theoreticians. During World War II he was in England, where as a Communist, he became the Economic Advisor to Foreign Minister Jan Masaryk at the international conference that created UNRRA, and played a leading role in planning the postwar economic reconstruction in Czechoslovakia with the government-in-exile. After the liberation, Dr. Loebl became a Deputy Foreign Trade Minister, was the UNRRA bureau chief in Prague, and a member of the Presidium of the Economic Commission of the Communist Party of Czechoslovakia.

Dr. Loebl was the first of the group of thirteen so-called "accomplices" to be arrested and arraigned before the State Court with the party's Secretary General and Deputy Prime Minister, Rudolf Slansky. Eleven of the accused were condemned to death and hanged; the other three, including Dr. Loebl, were sentenced to life imprisonment. Dr. Loebl was arrested in November, 1949; the trial did not take place until 1952, and it was not until 1961 that he was released conditionally. In 1963 he was rehabilitated unconditionally and made director of the Slovak State Bank. In 1968, he again left his country after the Russians invaded it, and is living in the United States. He has lectured extensively, taught at the University of Southern Illinois, and will begin to teach at Vassar in the fall of 1969.

About the Editor

The editor of the American Edition of this book, Herman Starobin, has been a student of the Czechoslovak economic and political scene for more than two decades, and first met Dr. Loebl in 1946. Mr. Starobin received his doctorate in economics from New York University.